Reading Mark,

Engaging the Gospel

Reading Mark,
Engaging the Gospel

David Rhoads

Fortress Press

Minneapolis

READING MARK, ENGAGING THE GOSPEL

Cover design: Ann Delgehausen
Cover image: Rock Cliffs at Zion National Park. Photo by Geoff Manasse. ©Getty Images. Used by permission.
Interior design: Zan Ceeley

ISBN: 0-8006-3649-X

08   07   06   05   04   1   2   3   4   5   6   7   8   9   10

To the faculty, students, administration, and staff
of the Lutheran School of Theology at Chicago
for their unwavering support and encouragement.

❖

Contents

Preface

My fascination with the Gospel of Mark has spanned three decades. Above all, it has been characterized by efforts to apply new approaches to illuminate the same text in different ways. Innovations in biblical studies have come primarily by asking fresh questions and employing new methods—most of them originating from secular disciplines and adapted to the biblical materials. This was true of the traditional historical-critical methods, and it applies equally to new approaches that have been developed over the past several decades. The essays included in this book are the result of such new questions and new methods—specifically, narrative criticism, social-science criticism, performance criticism, and intercultural criticism.

My journey with the Gospel of Mark began with my first teaching assignment at Carthage College in 1973. I was trained primarily as a historian, and I was revising my dissertation for publication as *Israel in Revolution*, a political history of Israel in the first century up to and culminating in the Roman-Judean War of 66–70 C.E., based on the writings of Josephus. At the same time, I was lecturing on the historical context of Mark. I suddenly realized in a new way the importance of the fact that Mark was written at the time of the Roman-Judean

War, either during the war or shortly thereafter. Moreover, Mark wrote either from Rome (where Josephus was located after the war!) or from some location in Palestine. In either location, Mark would have had intimate knowledge of the war and may have been directly impacted by it. The war was the most significant event for Jews in the first century, and it struck me that Mark, in part, was writing his own perspective on and response to the war by recounting the astounding events surrounding the person of Jesus that took place before the war. As I pondered the various themes and dynamics of Mark's story, it seemed to me that this Gospel fit the historical context of the war like a hand in a glove.

My interest in the historical context of Mark has never waned. But something else sparked my interest in Mark that led in another direction. I was teaching an introductory course on the New Testament, and what fascinated me most was the distinctive nature of Mark's Gospel. Here was a text that tended to thwart all the expectations that students generally brought to the New Testament—there were no birth narratives, Jesus was not divine, he kept his identity secret, he could not perform some healings, there were no resurrection appearances, the women left the grave speechless. I have loved to teach this Gospel at the beginning of a course on the New Testament because it constrains the students to read carefully to see what is really there in a Gospel and what is *not* there! When they have thoroughly digested Mark's Gospel, they are ready to go on to see each of the other Gospels as equally distinctive.

I was so intrigued by Mark's story that I asked an English professor at Carthage, Don Michie, if he would be willing to come into the class and show us what it would mean to read Mark like a short story. When he laid out an exciting scenario of reading that sounded nothing like any biblical scholarship I had ever read, I was stunned and exhilarated. It was like a bright light shining in an area of interpretation that had become lost for lack of use. Not only was Mark a historical document, but it was a real story, and a good one at that. Don Michie and I began meeting regularly to talk about Mark and about literary criticism. Before long, I had abandoned my *Gospel Parallels* and was telling my students to read each Gospel at one sitting and then to compare the Gospels as a whole rather than individual pericopes. For example, I would have students compare the characterization of Jesus or the disciples in the four Gospels or analyze the different settings that give structure to each narrative or identify the distinctive standards of judgment guiding readers in each Gospel.

While I was learning about the narratives of Mark and the other Gospels from teaching, there were major shifts going on in the Markan Seminar of the Society of Biblical Literature. During the late seventies various scholars were reading papers and publishing articles on narrative features and episodes of Mark's Gospel. Thomas Boomershine had written on the passion narrative, Bob Tannehill did character analyses of the disciples and Jesus, Joanna Dewey had written on concentric patterns, Norman Petersen looked at the narrator and introduced the idea of a "narrative world," Werner Kelber argued for the overall literary impact of the story, Mary Ann Tolbert analyzed the implied reader, and Robert Fowler worked with the rhetoric of Mark. These studies broke with the traditional historical-critical approaches to the narratives of the Gospels. The times were changing.

In the late seventies, as a member of the group, I was asked to write a statement about where we had come in the Markan Seminar. Chapter 1, "Narrative Criticism and the Gospel of Mark," represents this effort. It is an attempt to chart the shift that takes place when one goes from the traditional historical-critical method to a narrative analysis of Mark—the shift from history to story, from a redactional analysis of the text to treating the text as a whole, and from a focus on how the writer composed to the experience of a reader/hearer. I had spent many hours the previous year in the bowels of the Duke University library reading ancient and contemporary literary criticism, trying to put together a holistic approach to biblical narrative. At the end, I tried to chart the most recent methods for analyzing narrative in secular and biblical studies and to suggest how these methods might be applied to the Gospel of Mark. This study also resulted in a book on the narrative of Mark, *Mark as Story: An*

Introduction to the Narrative of a Gospel, written with Don Michie, and later revised in collaboration with Joanna Dewey.

Shortly thereafter, the work of the Markan Seminar began to take hold, and holistic interpretations appeared offering thoroughgoing treatments of the narratives of each of the other Gospels. Subsequently many books and articles have been published analyzing various aspects of the narratives of the four Gospels and the Acts of the Apostles, as well as the narrative features of different letters and of the Revelation of John. Mark Powell wrote a helpful introduction to the discipline, *What Is Narrative Criticism?* This employment of narrative criticism, begun by the Markan Seminar, burgeoned quickly into a fruitful field for New Testament studies.

From biblical narrative criticism, scholars doing literary criticism moved on to reader-response criticism, deconstructionist criticism, postmodern criticism, and postcolonial criticism, among others. Meanwhile, narrative criticism has established a firm foothold in biblical studies, and it continues to be a lively and productive discipline in Hebrew Bible and New Testament studies.

About twenty years after the end of the Markan Seminar, an opportunity came to take a fresh look at narrative criticism as a discipline. Chapter 2, "Narrative Criticism: Practices and Prospects," seeks to assess where we have come, what difference narrative criticism has made, and where we might go from here. I am convinced that narrative analysis will continue to be a vital part of biblical studies, in part because it is constantly evolving and in part because it works so well together with many other new methods—reader-response criticism, rhetorical analysis, social-science criticism, orality criticism, postcolonial criticism, as well as feminist and other liberationist approaches.

Throughout this time, I was seeking to look at overall features of Mark's narrative. One effort was to ferret out the Markan standards of judgment in an effort to lay bare the moral backbone of Mark. Chapter 3, "Losing Life for Others in the Face of Death," analyzes some of the beliefs and values of Mark, the norms that undergird the narrator's description of characters and events and that serve to draw the reader into the narrator's perspective. Shortly thereafter, a comparison of the standards of judgment in Mark's Gospel with those of other New Testament writings led to the publication of *The Challenge of Diversity: The Witness of Paul and the Gospels*.

In addition, there has been an ongoing interest in careful analyses of individual episodes in the context of a whole Gospel. Chapter 4, "Jesus and the Syrophoenician Woman," represents a narrative analysis of the story of Jesus' encounter with the Syrophoenician woman, a study that seeks to take into account not only the characters, settings, events, structures, and rhetoric of the episode but also the Markan themes, stylistic devices, and motifs that run through this episode, along with its place in the larger sequence of episodes. I have become convinced that only a detailed narrative exegesis of individual episodes can be an adequate basis for an overall narrative interpretation of a whole Gospel.

Meanwhile, in the early eighties, my work on Mark took a turn toward a social-science interpretation of the biblical writings. Bruce Malina's book, *The New Testament World: Insights from Cultural Anthropology*, opened up for me many new adventures in biblical studies and made me realize how far I needed to go to see Mark's story as a world construction of first-century Palestine. Thanks to Bruce's exceptional hospitality, I was able to go to Creighton University for a brief period and get an immersion in cultural anthropology. This experience set me on a path of study that has significantly affected my teaching, my interpretation of biblical texts, and my efforts to construct historical scenarios of early Christianity. In this endeavor, I have learned a great deal from members of The Context Group—S. Scott Bartchy, Dennis C. Duling, John H. Elliott, Philip F. Esler, K. C. Hanson, Bruce J. Malina, Jerome H. Neyrey, John J. Pilch, Douglas E. Oakman, Carolyn Osiek, Richard L. Rohrbaugh, among others.

Chapters 5 and 6 are efforts to illuminate Mark's narrative world using models from cultural anthropology. As heuristic devices, these models crack open our own cultural assumptions and lead us to see things from a fresh perspective, one much closer to the biblical world. Combining this approach with knowledge of the historical context of a Gospel offers many new insights for interpreting the narrative of a

Gospel. To this end, chapter 5, "Network for Mission: The Social System of the Jesus Movement," uses a number of different models to understand the Jesus movement portrayed in Mark's story-world as an expanding network that is wholly oriented to mission. Chapter 6, "Crossing Boundaries: Purity and Defilement," outlines and then applies four approaches to the social study of the New Testament (including models from anthropologist Mary Douglas and historian of religion Jonathan Z. Smith) to explore the dynamics of purity and defilement in Mark's story-world. Both of these essays are interdisciplinary expansions of narrative criticism, because they represent social-science analyses of the narrative world of Mark's Gospel.

Chapter 7, "Performing the Gospel of Mark," moves in a very different direction, namely, the experience of performing Mark. In the late seventies, I had occasion to memorize the Gospel of Mark and then, over the last twenty-five years, to perform it for more than two hundred audiences. The experience of performing Mark has enabled me to have a unique medium through which to understand and interpret Mark—not as a reader, not as a hearer, but in the role of the narrator of an oral story. Such an experience brings the text to life in ways that no other experience can do. Through this oral presentation of Mark and other New Testament writings, I have come to consider what performance criticism might contribute to New Testament studies. My work in this area has been stimulated by the work of Thomas E. Boomershine, David L. Barr, Joanna Dewey, Bernard Brandon Scott, Robert M. Fowler, Werner H. Kelber, and Arthur Dewey in the SBL Working Group, "The Bible in Ancient and Modern Media."

More recently, another development in biblical studies has become a significant part of my research and teaching. Through the eighties and nineties, there came a major turn in hermeneutics from a modernist to a postmodernist approach. Feminist criticism and postmodern interpretation in particular made it clear how much every point of view is limited and relative and how much each perspective bears dimensions of power. At the same time, there was an influx of new voices into academic publishing from many different social locations in the U.S. and globally. I was privileged to attend the first conference on "Cultural Exegesis" in North America, in which more than thirty scholars, representing cultures from all over the globe, shared their approach to biblical studies. This immersion was a transformative experience. Subsequently, interacting with diverse cultural perspectives has become an integral part of my research and teaching. In an effort to understand intercultural criticism, I have benefited greatly from the works of Brian K. Blount, Musa Dube, Elisabeth Schüssler Fiorenza, Benny Liew, Fernando F. Segovia, R. S. Sugirtharajah, Mary Ann Tolbert, and K.-K. Yeo.

As I have struggled with these issues, I have became acutely aware of the ways in which my own social location—white, male, Anglo-Saxon, Lutheran, heterosexual, middle class, educated, urban, modern, Western, U.S. citizen—has shaped and determined my interests, methods, interpretations, and appropriations in biblical studies. It quickly became clear how absolutely essential it is to interpret and appropriate the text with people from social locations other than my own. The last chapter of this book, "The Ethics of Reading Mark as Narrative," organizes reflections on intercultural criticism around the emerging discipline of the ethics of reading.

My struggle with Mark's fascinating and powerful story continues to deepen and broaden as new methods in biblical scholarship become available and as interpreters from diverse social locations bring their fresh insights to bear upon the meaning and rhetoric of Mark's Gospel.

❖

I am grateful to K. C. Hanson for his encouragement of me in this project and for the wisdom of his editorial help. It is gratifying to have an editor who is also a colleague and friend.

I wish to thank Britt Leslie, my graduate research assistant at the Lutheran School of Theology at Chicago for his expert hand in getting these essays into the proper format for publication. Joanna Dewey and Sandy Roberts have been incredibly faithful readers and have suggested many improvements in the text.

I am also deeply thankful to the Lutheran School of Theology at Chicago for their enthusiastic support of my teaching, my research, and my personal and family life.

Finally, I want to thank the many students through the years who have challenged me and who have collaborated in experimenting with new methods and new interpretations.

❖

Many of the chapters in this book originally appeared as articles in journals or books.

Chapter 1: "Narrative Criticism and the Gospel of Mark." *JAAR* 50 (1982) 411–34.

Chapter 2: "Narrative Criticism: Practices and Prospects." In *Characterization in the Gospels: Reconceiving Narrative Criticism,* edited by David Rhoads and Kari Syreeni, 254–85. JSNTSup 184. Sheffield: Sheffield Academic, 1999.

Chapter 3: "Losing Life for Others: Mark's Standards of Judgment." *Int* 47 (1993) 258–69.

Chapter 4: "Jesus and the Syrophoenician Woman in Mark: A Narrative-Critical Study." *JAAR* 62 (1994) 343–75.

Chapter 5: "Network for Mission: The Social System of the Jesus Movement as Depicted in the Narrative of the Gospel of Mark." In *Aufstieg und Niedergang der römischen Welt* II.26.2., edited by Wolfgang Haase and Hildegarde Temporini, 1692–729. Berlin: de Gruyter, 1995.

Chapter 6: "Crossing Boundaries: Purity and Defilement in the Gospel of Mark." In *Mark and Method: New Approaches in Biblical Studies,* edited by Janice Capel Anderson and Stephen Moore, 135–61. Minneapolis: Fortress Press, 1992.

Chapter 7: "Performing the Gospel of Mark." In *Body and Bible: Interpreting and Experiencing Biblical Narratives,* edited by Bjorn Krondorfer, 102–19. Harrisburg, Pa.: Trinity, 1992.

Abbreviations

AB	Anchor Bible
ANRW	*Aufstieg und Niedergang der römischen Welt: Geschichte und Kultur Roms im Spiegel der neueren Forschung.* Edited by H. Temporini and W. Haase. Berlin, 1972–
BETL	Bibliotheca ephemeridum theologicarum Lovaniensium
BibInt	*Biblical Interpretation*
BibIntSer	Biblical Interpretation Series
BibSem	Biblical Seminar
BLS	Bible and Literature Series
BTB	*Biblical Theology Bulletin*
BZNW	Beihefte zur ZNW
CBQ	*Catholic Biblical Quarterly*
CBQMS	CBQ Monograph Series
ConBNT	Coniectanea biblica. New Testament series
CurTM	*Currents in Theology and Mission*
ESEC	Emory Studies in Early Christianity
FCBS	Fortress Classics in Biblical Studies
GBS	Guides to Biblical Scholarship
HTR	*Harvard Theological Review*
HUT	Hermeneutische Untersuchungen zur Theologie
HvTSt	*Hervormde Teologiese Studies*
ILBS	Indiana Literary Biblical Series
Int	*Interpretation*

JAAR	*Journal of the American Academy of Religion*
JBL	*Journal of Biblical Literature*
JR	*Journal of Religion*
JRS	*Journal of Roman Studies*
JSNT	*Journal for the Study of the New Testament*
JSNTSup	Journal for the Study of the New Testament: Supplement Series
JSOT	*Journal for the Study of the Old Testament*
JSOTSup	Journal for the Study of the Old Testament: Supplement Series
LCBI	Literary Currents in Biblical Interpretation
m.	*Mishnah* tractates
Meg.	*Megillah*
Neot	*Neotestamentica*
NIGTC	New International Greek Testament Commentary
NovT	*Novum Testamentum*
NTL	New Testament Library
NTOA	Novum Testamentum et Orbis Antiquus
NTS	*New Testament Studies*
OBT	Overtures to Biblical Theology
PMLA	*Proceedings of the Modern Language Association*
PNT	Personalities of the New Testament
PTMS	Pittsburgh Theological Monograph Series
RB	*Revue biblique*
RevExp	*Review and Expositor*
RNTS	Reading the New Testament Series
SacPag	Sacra Pagina
SBEC	Studies in the Bible and Early Christianity
SBL	Society of Biblical Literature
SBLDS	SBL Dissertation Series
SBLMS	SBL Monograph Series
SBLSS	SBL Symposium Series
SJLA	Studies in Judaism in Late Antiquity
SNTIW	Studies in the New Testament and Its World
SNTSMS	Society of New Testament Studies Monograph Series
t.	*Tosefta* tractates
TS	*Theological Studies*
ZNW	*Zeitschrift für die neutestamentliche Wissenschaft*

1

Narrative Criticism

and the Gospel of Mark

Wayne Booth, a prominent literary critic of our time, has written: "I do not think that if the world is not saved, all is lost. For me, one good reading of one good passage is worth as much as anything there is, because the person achieving it is living fully at that time. . . . I don't see how any such person should prove useless to the world."[1] Most biblical critics would drink to such an affirmation (some would simply say "Amen!") despite our very weighty responsibility for "saving the world." Revering the written word, peering reflectively into a text, and being deeply satisfied with the insights that it yields are common experiences of biblical critics.

One who peers into texts would likely also champion a statement of Yogi Berra (a luminary more familiar to us than Wayne Booth), who once philosophized: "You can observe a lot just by looking." Were Berra a hermeneutician, he might have added: "And *what* you observe depends a lot on what you *look for*." Biblical studies has historically adopted new methods for "observing" the text, each method "looking for" different characteristics of the text and the world implied by it. Thus, new insights about old texts have come from posing fresh questions, questions that highlight what was previously unnoticed or that show the familiar in a new light.

Literary criticism, or more precisely the branch of literary criticism that looks at the formal features of narrative, is one such fresh approach with new questions for Gospel studies. Biblical scholars have long practiced literary criticism, sharing source criticism and redaction criticism and form criticism in common with literature scholars. But literary criticism is a broad field encompassing many approaches to a text, and only recently have biblical scholars begun to investigate the formal features of narrative in the texts of the Gospels, features that include aspects of the story-world of the narrative and the rhetorical techniques employed to tell the story. I shall refer to such investigative areas of literary criticism as "the literary study of narrative," or *narrative criticism*.[2]

In order to expand our range of literary tools, then, I address the question, What do literary critics of narrative, such as Wayne Booth, look for when they delight in "one good reading of one good passage"? It would be impossible to account for all the techniques and approaches of narrative criticism, so I will here define briefly some basic areas of literary investigation into narrative: plot, conflict, character, setting, narrator, point of view, standards of judgment, the implied author, ideal reader, style, and rhetorical techniques. In examining these narrative features I will also ask, What have biblical scholars observed when they have peered into the Markan text looking for these features of the narrative? Much scholarship has been done on the Markan narrative, albeit in piecemeal fashion. This chapter gathers and reviews these contributions in relation to each area of literary investigation into narrative. At the end, I pose questions that point to further issues and future directions.

Shifts in Perspective

The value of looking at the plot, the characters, and the conflicts in Mark's Gospel seems patently clear. After all, Mark is a story, and a very good one at that. I had an early reservation about the narrative approach to Mark: Should we read ancient literature with methods developed primarily to read contemporary literature? I have discovered, however, that literary critics deal with features characteristic of many narratives. In addition, the better critics seem to take seriously the uniqueness of each narrative and also to interpret each story in the context of the age in which it was written.

Embracing the literary approach to the Markan narrative has involved for me two major shifts of perspective: one a shift from fragmentation to wholeness, the other from history to fiction.

From Fragmentation to Unity

The first shift has involved moving toward an emphasis on the unity of the narrative. Redaction criticism, form criticism, source criticism, and even composition criticism break up the narrative in order to get at the questions they pursue. Distinctions between redaction and tradition, between history and tradition, naturally fragment the text, a tendency that is reinforced by the designation of chapters, verses, and pericopae. By contrast, literary questions about narrative features tend to reveal Mark's Gospel as whole cloth.[3] For example, the narrator's point of view is consistent throughout. The plot has closure; that is, anticipated events come to pass, conflicts are resolved, predictions are fulfilled.[4] The characters are consistent from one scene to the next, fulfilling the roles they take on and the tasks they adopt.[5] Some rhetorical techniques, along with elements of style and organization, unify the narrative at many levels: phrase, sentence, grammar, episode, structure. And at a conceptual level, there is a consistent view of the human condition, sin, faith, ethical choices, God's rule, and the possibilities for human change. One can discover the unity of this Gospel in terms of the remarkable integrity of the "story" it tells, and one can come to trust that many apparent enigmas and discrepancies may be satisfactorily solved within the larger whole of the story. We know how to take the text apart to analyze it; employing narrative criticism in our study is an opportunity to reaffirm the original achievement of Mark in creating a unified story.

From History to Fiction

The other shift, from history to fiction, follows the first. By emphasizing the integrity of the narrative, one is able to enter the fictional
world of the story. By using the term "fiction" I do not mean to deny
that Mark used sources rooted in history or that his story does not
reflect historical events of Jesus' day. Rather, by "fiction" I mean to
suggest that the narrative world of the story is a literary creation of
the author and has an *autonomous integrity*,[6] quite apart from any
resemblances to the real world of Jesus' or Mark's time, in much the
same way as Leonardo da Vinci's portrait of Mona Lisa exists inde-
pendently as a vision of life quite apart from any resemblance or non-
resemblance to the model who posed for it. When looking at Mark as
literature, it is a referential fallacy, as Norman Petersen has shown, to
think that the statements expressed or implied in the narrative of
Mark are a "direct" representation of events in Jesus' day. Rather, the
narrative statements refer to the people, places, and events *in the story*
being told by the author.[7] The author has not simply collected traditions, organized them, made connections between them, and added
summaries; the author has told a story, a dramatic story, with characters whose lives we follow to the various places they travel and
through the various events in which they are caught up.

This shift to grasping the autonomy of the story-world is of fundamental importance, because narrative criticism works with the text as
"world-in-itself." Other approaches tend to fragment, in part because
their purpose is to put elements of the text into contexts outside the
text; so, for example, biblical scholars may identify the feeding of the
five thousand as a historical event in Jesus' time or as an oral story
emerging from the early church or as vehicle for a theological truth[8] or
as a story that reveals the author's intention, or as instructions to
Mark's community. Narrative criticism brackets these historical questions and looks at the "closed" universe of the story-world. (Of course,
knowledge of the history and culture of the first century is a crucial
aid to understanding Mark's story-world, but that is a different matter from using elements of a text to reconstruct historical events.) Recognizing the conceptual autonomy of the narrative world created by

the author of Mark is absolutely essential to the study of Mark as narrative. The feeding of the five thousand is a dramatic episode *in the continuum of Mark's story*—a miraculous feeding and a conflict between the teacher and his disciples, every detail vivid and relevant. The exorcisms, the healings, the journeys, and the trial and crucifixion are all events in the narrative world of Mark's story, each element important and integral. In the same way, Jesus, the disciples, Herod, and the centurion are all characters in the story-world of the Gospel. And the desert, the mountains, Nazareth, and Jerusalem are all settings in the narrative world of Mark's story.

When we see the narrative as containing a closed and self-sufficient world, with its own integrity, its own past and future, its own sets of values, its own universe of meaning, we are able to enter the marvelous world of this story. Boris Uspensky has articulated well the experience of entering a fictional world. He writes:

> In a work of art, there is presented to us a special world with its own space and time, its own ideological system, and its own standards of behavior. In relation to that world, we assume (at least in our first perceptions of it) the position of an alien spectator, which is necessarily external. Gradually we enter into it, becoming more familiar with its standards, accustoming ourselves to it, until we begin to perceive this world as if from within, rather than from without. We, as readers or observers, now assume a point of view internal to the particular work. Then we are faced with the necessity of leaving that world and returning to our own point of view, the point of view from which we had to a large extent disengaged ourselves while we were experiencing (reading, seeing, and so forth) the artistic work.[9]

Whatever Mark's Gospel may yield for us about historical events of Jesus' day or the circumstances of Mark's community or the values and beliefs of early Christians, as literature it represents first and foremost a story-world created by the author.

Story and Discourse

We return to the questions: What do critics of narrative look for? And what have Markan scholars observed? For an outline of narrative categories investigated by literary critics, I have followed Seymour Chatman. Chatman distinguishes the "what" and the "how" of narrative. The "what" is the *story*, apart from how it is told, including the chain of story events (stated or implied by the narrator, in chronological order), the characters, and the details of setting. The "how" of the narrative is the *discourse*, the particular way in which a given story is told, including the arrangement of events in the plot, the type of narrator, point of view, style, and rhetorical devices. The "what" and the "how," story and discourse, content and form, are obviously inseparable in narrative, and their interrelation is integral to the impact of a narrative. Only for purposes of analysis do we legitimately isolate a feature of narrative, such as character or point of view, and then only to interpret it in light of the whole narrative. But this fragmentary analysis, no matter how exhaustive, can never replace the unitary impact of the narrative itself.

We see the "what" and the "how" of Mark's narrative in Norman Petersen's distinction between *story time* and *plotted* (discourse) *time*.[10] Story time is part of the "what" of a narrative, while the plotted or discourse time reflects "how" the events are presented in the narrative. To reconstruct the story time, we simply take the references to all story events mentioned or represented in the narrative and rearrange them into their chronological order, from "the creation which God created" to the coming of the Son of Man (within a generation after the time of the character "Jesus"). This recounting of events represents the basic story in chronological time. By contrast, the time of the discourse or plotted time is the particular order or arrangement of these events in Mark's narrative. Hence, story time is the order in which events occurred in the story-world, while plotted (discourse) time is the order in which the reader learns of the events. By contrasting the sequence of events as introduced in the narrative with the implied chronological sequence in the story-world, Petersen is able to identify the devices Mark uses to plot the events of the story-world. These plot devices include anticipation, prediction and fulfillment (which Petersen considers the major device), recollection, flashback, repetition, and so on. If we attempt to read Mark's plotted narrative as if for the first time, asking what the reader knows and when the reader knows it, we can see how Mark's emplotment of events creates tension and suspense,[11] maintains interest, and conveys a sense of resolution or lack of resolution for the reader.

The Story

Chatman identifies the three elements of the story as plot (events), characters, and settings.[12] Plot refers to the order and movement of events in the story. Characters include all figures who appear in the story, including such forces as God and Satan. Settings involve not only spatial but also temporal settings.

Events: Conflict Analysis of the Plot

The basic story includes, first of all, the *events*. The movement of events in a story may be dealt with in a variety of ways. One way to approach events in a story is to focus on the conflicts. When conflicts are central to a story, it is important to understand their origin, the causes of their escalation or defusion, their climax, the resolution or lack of resolution. The protagonist of a story may be in conflict with nature or with supernatural forces or with other people or with society in general or within himself or herself. We see each of these types of conflict in Mark's story. In the Gospel, all these conflicts occur within the larger context of God establishing his rule over (against) all other powers and claims to authority, and the conflicts come to focus on the protagonist Jesus, the agent of God's rule. Furthermore, these conflicts are carried out on different levels. In direct conflict with demons, Jesus clearly has the upper hand and uses his authority from God to destroy them. Likewise, in direct conflict with the forces of nature, Jesus readily subdues or controls them. But Jesus has no authority from God to subdue people. He can heal only when people have faith. He cannot make them keep quiet. He cannot make his disciples understand, nor can he stop the society from executing him (except by ordinary means, which he does not employ). So Jesus' conflicts with people, being more evenly matched than those with nature or the supernatural, are the central and suspenseful conflicts in the story.

Jesus is in conflict with the authorities. Here Jesus is vulnerable because he has no authority to lord over people. Yet he is superior to the authorities because of his courage and cleverness in debate. Time and again he conveys his message while at the same time eluding their efforts to indict or destroy him. Joanna Dewey has charted the careful development in Mark's narrative of Jesus' conflicts with authorities, first in Galilee and then in Jerusalem.[13] She illuminates many specifics by showing each debate in its chiastic relation to other debates. In the Galilean debates, the opposition escalates to a climax with the opponents plotting to destroy Jesus, while, in the Jerusalem debates, the opposition diminishes and withdraws in defeat until there is no one left for Jesus to confront. The stories of debate vindicate the protagonist's understanding of God and Israel and display the illegitimacy of the authorities' subsequent execution of Jesus. Dewey's study also details the substance of the conflicts: legal issues, interpretation of the scripture, views of God's rule, authority, and so on. Seen within the values of the story, the running conflict between Jesus and the authorities (in terms both of issues and tactics) is consistently a stark clash between "thinking the things of God" and "thinking the things of humans."

Tannehill has shown that the key to the conflict between Jesus and the authorities is the irony of its resolution.[14] The authorities executed Jesus, but Jesus, for different reasons, wanted the same resolution that the authorities sought and even cooperated to make it come about. The authorities, who believe they are vindicated by Jesus' death, are really blindly carrying out a divine plan that ultimately seals their own destruction. The reader is aware that the ultimate resolution to the conflict within the story-world is not the death of Jesus but the reversal of this apparent defeat for Jesus when he is to return (within the story-world), this time in power, within a generation after his death.

Jesus is also in conflict with the disciples, but in this conflict he is not so superior. His task is more difficult and his efforts to get his disciples to understand and follow him are more than equally matched by their impenetrability and their fear. The details of the conflict have been traced by many. The substance of the conflict parallels the conflict with the authorities: the clash between thinking the things of God and thinking the things of humans. But the challenge is different. The one conflict is with people in determined opposition to him, the other with those who are trying to be his followers. Despite Jesus' best, almost desperate efforts—teaching, correction, example, demonstration, and so on—it is always uncertain, at best, whether Jesus will succeed in leading them to be faithful disciples.

Perhaps it is the subtlety and ambiguity of Mark's marvelously exasperating ending that explains why so many studies of Mark focus on the disciples. What is the resolution to this conflict? Theodore Weeden, Werner Kelber, Robert Tannehill, Thomas Boomershine, Joanna Dewey, Kim Dewey, Norman Petersen, and others, using literary methods, have dealt with this. There is no consensus; opinions differ radically. Most consider the conflict resolved favorably by the implied reunion of the risen Jesus with his disciples in Galilee. Others argue that the resolution is negative; the message to the disciples never gets through to them. Still others argue that the conflict is deliberately left unresolved by the narrator, who does not give enough information (or who gives information that is too ambiguous) for the reader to be able to determine the ultimate fate of the disciples (as characters in the story) in the rule of God.[15] A fascinating question: What is it precisely about each critic's interpretation of Mark—the literary methods involved, the evidence garnered from throughout the story, how the evidence is weighed—that leads to such diverse conclusions? We are not finished with this puzzle yet.

As Mary Ann Tolbert has reminded us, none of the lines of conflict in this story is to be seen in isolation from the others.[16] They weave in and out, crossing each other, while the narrative makes explicit and implicit connections, enriching each conflict by comparison and contrast with the others.

Characters

The "what" of narrative also includes *characters*. Characterization refers to authors' bringing characters to life in a narrative by "telling" about them and/or by "showing" them through (1) what they say, (2) what they do, and (3) how other characters perceive them or react to them. Understanding the characters is essential to comprehending the story. One major way to analyze characters is to focus on the characters' actions, evaluating the functions of their actions in relation to the plot of the story. This approach is most appropriate to narratives like Mark in which the development of plot predominates over the development of character. The other major way to analyze characters is to treat the characters as autonomous beings and to assess them in the same way we evaluate real people. Chatman argues for such an "open theory of character" based on the notion that we recall Huck Finn and Hamlet as we recall real people, not simply as a set of narrative functions.[17] In this approach, we analyze not only what characters do but also who they "are." The interpreter constructs what kind of "persons" the characters are from the narrator's descriptions and characterizations, the characters' interactions with others, their motives, and so on, then assigns them traits, noting how the traits are revealed and whether they change in the story. The interpreter constructs characters only from evidence suggested within the boundaries of the narrative world.

Chatman considers the assigning of traits to be an important part of the construction of characters. A trait is a personal quality of a character that persists[18] over whole or part of a story. The interpreter will find some traits named in the narrative and infer others from the characterization. Traits assigned to characters come from within the realm of traits familiar to the culture during the era of writing. The open approach to characters applies even to action-centered narratives like Mark, since traits derive in part from the actions of a character. E. M. Forster dubbed as "round" those characters with many and conflicting traits, characters who are complex and unpre-dictable.[19] By contrast, "flat" characters have fewer, usually consistent traits and are generally predictable. "Stock" characters are completely flat, having only one trait (e.g., "a crooked lawyer").

The protagonist is of course Jesus. Tannehill made a major break-through in the treatment of the character Jesus. To give content to the titles of Jesus, he looks at the narrative—the roles and tasks Jesus takes on and how he carries them out in relation to other characters. Tannehill shows how Jesus' commission from God comes not in the form of instructions that define the character but only as a designa-tion, "Son of God." So we must look to the way Jesus functions in the subsequent narrative as ameliorator, influencer, protector, and cor-rector in order to see what his character role is.[20] Tannehill focuses primarily on the functions of Jesus' actions in the plot.

By contrast, the "open view of character" advocated by Chatman would take a somewhat different tack, focusing on the character him-self, and reconstructing the character from descriptions by the narra-tor, what Jesus says and does, how others react to him, his motives and the causes of his actions,[21] how he compares and contrasts with other characters, his conflicts with others. From these we would con-struct a picture of the character "Jesus" in this story—his personal traits, his values and worldview, his attitudes, his style and the dynamics of his relationships, the integrity of his words and actions, his struggle and possible development of character. In addition to attributes like "authoritative," "innovative," "charismatic," Jesus' traits might include "clever," "abrasive," "frustrated," "impatient," "determined," "loyal," and so on. Although Jesus is not a round char-acter in the sense of having conflicting or changing traits, he certainly has a rich complex of many traits, the full extent of which only grad-ually unfolds in the course of the narrative. Such an open approach to character also liberates traditional studies of Jesus from the reduc-tionistic category of a "Christology," for even the so-called titles of Jesus may be considered epithets depicting his character.

The major antagonists of Jesus are the authorities. The opponents of Jesus, the religio-political authorities, are rather flat characters with a few consistent traits and predictable behavior. Anitra Kolenkow, followed by Joanna Dewey, has noted their consistent traits: they desire power and status, fear Jesus, defer to public pressure, and are destructive.[22] Robert Mulholland, in a dissertation that is only partly literary in its approach, has done the most complete study of Jesus' opponents in the Gospel of Mark. Further narrative analysis reveals additional carefully constructed patterns in the characterization of opponents: the different groups are connected by association with each other; the escalation and intensity of opposition to Jesus are carefully plotted; and the narrator's views into the minds of the opponents offer consistently negative portrayals. The opponents exemplify in attitude and behavior the negative values of "thinking the things of humans."

The disciples, who have many and conflicting traits, are the most rounded characters in the story. On the one hand, they are loyal and courageous, with a capacity for sacrifice, and perceptive enough to follow Jesus. On the other hand, they are afraid, self-centered, and dense, preoccupied with their own status and power. Ever since Theodore Weeden highlighted the predominantly negative portrayal of the disciples, Markan scholars have struggled to determine the precise nature and balance of Mark's characterization. Some literary approaches have incorporated historical information about the apostles to fill in the characterization of the disciples. Other recent studies have emphasized analysis of the narrative itself. Mary Ann Tolbert argues that the few positive characteristics of the disciples are present, in part, in order "to make a good story."[23] Joanna Dewey explains that, due to their negative portrayal, the disciples serve as foils for the character "Jesus" and provide questions or problems in the story as a way to maintain reader interest.[24] Thomas Boomershine thinks distance in characterization is crucial to an assessment of the disciples, the narrator maintaining a close distance between disciples and readers, a distance close enough to transcend the negative characterization. Obviously, the characterization of Jesus' disciples in this Gospel will continue to be debated.

There are also the minor characters. In his article on Jesus, Tannehill gives a depiction of those minor characters who are supplicants, correctly observing that although they may be treated together, they do not function as a group-character in developing interaction with Jesus (as the disciples and opponents do).[25] Almost all the minor characters (not just the supplicants), from Simon's mother-in-law to Joseph of Arimathea, share similar traits: a childlike faith, capacity for sacrifice, and a disregard for personal status and power. The literary function of the cameo appearances of these minor characters changes in relation to developments in the plot, the minor characters exemplifying emerging standards of judgment and serving as foils or parallels to other characters in various situations. Regarding other characters, Rebecca Patten has written about the role of the crowds in Mark's Gospel, and Ron Kittel has offered a literary treatment of John the Baptist. Also, by Chatman's definition of character, "an agent who takes plot-significant action," God as well as Satan qualify as characters. In our discussions of the theology of Mark, we might well analyze God's role in the story-world of the narrative.[26]

Settings

As an element of the "what" of narrative, *setting* is often quite integral to a story. Chatman says that settings can serve multiple functions—shaping atmosphere, contributing to a conflict, bringing out traits in a character, or providing symbolic commentary (sometimes ironic) on the action.[27] In Mark, setting is almost never irrelevant. Temporal settings (such as Sabbath, nighttime, and Passover) and spatial settings (such as desert, sea, mountain, synagogue, house, the way, Galilee, Jerusalem, and Temple) are all either indispensable to the drama of the story or, at minimum, greatly enrich it.

Most studies of Mark refer to the meaning and importance of at least some settings. Some studies have seen settings as central to the interpretation of the story. Werner Kelber sees the movement in the story from Jerusalem back toward Galilee as the means by which the author established a new place for his readers after the destruction of Jerusalem.[28] Kelber also views the sea as symbolic of the stormy passage from a Jewish to a Gentile mission, a view that has been challenged by Robert Fowler. Kelber later focused his retelling of the

Gospel around the setting of "the way."[29] Donald Juel, among others, has shown the central role of the Temple setting in Mark's Gospel. Willard Swartley has dealt with the interrelation of many settings, attempting to establish a narrative function for settings such as sea, mountain, wilderness, way, and Temple in light of the associations of these settings with Israel's history. We will do further studies on the narrative functions of settings as we establish a more thorough-going approach to the Gospel narrative.

The Discourse

The "how" of the narrative is discourse, the execution of the story into a narrative. An author might tell a story in any number of ways. At each point, the author chooses, consciously or unconsciously, how he or she will tell it. Wayne Booth uses the word "rhetoric" to depict all the choices and techniques an author uses to impose his or her fictional world upon the reader.[30] These choices and techniques include plot (arrangement of events), which we have discussed, narrator, point of view, standards of judgment, implied author, ideal reader, style, and rhetorical techniques.

The Narrator

Narrator is a literary term designating the storyteller of a narrative. The narrator is not the author but a rhetorical device the author uses to get the story told and to get it told in a certain way. The narrator may be a character in the story, perhaps the protagonist or a peripheral bystander. Or an unnamed narrator may be outside the story being told (but implicit in the narrative as storyteller): one who narrates in an object-style report; or one who, displaying limited omniscience, is able to narrate what is in the mind of the protagonist; or one who, displaying full omniscience, is able to narrate what is in the mind of any character at any time and place.[31] Once aware of the role of the narrator, the critic can observe carefully how the narrator guides the reader through the story.

Petersen has identified the salient characteristics of the narrator in Mark: the narrator exists outside the story being told; speaks in the third person; is an implied invisible presence in every scene, capable of being anywhere—with Jesus alone or with his opponents—to "report" the action; displays full omniscience by narrating the thoughts, feelings, or sensory experiences of many characters; often turns away from the story to give direct "asides" to the reader, explaining a custom or translating a word or commenting on the story; and narrates the story from one overarching ideological point of view. Regarding the persistence of these characteristics throughout the story, Petersen notes: "The rhetorical consistency of Mark's narrative is nothing short of remarkable."[32]

Understanding the role of the narrator unlocks many a mystery in the Gospel. Petersen encourages us to see that the Markan narrator has a different relationship with the reader than with the characters in the story being narrated. The narrator gives information to the reader that is not available to the characters in the story.[33] The omniscient narrator tells the reader in the first line (an "aside" to the reader) that Jesus is the Christ, while the characters in the story must yet discover this for themselves. The reader's inside knowledge in turn affects the reader's relationship to the characters; the reader, who knows about Jesus, experiences a tension in relation to the characters, who do not know about him. Hearing Mark's story for the first time is like watching a Hitchcock movie in which the viewer becomes aware of a threatening situation at the opening of the film, then nervously watches the unsuspecting characters in the story find out for themselves. Since the narrator is "the reader's guide through the imaginative world of the story,"[34] paying careful attention to the narrator's presence will illuminate every episode of this story.

Point of View

Point of view is also a part of the "how" of the narrative. The narrative reveals the point of view of the narrator, and the narrator in turn shows us the points of view of the characters, in the course of telling the story. We therefore distinguish between the narrator's point of view (narrator's voice) and a character's point of view. Uspensky offers a comprehensive analysis of point of view in narrative. He shows how point of view is evident in narrative on four different planes: (1) the ideological (the general evaluative system of viewing the world conceptually); (2) the phraseological (the use of words that introduce or identify point of view in dialogue); (3) the spatial and temporal (the physical place or the point in time from which someone views something); and (4) the psychological (states of the characters' minds, such as thinking, feeling, or experiencing). Using these distinctions to analyze point of view in Mark's narrative yields many insights. We can more clearly distinguish the narrator's point of view from those of the different characters, enabling us to portray more accurately the narrator and each character. We can see how the narrator guides the reader through the narrative, "showing" us what the opponents *think* about Jesus or how Jesus *sees* the faith of a cripple or that the disciples are too *afraid* to ask questions or *why* Herod protected John. Also, by showing a character's point of view or by showing it in an unsympathetic way, the narrator controls the reader's distance from or identification with various characters. Furthermore, by distinguishing the point of view of the narrator from that of the characters, we can see how the points of view of the various characters are encompassed within the overarching, consistent point of view of the narrator, who, as the storyteller, controls and often assesses the points of view of the characters.

Standards of Judgment

Reconstructing *ideological points of view* is fascinating. Every one of the ideological points of view in a text "claims to be the truth and each struggles to assert itself against the opposing ones."[35] Among the characters of the Markan story-world, there consistently seem to be only two basic ideological points of view, two mentalities, represented by the expressions "thinking the things of God," evident in Jesus and most minor characters, and "thinking the things of humans," reflected by the opponents of Jesus.[36] The disciples vacillate between the two points of view. The tightness and consistency of the Markan narrative in this regard is really quite extraordinary; Jesus' teaching establishes the values, attitudes, and actions involved in thinking the things of God, and the characters either exemplify that teaching or illustrate the contrary.

In order to fill out the full picture of these two basic ideological points of view, we can analyze the words, values, attitudes, beliefs, and actions of the various characters. We can also determine the ideological point of view of the narrator by analyzing the narrator's "asides" or comments on the story, explanations, descriptions of characters and events, view of scripture as authoritative, and establishment of characters as reliable or unreliable. The narrator's ideological point of view, or system of values and beliefs, represents the *standards of judgment* in the story, the overarching standards by which the reader is led to evaluate and judge all subordinate points of view (those of the characters) in the story. Petersen observes that the Markan narrator's ideology is consistently that of "thinking the things of God," a point of view the narrator shares with the central and reliable character Jesus.[37]

Implied Author

Closely related to the notion of narrator is the idea of the *implied author*. The implied author is reconstructed from a narrative by uncovering the "core of norms and choices" (standards of judgment) implicit in a work; that is, the implied author is equivalent to the overarching beliefs and values of the story along with the choices implicitly involved in "what" story is told and "how" it is told. The implied author is distinct from the *actual author*. The reconstructed viewpoint of the implied author is "not that of the (actual) author's world view in general, but only the viewpoint which the author adopts for the organization of the narrative in a given work."[38] We see this clearly when we contrast an actual author with the different cores of norms and choices implicit in several works by that same author. As Booth says, the implied author is the author's "second self," which the author creates in the course of writing a story and which is implicit in and not external to the work itself.[39] The implied author is also distinct from the narrator of a story. This is especially clear when the overarching norms of a story (the implied author's norms) lead the reader to consider that the narrator of that story is unreliable and cannot be counted on to give a valid interpretation of the events she or he is narrating. On the other hand, in a narrative like the Gospel of Mark, with a wholly reliable narrator, there is little or no difference (or distance) between the norms and choices of the implied author and the point of view of the (reliable) narrator.

Readers

The *ideal reader* is something of a mirror image of the implied author, seen from the receiving end of the communication of the story. Like the implied author, the ideal reader is implicit in the text and is distinct from any actual reader, ancient or modern. The ideal reader is a reconstruction of all the appropriate (ideal) responses suggested or implied by the text, whether it be surprise or suspense or puzzlement or understanding or whatever. Robert Scholes[40] defines the ideal reader as a "property of the text itself, each text implying a particular ideal reader, equipped with certain kinds of knowledge and experience, and capable of being manipulated in certain ways." In a sense, the ideal reader is "the image in the literary text of the reader as the (implied) author desires him [or her]."[41] Booth argues that the aim of literature is to make the actual reader conform to the image of the fictional ideal reader implied by the text. As the actual author creates a "second self" in writing, so also the reader, by entering a fictional world through reading, becomes "the self whose beliefs must coincide with the (implied) author's" if the work is to have its full effect.[42]

Study of the ideal reader implicit in Mark's narrative will not tell us about the actual first readers, but it may show us what image—of attitudes, values, beliefs, and actions—the author wanted the readers to become. Scholars have not done an extensive construction of the ideal reader in Mark's narrative, but several have suggested some overall patterns. Mary Ann Tolbert shows how Mark's story "creates its 'ideal reader' as it proceeds."[43] The story leads the ideal reader to identify with the hero, Jesus. So when the disciples betray Jesus by abandoning him, they also implicitly betray the ideal reader. Unlike the disciples, the ideal reader stays with Jesus through the trial and crucifixion to the tomb. By staying with the story to the end, the reader is more faithful than the disciples or the women at the tomb. Thus, the implied author has made of the ideal reader a faithful disciple in the process of narrating the Gospel. Presumably, then, this is the ideal image that the author wishes to impose on the actual reader. Joanna Dewey agrees that the ideal reader identifies with Jesus but is not so much betrayed by the disciples as left in doubt about their fate. Because the text alternately gives favorable and then unfavorable depictions of the disciples, the ideal reader is led to retain interest in the fate of the disciples to the end, even when their fate is still left somewhat in doubt.[44]

Robert Tannehill works with Wolfgang Iser's model of the *implied reader*, a concept somewhat different from the ideal reader. The implied reader incorporates not only "the prestructuring of the potential meaning by the text" (the ideal reader?) but also a real reader's "actualization of this potential through the reading process."[45] Tannehill argues that the text leads the reader initially to respond favorably to the disciples and to identify with them, but then to reject them along with their values. Through the negation of the accepted values of the disciples, the text leaves a gap for the actual reader to fill by seeking "a positive counterbalance elsewhere in the world familiar to him [or her]," which in this story-world is the value system of Jesus.[46] The negation of what might have been expected by the reader thus encourages the reader to take an active part in producing the meaning of the text by embracing the values of Jesus and deciding to follow his way.

Consonant with a major shift in literary criticism in the last two decades, the literary studies of Mark may focus less on the author and the author's intention (or even perhaps on the intention of the text) and more on the readers and the readers' responses. Clear distinctions between the ideal reader, the implied reader (of Iser's model), hypothetical "historical" readers of the first century, and actual contemporary readers (whose responses are valued apart from the prestructuring meanings of the text), will help to facilitate our debate on these matters.

Style and Rhetoric

Stylistic features and rhetorical techniques also point to the "how" of a narrative. Peter M. Wetherill shares a wealth of methodological resources for dealing with narrative *style*.[47] A narrative approach to style focuses on style as integral to the rhetorical act of communication between author and reader. How does the style of a story, as a part of "how" the story is told, affect the reader's experience of a story? Wetherill deals with sounds, grammar, vocabulary, meaning, stylistic techniques, rhetorical devices, and structure. Here we will deal briefly with Mark's style and rhetorical devices.

Mark's style is terse, words being suggestive rather than exhaustive, concrete rather than abstract. The narrator "shows" us the action directly and seldom tells about it indirectly. Most of the narrative is a representation of action, with little summary. The action moves quickly from scene to scene conveying the urgent *tone* by which the narrator addresses the reader. But the *tempo* varies; whereas early in the narrative the action shifts rapidly from one location to another and covers longer periods of time, the end of the journey slows to an hour-by-hour account of the crucifixion in a single location, Jerusalem. The choice of words throughout the story is simple and limited, yet the many key words that recur through the text (e.g., "handed over," "the way," "send," and so on) form verbal threads, enriched by repetition and deftly woven through the text to create an intricate design of motifs.

Also, the narrator uses many *rhetorical devices* to tell the story. The list that follows does not do justice to the work of many Markan scholars who have discerned patterns in the narrative: repetition of words within episodes for emphasis and thematic development;[48] repetition of words to form verbal threads or motifs through the story;[49] duality, a two-step progressive device found at every level of the narrative (description, dialogue, structure of episodes and the story as a whole);[50] repetition of similar episodes in series of three;[51] framing of one episode by another;[52] chiastic patterns within episodes; episodes (and description) in a pattern of concentric rings;[53] the use of rhetorical questions in the dialogue;[54] and the extensive use of various kinds of irony,[55] among others. The rhetorical devices uncovered by scholars constitute some of the most significant grounds for appreciating how carefully and cleverly Mark has told this story.

Parables and Quotations

Two further aspects of the style and rhetoric deserve mention: parables (riddles) and quotations from the scripture. A narrative analysis of all the parables in Mark suggests they are allegories that refer to actions and people and happenings in the past, present, and/or future of the story-world. Jesus tells parables either to obscure or clarify the meaning of those actions and happenings for other characters. Put another way, the parables are cryptic allegories about a hidden reality, or riddles about the kingdom of God. If some characters already perceive the hidden reality of the kingdom of God in the events surrounding Jesus, Jesus expects that the riddles will further explain God's rule for them. On the other hand, if characters do not discern the presence of the kingdom of God, Jesus expects the riddles will further obscure matters for them.[56] Thus, for the characters and indirectly for the readers (who have inside information about the presence of the kingdom of God in Jesus), the riddles of the sower, the strong man, the clean and unclean, the vineyard, and so on, all offer commentary and explanations about the meaning of actions and people and happenings in the story-world of Mark's Gospel. Likewise, the quotations from scripture function first and foremost for the characters in the story and only indirectly for the readers. All but two quotations appear in dialogue, where they reveal character and define conflicts. Jesus often quotes the scripture to explain to other

characters the meaning of actions and people and happenings in the
story-world. This device, putting on the lips of the protagonist riddles and quotations that explain the story-world, also serves to reveal
Jesus' knowledge and understanding while at the same time exposing
the ignorance and blindness of other characters, especially the opponents and disciples.

Conclusion

Based on an analysis of these many narrative features, the critic is
readily able to see the many themes and motifs running through
Mark's story. And putting the narrative back together, story and discourse, form and content, in order to show just what the story is
about represents a great challenge. Perhaps in terms of narrative criticism of Mark's Gospel, we are not yet ready to make these kinds of
integrative conclusions. While reporting on Markan scholarship,
our discussion has emphasized the need for further study of Mark's
narrative. And since literary criticism of narrative encompasses so
many resources and approaches (I have discussed here only some of
the standard areas of investigation), we can draw upon further
methodological procedures in order to broaden what we look for in
the narrative.

2

Narrative Criticism:

Practices and Prospects

Narrative analysis of New Testament writings had its beginnings in the 1970s with the seminal works of Norman Perrin, Thomas Boomershine, Joanna Dewey, Werner Kelber, Norman Petersen, Robert Tannehill, and Mary Ann Tolbert. It came into its own in the early 1980s with efforts to produce narrative analyses of each of the Gospels as a whole. Since then it has become popularly known among New Testament scholars as narrative criticism and has generated many fine studies of the narratives of the New Testament.[1]

The purpose of this chapter is to consider the practices and prospects of narrative criticism. After a brief introduction, I will proceed (1) by reflecting on critiques of narrative criticism (2) followed by some ways narrative analysis of the New Testament is being sharpened and broadened, (3) then by showing how some traditional disciplines and (4) some newer methods in biblical studies are being incorporated into the practice of narrative criticism, and (5) finally by dealing with the relationship between narrative interpretation and the ethics of reading.

Introduction

Narrative criticism has come to be understood as the analysis of the story-world of a narrative along with the analysis of its implied rhetorical impact on readers. First, the analysis of the story-world focuses on the world inside a narrative with its own times and places, its own characters, its past and future, its own set of values, and its series of events moving forward in some meaningful way. This story-world is neither the historical world depicted by the story nor the historical world of the situation in which the story was first told.[2] Rather, it is the imaginary world created by the narrative in its telling. Second, the analysis of a narrative's rhetoric focuses on the implied impact of a narrative both from the *story itself* as well as from the *way* it is told—with its distinctive style and point of view, set of literary techniques, and order of recounting.

Narrative criticism has been one of many new methodologies to arise in biblical studies in the last several decades. Narrative criticism has recovered the text as a story to be experienced, an experience that had been all but lost during the last two centuries of biblical studies.[3] As such, narrative criticism has recovered the story as a whole, instead of the fragmented pieces of historical criticism. In this way, narrative criticism has opened up new questions and areas of analysis of the text. It has helped to establish literary rhetoric as a legitimate way to study New Testament narratives and to pave the way for the development of reader-response criticism.

Narrative criticism's major contribution to biblical scholarship in general has been the establishment of the surface narrative of the text as a legitimate object of study. Many writers of monographs, commentaries, and articles now regularly deal with the narrative in its final form and of the story-world of the New Testament narratives without sorting out tradition and redaction or engaging in historical reconstruction from the text.

Critiques of Narrative Criticism

Narrative criticism arose in the context of the predominance of traditional historical-critical methods employed in Gospel studies—source criticism, form criticism, and redaction criticism. These methods generally explored the text for layers of tradition in order to construct the history of the early church from the time of Jesus to the time of the evangelists. Narrative criticism provided an alternative approach by shifting the focus from the world outside the Gospel to the world of the story itself. It involved other shifts as well: from the study of brief form-critical units to the study of a Gospel narrative as a whole; from reconstructing the layers of tradition and redaction to the analysis of the single surface layer of the final story; from the author as redactor to the author as creator of a story; and from how the author may have constructed the Gospel to how the readers may have experienced it.

In general, these shifts have meant the bracketing of earlier methods, because treating the reader's experience of the narrative in the integrity of its final form was methodologically incompatible with the layering of the text into redaction and tradition. Because the several methods could not easily be mixed into one method, there was need for narrative critics to embrace the new method as a discrete discipline.

Some critiques of narrative criticism, then, have come from those who use traditional methods. Other critiques have come from those who have moved beyond narrative criticism to postmodern literary methods. I would like to reflect briefly on four critiques of narrative criticism.[4]

Coherent Narratives?

Some scholars using traditional methods have argued that the Gospels are really such a patchwork of embedded traditions and authorial redactions that they cannot legitimately be treated as whole cloth. They argue that narrative criticism emphasizes too much the coherence of the narrative or assumes a unity that is not really there.

Therefore, although redaction criticism is itself far from exact, some scholars will continue to use redaction criticism as the primary basis for recovering the purposes of the Gospel writers, in some cases combining it with composition analysis. This is an important enterprise that will allow for helpful comparisons of the results of the two methods.

Narrative critics have used the coherence of the text as a working hypothesis, a heuristic device to discern fully the coherent patterns of storytelling on the surface level of the final narrative. In the case of Mark, some narrative critics have been so impressed with the pervasive signs of the coherence of the narrative world as to argue that it will be difficult now for scholars to distinguish tradition from redaction. Narrative critics might say the same with regard to Matthew or Luke, except that, with the Markan source in hand, they can see how these authors have changed their traditions. Nevertheless, narrative criticism does not necessarily weigh differently what authors of the Gospels have kept from their traditions and what they have added from their own hand. Matthew's free editorial hand, for example, could have omitted any part of Mark; as such, the author of Matthew may have kept parts of Mark precisely because they served his purposes every bit as much as his own redactions of that material. At a minimum, the evangelists have included or omitted material, modified it to a greater or lesser extent, and ordered it into a consecutive narrative. In the end, then, both tradition and redaction combine together to create something that is more than the sum of its parts, the narratives of the Gospels as the subject matter for interpretation.

Narrative analysis can certainly be aided by information about an author's redaction of sources. In many cases, such observations will confirm and inform a narrative analysis. We would be foolish to ignore insights that come from an integrated approach with form and redaction criticism. And attention to tradition and redaction can helps to reconstruct the trajectories in the tradition.

Nevertheless, the shift in narrative criticism from author to reader/hearer makes the study of redaction somewhat limited in value, for narrative criticism seeks to recover the final story the author has created for the reader. A first-century audience hearing a Gospel would have experienced it as a whole and not as pieces of earlier tradition. Readers/hearers of a Gospel were surely not listening to sort out tradition from redaction. Nor does the narrative reveal what its author rejected of its sources, Rather, hearers were absorbed in the story as it was being presented to them. And, in general, the Gospel writers succeeded in creating rather coherent reading/listening experiences for their audiences.

So, narrative criticism deals with how a reader experiences the story in its final form, even when there are places in which the story does not cohere so well. Thus, narrative critics may show where they find the narrative to be coherent and at the same time be open to its lack of coherence as a narrative. We see the problem most clearly, for example, in the Gospel of John, where there are awkward breaks in the narrative and where some characters are first mentioned as if they had already been introduced. Nevertheless, instead of returning to redaction criticism, narrative critics still take seriously the final form of the narrative as an audience might have experienced it—with all its faults and failures as a narrative. We need to develop a narrative poetics for each Gospel so as adequately to take into account all the peculiarities of that narrative without forcing it into a straitjacket of coherence.[5]

Detached from History?

Some critics argue that narrative criticism, by focusing on the story, has detached the narrative from its historical moorings. After all, the Gospels were about historical events, and the Gospels indirectly reflect historical events and circumstances at the time of their writing. As we have noted, before narrative criticism, the literary methods of source, form, and redaction criticism were pursued primarily in the service of historical reconstruction. Narrative criticism has succeeded in showing the value of the narrative in its own right, without serving as a handmaid to historical reconstruction. Nevertheless, narrative criticism affirms that a Gospel narrative is a historical artifact, a first-century contextual document fully conditioned by its time and place and representing one person's (one community's) conception of the world. More than ever, interpretations of the Gospel narratives are drawing upon our knowledge of the history, society, and cultures of the first-century Mediterranean world as a means to help us understand the story better.

As the fruits of narrative criticism become evident, it will be important to reassess traditional historical-critical disciplines in light of the results of narrative criticism. Rethinking redaction criticism and source criticism will be appropriate. It may also be possible for narrative criticism to contribute to historical criticism by finding some new ways to make inferences from the Gospel narratives and their rhetoric about the authors, audiences, and circumstances of the Gospels.

Narrative critics treat the Gospels as discrete "fictionalized versions" of the events they are depicting. At some level, therefore, the accuracy or inaccuracy of the events as recounted is not essential for an appreciation of the Gospels as first-century narratives. Nevertheless, it is an important part of the rhetoric of the Gospels that they do in fact make implied or explicit claims to be faithful depictions of actual people and events. Consider, for example, the explicit claims to historicity made by the Gospels of Luke (1:1-4) and John (21:24). As such, we can only fully understand the rhetorical impact of the Gospels when we see them as narratives presented as being about real events.

An Autonomous Narrative World?

Narrative criticism arose when New Criticism was prevalent among secular literary critics. New Criticism argued for the study of the text in its own right apart from authorial intention or reader responses. Texts were seen to have an independent autonomy, a kind of life of their own. However, even though we cannot recover the intentions of an author,[6] subsequent literary studies have made clear that there is no story-world apart from social context, and there is no story-world apart from the reading experience. This is equally true of ancient readers and modern readers. Apart from the reading experience, the text is only a series of marks on a page.

Hence, readers who are engaged in the act of reading give meanings to words, use their imagination, attribute emotions, fill in gaps, make connections, among many other tasks. For example, the sparseness of language in characterizations by the Gospel writers especially invites reader participation.[7] One of the results of such reader participation is that there is no single authoritative reading, only various readings. As such, narrative critics will deal with the role of a reader in analysis and interpretation—both in the construction of ancient readings as well as in the readings of modern readers, including critics. At the same time, it is important to remember that when narrative critics are constructing the reading experience of a hypothetical "ideal reader" or the imaginative reading experiences of ancient audiences, it is, of course, the narrative critics themselves as readers who are constructing these imaginary reading experiences of the first century.

Unified Narratives?

While the earlier critique about coherence comes from traditional historical critics, a somewhat different concern about unity comes from literary postmodern critics. As we have said, narrative criticism tends to look for the unifying patterns of a text as the basis for interpretation. Each line is interpreted in the context of the whole. Where paradoxes and contradictions occur, the narrative critic seeks to relate them to each other in light of the whole. However, postmodern critics point out that by its very nature, at a fundamental level, narrative is not unified—not just ancient Gospels, but even carefully crafted modern fiction.[8] Narratives overflow with a surplus of meaning, and they are full of gaps, fissures, contradictions, ambiguities, multiple meanings and connotations, and a lack of connection between possible causes and consequences. Therefore, any effort to provide an airtight unified interpretation of a writing will be illusory; indeed, it may do violence to the complexity and multi-valence of that narrative. So, postmodern critics read and interpret "against the grain" of standard interpretations in order to expose the gaps and contradictions in texts and interpretations.

Narrative critics will do well, therefore, to acknowledge the complex nature of narrative. Perhaps the goal of narrative criticism is not so much to discern the unity of a text as it is to assess its impact—to see in what ways a narrative coheres adequately to give a satisfying reading experience. With this more modest goal in mind, narrative critics will continue to look for patterns of coherence and at the same time be aware of what they notice and also learn from reading against the grain. They will continue to interpret portions of narrative in light of the whole, seeking to avoid imposing unity where it does not exist and with the recognition that the goal of finding total unity in texts are clearly illusory.

Sharpening and Broadening of Narrative Criticism

The parallel to narrative criticism in secular literary criticism is the discipline of narratology—the theory and practice of narrative analysis. There are many works in narratology dealing with narrative as a whole, and there are works that represent particular developments in the understanding of character, plot, setting, standards of judgment, point of view, and literary-rhetorical analysis.[9] These developments in narratology will continue to be of benefit to narrative critics of the Bible.

Strengthening Narrative Criticism

Thus, narrative critics of the Bible may continue to sharpen their capacity to do narrative analysis. For example, narrative critics continue to grow in the discernment of patterns of storytelling, such as parallelism, forms of repetition,[10] and irony.[11] Work is being done with the symbolic language of the Gospel of John.[12] Style could become a greater focus of attention. Point of view can be informed by a treatment of the narrator's tone in addressing the audience. The concept of standards of judgment is yielding many insights into the moral world of a narrative. The study of setting is taking greater account of all the structures of the narrative world, including the sociopolitical ethos and the cosmology.[13] The analysis of character can enable critics to clarify an author's view of the human condition.[14] There could be greater efforts to understand the interrelation between plot, conflict, setting, and tone as a way to see more clearly the "world" offered by the narrative to the reader.[15]

In general, narrative critics have tended to aim their work at the whole narrative of a Gospel.[16] However, there are now also appearing detailed and careful treatments of particular episodes, as they can be understood in their context in the whole Gospel.[17]

Reader-Response Criticism

Narrative criticism will continue to give greater attention to the reader by combining its treatment of narrative with *reader-response criticism*.[18] Reader-response critics range across a spectrum, from a text-centered approach (the text determines the reading experience) to reader-centered approach (the reader determines the reading experience). Narrative critics lean toward the text-centered approach, because they want to understand the narrative better as a means to assess what impact the narrative might have had on first-century readers. In this regard, various theories about ideal readers have become useful—the ideal reader being not a real reader but a construction of the possible implied responses of an ideal reader through the course of the narrative.[19] The ideal reader represents what the author wants the real reader to become in the course of reading. Reader-response critics can help us to revise our understanding of the ideal/implied reader, because we have tended, inappropriately, to construct these imaginary readers as readers without a social location.

Thus, text-centered reader-response criticism is interested in the *literary rhetoric* of a story. Initially, relying on the work of Seymour Chatman, narrative critics limited the definition of rhetoric to the style of discourse an author used to tell the story, distinguishing the "what" of a narrative (story) from the "how" of a narrative (discourse or rhetoric). Now, however, there is reason to rethink this approach:

the rhetoric of a narrative refers to the overall impact of a story in its telling. As such, rhetoric is more than the impact of the events of the story. It is more than the stylistic features and literary devices by which the story is told.[20] Rhetoric is a combination both of the content of a particular story and of the literary style and devices used to tell it—in the diachronic experience of the narrative by the readers. Thus, rhetoric has to do not only with what the story *means* but also with what the story *does* to the hearers in the course of its telling. A narrative like one of the Gospels affects the readers in the process of reading so that readers are led to become something different as a result—people who embrace certain beliefs or values, become faithful followers of Jesus (Mark) or disciples who teach what Jesus has taught (Matthew) or followers who will share their wealth (Luke) or people who believe and have eternal life (John).

The New Testament narratives offer a significant challenge to critics seeking to understand the dynamics and power of their rhetoric, for they were composed as part of an effort to create and shape communities, to make available divine resources for transformation, and to announce judgment and salvation. One of the tasks of narrative criticism, then, is to deal with these questions: What are the New Testament narratives doing? And, literarily, how do they do it?

Reception Criticism

Also, *reception criticism* can be of assistance here as a helpful way to discern how actual readers from ancient times to the present have reacted to a particular writing. Reception criticism can thus be seen as a branch of reader-response criticism, because it looks at the way in which readers down through the ages have received, understood, and appropriated a Gospel—often evident in the history of commentaries on a particular writing. For example, insights into the Gospel of Mark come by seeing how Matthew and Luke reacted in their reading of Mark—as implied by their revisions of Mark. In a time when so many international scholars are entering biblical studies, reception criticism can now expand to encompass not only reception of a biblical writing through Western history but also the diverse receptions of it in contemporary global arenas.

Speech-Act Theory

Further insights about the impact of a narrative on the reader may also come from the literary branch of study called *speech-act theory*. Speech-act theory assesses the whole range of performative functions of language in the interaction between speaker and receiver.[21] This approach began in the philosophical analysis of language. In literary criticism, it has been applied to interpret whole pieces of literature as speech-acts. Speech-act theory has many important implications for the study of biblical narrative and dialogue.

Application to Other Genres

Finally, narrative criticism is broadening its scope and proving to be useful in analyzing literary works that are not primarily narrative in nature but which have narrative dimensions. For example, it is possible to analyze the occasional letters of Paul by reconstructing the chronological story of the past events that are portrayed or mentioned in the letter and the potential future events projected by the letter, and then to see the letter as a moment in the story surrounding the letter—with its own plot, characters, settings, point of view, tone, standards of judgment, and rhetoric.[22] Also, writings such as the book of Revelation may be analyzed for the same formal features of narrative.[23]

Incorporating Some Traditional Disciplines

Ancient Narrative

Narrative critics enhance their analysis of biblical narratives by comparison with other ancient literature. They begin by consulting treatments of narrative in ancient literary handbooks, such as Aristotle's *Poetics*, and then they study the features of narrative expressed in ancient writings that are parallel to the New Testament narratives.[24] Also, the presentation of characters in ancient biographies and novellas can be an important means for understanding New Testament narratives.[25] Not only analogies with Greco-Roman literature but also recent narratological studies of the Hebrew Bible should be explored more extensively as ways of enhancing our understanding of the dynamics of New Testament narratives.[26]

Genre Criticism

In addition, genre criticism is increasingly important for narrative analysis. Seeing a Gospel as representing a particular genre—whether tragedy or biography or romance or apocalypse—helps to identify an implied audience, the social ethos, the issues being dealt with, and the expectations that an audience brings to a story.[27] Thus, genre studies help to imagine contexts for the reception of the Gospels in antiquity. Genre studies are complex, because narratives seldom fit into a single category of genre. One may decide that a Gospel represents a mixed genre or a subversion of a familiar genre or even a new genre. Nevertheless, any comparisons and contrasts with other similar writings of the time can be helpful in clarifying the nature of a Gospel.

For example, a recent approach to genre analysis of the Gospel stories deals with rhetorical criticism and employs classical, Greco-Roman rhetoric of argumentation.[28] Critics take individual stories from the Gospels and analyze them as the narrative equivalence of speeches—representing species of argumentation, showing an order of argumentation, and manifesting techniques of ethos, pathos, and logos.[29] Such analyses may be a helpful way to inform an understanding of plot and character, point of view, standards of judgment, and the narrative rhetoric of persuasion. The fruitfulness of this approach is just beginning to be apparent, and it is not yet clear if the approach can be sustained over the narrative of a whole Gospel.[30]

Incorporating Some New Disciplines

While narrative criticism has many parallels to narratology, narrative criticism is taking its own unique shape because of the particular nature of the literature under study. For example, the Gospels are examples of oral/aural literature that was designed to be heard and not read. Also, the Gospels originated from a culture very different in time and place from our modern world. In addition, the Gospels were all shaped by their political context under the aegis of the Roman Empire. As a means to take full account of such factors, narrative critics are incorporating insights and approaches from other fresh disciplines in New Testament studies.

Orality Criticism

Orality criticism focuses on the aural reception of oral performances of literature in an oral culture. It is clear that the Gospels were written to be performed to audiences in a predominantly nonliterate culture. Considerable work has been done on the qualities and features of oral literature and on the context and impact of the aural reception of it.[31] Most of the work has been done on the Gospel of Mark,[32] but all the narratives of the New Testament were written to be performed aloud to a listening audience.[33]

The connection with narrative criticism (and reader-response criticism) is immediately obvious. Critics are reframing narrative criticism by conceiving of the narrator as a performer, of a temporal rather than a spatial (on the page) experience of a Gospel, of forecasts and echoes rather than foreshadowings and retrospections, of hearers (probably in a group as an audience) rather than private readers, of type scenes rather than forms, and of diverse examples of repetition with variation.

Hearers of a Gospel can listen to the narrative for its sounds and rhythms.[34] Here careful attention is given to word order—foregrounding, backgrounding and elision, as well as to synonymous and antithetical parallelism and chiastic patterns. The development of "sound charts" to identify repetitions and alliteration help to bring out the aural experience of the text.[35] The Gospel of Mark, for example, offers a hearing experience of verbal echoes both within and between episodes. The teachings in the Sermon on the Mount reveal parallel and chiastic patterns of sound and rhythm. The alliteration and lilt of the Gospel of John may be part of a rhetorical aesthetic designed to draw hearers into the experience of eternal life. Also, *hearers* of narrative will have a different experience of characters in a Gospel than *readers* do. Because the performer addresses the hearers directly with the speech of each character, hearers are led to identify with as well as be addressed by *all* the characters. In this way, the story also becomes an emotional experience (similar to viewing a film), rather than simply a source of information.

Performance Criticism

The interpreter may also relate to narrative in terms of *performance criticism* and may even practice being the narrator as performer.[36] Preferably, this is done in the Greek language, but the experience also bears much fruit by performing translations that attend to the oral/aural features of the narrative.[37] Such an experience of performing recovers a new level in the analysis of narrative, because oral performers must make interpretive decisions not only about what a line *means* but also decisions about *how* a line is to be delivered. Every line has a *subtext*—the message that is being conveyed by *how* the line is said. Every subtext is determined from the lines themselves in the context of the episode and of the story as a whole, as if one were discerning stage directions in the script of a play. Oral performance can be a test of interpretation, because it is difficult to find a way to deliver some lines with the meanings attributed to them in some interpretations.[38]

One can readily see the applicability to character analysis, for example. Performers will place themselves in the position of each of the characters and clarify the differing points of view in a narrative. Performers will notice the distinctive speech patterns of the different characters and will attempt to identify subtexts for the lines of the characters that are suggested by the text. Also, the interpreter as performer will bring out emotive dimensions of the text in new ways, because characters speak with amazement or fear or surprise or irony. Recently, efforts have been made to construct the manner of an ancient performance of Mark, based on suggestions culled from rhetorical handbooks from antiquity.[39] It remains to be seen how this may help us in the interpretive process.

Social-Science Criticism

Narrative critics can also benefit from the discipline of *social-science criticism*. The world of the story represents one example from antiquity of a social construction of reality. It is crucial, therefore, to use all the tools we have to understand the nature of that social construction. Because the narrative worlds of the Gospels reflect ancient society, interpretation becomes a cross-cultural process. The question is, how can we begin to construct the shared cultural assumptions that enabled ancient readers to understand the story and to fill in the gaps of the texts? In order to address this question, narrative critics turn not only to the knowledge we have about the first century from literary and material artifacts but also to the use of cultural models that help to organize and interpret the ancient cultural information in the narrative—thus helping us to avoid imposing the conceptions of the world we bring from our experiences in the twentieth century.

Social-science criticism employs models from sociology and anthropology as heuristic devices to enhance our understanding of ancient biblical cultures.[40] The Mediterranean societies of antiquity had parallels to current Mediterranean cultures. Therefore, models based on studies of contemporary Mediterranean cultures—models dealing with honor and shame, dyadic personality, purity and defilement, economy of limited goods, patron-client relations, kinship patterns, among others—are helpful in understanding ancient society. Because a Gospel narrative is a relatively coherent slice of life from cultures that these models reflect, it is possible to use these models to unpack the dynamics of the story-world. The use of the models helps to articulate reading scenarios, representing the framework of assumptions and expectations that first-century readers might have brought to their experience of the story.[41]

The social-science approach has been employed fruitfully to illuminate the narratives of the Gospels.[42] Issues of honor and shame illuminate the conflicts in the plot.[43] An understanding of ancient economy informs the standards of judgment regarding wealth and poverty.[44] Studies of purity and defilement help to clarify the ethos of the setting.[45] So also do cross-cultural treatments of sickness and healing.[46] Models about the importance of eating and food shape our understanding of meal settings. Models of social change distinguish the features of the Jesus movement depicted in the various Gospels.[47] Social-science commentaries on the Gospels have helped to integrate many of these models into a greater understanding of the narrative.[48]

Especially in relation to characterization in the Gospels, the social-science approach is helpful as a means to understanding the dyadic cultures of ancient Mediterranean societies, that is, cultures in which people depend on the group to which they belong for their identity. Features of dyadic cultures include the tendency to stereotype, the importance of kinship (both natural and fictive), a contrasting treatment of insiders and outsiders, the lack of introspection—all of which provide important heuristic insights into the portrayal of characters in the Gospel narratives.

Narrative criticism and social-science criticism work well together.[49] Social-science criticism helps to clarify the common assumptions made by author and hearers in the act of communication. At the same time, the detailed attention to the text offered by narrative criticism helps to give specificity and qualification to the abstract and generic nature of the models. And it applies social-science criticism to the narrative *as a narrative world.*

Social Location

One of the most helpful aspects of the social study of the narrative worlds of the Gospels is the identification of *social location* within the structure of ancient society and its cities.[50] Pre-industrial, agrarian societies were organized hierarchically with (1) a small ruling elite (2–3 percent) along with (2) their scribal and mercantile retainers, below which were (3) the masses of peasants (about 95 per cent) living at a basically subsistence level, in addition to (4) a small percentage of "expendable" people comprised of unclean and other marginalized groups.[51] This economic and political ordering of an honor-shame society, without a middle class, becomes an important framework for interpreting the narrative world of a Gospel—the ethos of the settings, the nature of the conflicts that comprise the plot, and the social location of the various characters.

In studying the narrative world, attention to social location especially helps to amplify character analysis, because characters can be identified by their cultural origin, social status, economic level, kinship identification, gender, honor rating, state of purity or defilement, health, occupation, education, religious allegiances, urban/ rural origin, and so on. The idea is not simply to identify the social locations of the characters, but to use what we know of the society as tools to interpret better the narrative and the characters and conflicts in it.

Analysis of social location and power relations can also helpfully be applied to the authors and audiences of the New Testament narratives.[52] Rather than simply identifying geographical origin and date of a biblical writing, scholars can seek to infer from each Gospel a range of factors that help to identify the social location of the narrator/author and the implied audience of a writing. Where does this writing fit into ancient society? Whose interests do the beliefs and values promoted by the narrative serve? What power or rhetorical force does the narrative use to have its way? What kind of society does the narrative serve to subvert or reinforce or shape or generate? All these questions increase our capacity to clarify the rhetoric of a Gospel in relation to its audience.

In addition, a model of social location in antiquity may be a helpful heuristic device to imagine the responses of imaginary readers from many different social locations in the society of the audience—elites, a slave, peasants, a Roman soldier, a leper, and a Pharisee. Placing oneself in such imaginary roles of reading will better show how the text might have worked rhetorically in its ancient context—that is to say, what values and beliefs does the narrative reinforce and which ones does it seek to subvert and replace.

Ideological Criticism

Ideological criticism goes hand in glove with the identification of social location,[53] because it asks questions of power. Ideological criticism assesses the power relations between and among the characters from different social locations as the plot develops. What are the values and beliefs of the different characters? What access to differing kinds of power does each character and character group have? Who oppresses and who is being oppressed? Whose interests are served by the beliefs and values and the exercise of power of the different characters? These questions have led to studies that recover the political dimensions of the Gospel narratives.[54] Feminist critical studies in particular have unpacked the power dynamics between females and males in the world of the story and asked whether the plot works to overcome or to reinforce patriarchy, and in what ways.[55]

Postcolonial criticism

From the larger number of international scholars active in biblical studies has emerged *postcolonial biblical criticism*. At first, the focus was on the ways in which interpretations of the Bible have served the interests of colonial powers in their domination of colonized societies and the ways in which people from colonized countries can now find their voices in biblical interpretation after a long history of colonization. More recently, the focus has shifted to show how the biblical texts themselves are colonial or anti-colonial documents (or a mixture of the two) in relation to the imperial domination of the Roman Empire in the first centuries. Initial studies have shown the ways in which biblical writers seek to subvert the empire by adopting the dynamics of empire and depicting God as a superior imperial force. Such an analysis of the political dynamics of the Gospels will sharpen and make more complex our grasp of the narrative depictions of the kingdom of God. In this way, narrative criticism can deepen its understanding of the imperial and anti-imperial dynamics within the narrative worlds of the Gospels as well as in regard to the overall rhetorical impact of the Gospels vis-à-vis the audience as subjects of the Roman Empire.

Responsible Interpretation

Narrative criticism is also beginning to benefit from reflection on the relatively new field of the *ethics of* reading—reflection on the moral responsibility involved in the process of reading and interpreting as contemporary readers.[56]

Contemporary readers may think of reading as a dialogue—a meaningful exchange between the story and the reader.[57] Each partner has power and influence on what happens in the dialogue. On the one hand, a story seeks to influence readers—to affect them for good or for ill, to change people, and to shape communities. On the other hand, a reader also has power in this dialogue with the story. Readers can take a story seriously and be affected by it or they can be indifferent or resistant and have strong objections to the story. A reader can also use the story in ways that may be helpful or harmful to others.

In the dialogue with the story, narrative interpreters are responsible to allow the story of a Gospel to have its influence in this dialogue, by reading the story on its own terms and for its own time. In this dialogue with a story, the reader has the responsibility to treat the story with respect, to listen carefully over and over again—seeking to limit our tendency to impose alien ideas and images onto the story. It is important to assume that the story will be different from what we expect it to say or want it to say or fear it might say. Aware of our limited and relative perspective, we can make our social location, our reading communities, our assumptions, and our perspectives explicit from the start,[58] thereby helping us to avoid inappropriately reading them into the story. Also, it is important to identify the strengths, limitations, and liabilities in the methods we are using.

Of course, every interpretation will be only one interpretation in a range of faithful interpretations.[59] Given the multivalent nature of language and the limitations of reader perspectives, it is not possible (or even desirable) to provide one correct and objective understanding of a story. The goal is to be faithful to the narrative (given the parameters of the methods and criteria we are using) and to learn from other interpretations as well.

Once we have allowed a Gospel to address us on its own terms, the dialogue can begin to move to the modern reader's side of the equation: How does the story relate to contemporary life? On the one hand, we may resist many parts of a Gospel narrative—certain beliefs, depictions of demons, a compromising duality, an anti-Jewish thrust, patriarchy, or a glorification of suffering. Where the interpreter differs with the story, the idea is not to reinterpret the story to make it look acceptable, but to let the story say what it says and then to object honestly to those aspects of the story we find disagreeable or abhorrent.

At the same time, because this is a genuine dialogue, we need to be open to the ways in which the story as a whole may be potentially transforming for us.[60] Real dialogue involves risk, the possibility of being changed by our encounter with the text. We modern readers can enter the story-world in imagination and by immersion can allow the story to work its magic on us, as well as be careful not to use the story in ways that can harm others. Thus, whatever our interpretation, readers have an ethical responsibility for their interpretations— to promote the ways in which interpretations may serve the good and to counter those interpretations that will bring harm and oppress people.

Narrative critics are also learning the importance of reading and interpreting with others from different social locations. Every reader has a relative perspective due to national identify, social location within that society, and personal experiences, beliefs, and values.[61] Each perspective has its own angle of vision that will enhance understanding but that may also inhibit understanding.[62] By reading together we can learn from what others notice, we can correct each other, and we can guard against universalizing an interpretation. Again the ideological questions apply: Whose interests are being served by this or that interpretation? How can interpreters take responsibility for their interpretations? The recent discipline of *cultural exegesis* recognizes the importance of reading with people from many different cultures and social locations at a round table in which no positions are privileged or no positions are marginalized, with each participant bringing unique insights and understandings from their perspective.

Conclusion

There are many exciting new directions taking place in narrative criticism that are enabling students of biblical narrative to become even better practitioners of narrative analysis and at the same time to have that practice enhanced by integrating insights and methods from other approaches to New Testament. All the writings of the New Testament, as well as many writings outside the canon, provide opportunities to bring narrative analysis to bear upon a better understanding of a wide range of ancient literature.

3

Losing Life for Others in the Face of Death: Mark's Standards of Judgment

One way to understand the purpose of the Gospel of Mark is to discern the standards of judgment for human behavior that govern the narrative.[1] The standards of judgment are the values and beliefs implicit in the narrative world by which readers are led to judge the characters and the events.[2] The narrator does not "tell" us what these standards are. Rather, the narrator "shows" us these standards in the depiction of characters and the description of events.

Thus, we infer the standards of judgment from features of Mark's narrative, such as evaluative comments by the narrator, the teachings of Jesus, the actions and fate of the characters, the words of God, quotations from scripture, and so on. From these, we can see the positive standards that the narrative promotes as well as the negative standards that the narrative condemns. Mark engages in a rhetoric of contrast whereby he promotes one set of standards and at the same time condemns the opposite set of standards. Seeing the positive and negative standards in juxtaposition to each other is illuminating. From the standards of judgment, we get a picture of the moral backbone and purpose of the Gospel.

The Two Ways: Saving One's Life
or Losing One's Life for Others

A study of standards of judgment shows that the Gospel of Mark is a tightly woven narrative reflecting two contrasting ways of life. At one point in the narrative, Jesus rebukes Peter, saying: "Get behind me, Satan, because you are not thinking the things of God but the things of humans" (8:33). Here is a contrast between two sets of values, two orientations to life: (1) the things of God, that is, what God wills for people and (2) the things of people, that is, what people want for themselves (what people think in their fear and blindness is best for themselves).

The Markan Jesus states these contrasting standards at the beginning of the journey to Jerusalem (8:22–10:52). On the way there, Jesus elaborates these standards in teaching to his disciples. The disciples resist Jesus at every point, even though they eventually accept his teachings. So the journey becomes a clash of values between Jesus who teaches what God wills for people and the disciples who exemplify what people want for themselves. On the way, Jesus prophesies three times to the disciples about his impending persecution and death (8:31–9:1; 9:30-50; 10:32-45). After each prophecy, the disciples show that they do not understand or accept his teaching. After each of these reactions, Jesus explains to his disciples the values of the rule of God that underlie his words and actions.

The teachings that follow these three prophecies on the way to Jerusalem are the core standards of Mark's Gospel. After the first prophecy, Jesus says, "Those who want to save their lives will lose them, but whoever will lose their lives for me and the good news will save them" (8:35). After the second prophecy, Jesus teaches: "If anyone wants to be great among you, that person is to be least of all and everyone's servant" (9:35). After the third prophecy, Jesus says: "Whoever wants to be great among you will be your servant, and whoever wants to be most important is to be everyone's slave. For even the son of humanity came not to be served but to serve and to give his life as a ransom for many" (10:43-45).

Each of these teachings involves a contrast between acquisition (saving one's life) and relinquishment (losing one's life for the good news).[3] People who follow the world's standards seek to acquire wealth, status, and power for themselves. This way of life is motivated by fear. By contrast, people who follow Jesus' standards welcome the blessings of the kingdom and are thereby enabled to relinquish life, status, and power in order to bring the blessings of this kingdom to others. This way of life is made possible by faith and grants courage. Thus, for Mark, the two ways of life are "saving one's life out of fear" or "losing one's life for others out of faith." The one way involves securing one's life for one's self, and the other way involves risking one's life for others. The following chart shows the characteristic Markan standards of these two ways.

What People Want for Themselves	*What God Wants for People*
self-centered	other-centered
save one's own life	lose one's life for the good news
acquire the world	give up possessions
be great	be least
lord over others	be servant to all
be anxious	have faith
fear	courage
harming others	saving others
loyalty to self	loyalty to God for the world

Mark's narrative consistently promotes the one way and condemns the other.[4] As such, the characters in Mark's narrative are stereotypical figures who embody one or the other of these two ways.[5] Jesus embodies "what God wills for people." He heals, drives out demons, pardons sins, feeds hungry people, confronts oppressors, and dies as a result of being persecuted for this mission. Also, the minor characters who come to Jesus for healing often exemplify "the things of God." They have faith and are willing to serve and to be least. By contrast, the Jewish and Gentile authorities embody "what people want." Because they are afraid, they seek to save their honor and to maintain their positions of power.[6] They aggrandize themselves at the expense of others. Finally, the disciples vacillate between the two ways. They are torn between following Jesus in service to the good news, on the one hand, and following Jesus in order to acquire status and power for themselves, on the other. In these characterizations, Mark promotes the values and beliefs of the kingdom by positive example, and Mark rejects the opposite values and beliefs by negative example. Mark means to persuade hearers of his Gospel to embrace values that will create a society of mutual service, free from oppression.

The Way of the World: The Fearful Saving of Self

The negative standards reflect Mark's view of human sinfulness, namely, that people are self-oriented and self-serving. People want to "save their lives" (8:35), to "acquire the world" (8:36), to "be great" (9:35), and to "lord over" people (10:43-44).

The Judean and Gentile Authorities

As indicated, the authorities are given a stereotypical characterization to illustrate the negative standards. As depicted in the narrative, they exemplify the fearful saving of self.[7] They have status, power, and security, and they are bent on maintaining them. They have taken control of the vineyard of Israel for themselves and do not bear the fruit on behalf of Israel's people, which God requires of them (12:1-12). They love their importance and they abuse their power: They love to be greeted in the markets; they want the best seats in the synagogue and at the banquets; and they devour the houses of widows (12:38-40). At the crucifixion, they ridicule Jesus because he "cannot save himself" (15:31).

For Mark, the quest to maintain power and status is motivated by fear (11:18). In the Markan portrayals, the Jewish and Gentile authorities are afraid. Herod fears John the Baptist (6:20). Pilate defers to the crowd (15:15). The leaders in Israel fear Jesus' popularity (15:10).

They fear losing their position as a result of Jesus' activity (12:7), and they fear losing face with the crowds (6:26; 12:12). Such fear is the opposite of faith/trust in God, which brings courage in the face of threat and loss.

To protect their power and status, the authorities destroy others. Although Herod considers John the Baptist to be a righteous man, he nevertheless executes John because he does not want to break his oath to Herodias's daughter, for fear of losing face before "the most important" and "the greatest" people of Galilee (6:26). Although Pilate thinks that Jesus is innocent and that the high priests have handed him over out of envy, he nevertheless executes Jesus in order to "do the satisfactory thing" for the crowd (15:15). Also, out of envy, the Jewish leaders seek to trap, discredit, and destroy Jesus. They bend the law, arrest Jesus surreptitiously (14:7), suborn witnesses (14:55), hold a kangaroo court (15:3), and stir up the crowd to release Barabbas (15:11)—all in order to maintain their status and their authority over the people.

The Disciples

The disciples often reflect the same values. Although the disciples leave all to follow Jesus, they desire to acquire status and power from following Jesus. Early on, the disciples are enamored with the crowds (1:37). On the journey to Jerusalem, they argue about who is greatest among them (9:33-34). James and John ask if they can sit on the right and left of Jesus in his glory in the age to come (10:35-40). When the other ten disciples find out about this, they become angry (10:41). The disciples have followed Jesus in the hope of acquiring glory and power.

So, too, are the disciples fearful. They are afraid in the storm on the lake (4:40). They are anxious about how to feed people in the desert (6:34-37; 8:4). They are afraid to ask Jesus about his death (9:34). They betray, flee, or deny Jesus, presumably in order to save themselves. Fear for themselves underlies their resistance to understanding, their lack of faith, and their failure to be faithful to the end.

In their anxious quest to acquire honor and power, the disciples harm others and generate dissension. They argue with one another about who is greatest (9:33; 10:41); they stop an exorcist from driving out demons in Jesus' name (9:38); they rebuke the people who bring little children to Jesus for a blessing (10:13); and they vie for honors from Jesus (10:35-45). In response to Jesus' predictions of death, they seek to secure themselves. They become arrogant, exclusive, competitive, and domineering. The disciples have bought into the values of the culture as depicted in the story. The disciples do not have the power and status that the authorities have, but they want them and they strive to attain them.

Mark's Gospel condemns the self-oriented, fear-filled quest for security, status, and power as contrary to what God wants people to be. People who embrace these standards are destructive of others and ultimately of themselves. The result is a society of conflict and oppression. In Mark's view, the ultimate consequence of a destructive life is to incur God's judgment against them (9:42-48; 12:40; 14:62).

The Vision for Life:
The Courage to Risk for Others

Characters who live the standards of the rule of God are willing to "lose their life for Jesus and the good news" (8:35), to "be least of all and a servant of all" (9:35), and to "be everyone's slave" (10:43-45). These sayings represent what God wills for people. While the Jewish and Gentile leaders, in Mark's portrayal, think that acquiring status and power over others makes them great, by contrast Jesus considers that the truly great human being gives up the status and power that one has, or feels entitled to, on behalf of those with less power and status.

In Mark, Jesus lifts up particular metaphors as paradigms of these standards. The metaphor for being least is a child or a house servant (9:35-37). The metaphor for the use of power is a servant or slave (10:44), because the role of "slave" exists to benefit others and offers no opportunity to use power over others for self-aggrandizement. These models of greatness are a contrast to the leaders of the Gentile nations who lord over people (10:42-43). The values of the kingdom turn the world upside down, so that the roles on the bottom become the moral paradigm for all human relations. Jesus does not give these models to people who are forced to serve or be least—slaves or women or children. Rather, Jesus gives these models of relinquishment to people (the authorities) who already have status or power and want to maintain it and to people (the disciples) who do not have status or power but who want to acquire it for themselves. In thus turning the world upside down, Jesus clearly opposes oppression. He means to stop the cycle of oppression and replace it with a cycle of service. As such, Mark promotes service, not servitude.

Minor Characters

Minor characters embody these positive standards of judgment. Suppliants serve by bringing others for healing (2:3; 7:32; 8:22) or by coming on behalf of a relative (5:23; 7:26). The Syrophoenician woman is least by being willing to accept Jesus' designation of her as a "little dog" in order to get her daughter healed (7:28). The poor widow gives out of her need, "her whole living" (12:41-44). An unnamed woman uses expensive ointment to anoint Jesus ahead of time for his burial (14:3-9). Joseph of Arimathea takes courage and approaches Pilate for the right to bury Jesus (15:43). Women go to anoint Jesus' body at the grave (16:1-3). Throughout the Gospel, women in particular not only embody the Markan standards of judgment but also serve as models for the disciples.

The Disciples

The disciples sometimes exemplify these standards. They leave their homes, families, and occupations to follow Jesus in the service of the good news (1:14-20; 10:28-29). They serve Jesus in many ways: They protect him from the crowds (3:9), provide a boat for him (4:1), distribute food in the desert (6:34-44; 8:1-10), obtain a donkey (11:1-8), and prepare the Passover meal (14:12-16). Also, as "fishers for people," they go from village to village depending on others for hospitality—food and shelter and clothes—in order to drive out demons and anoint the sick for healing (6:7-13). They continue to follow Jesus until confronted with death.

Jesus

For Mark, Jesus is the primary example of the standards of the kingdom. He serves people in his healings, his exorcisms, his pardons, his feedings, and his preaching, without seeking acclamation for himself (e.g., 1:43; 5:34). He speaks the truth of God whether people favor him or reject him (12:14). He refuses to lord it over others. As a result, he is persecuted by those whom he condemns. In his execution, Jesus manifests the standards of the rule of God (15:1-37): He is least in the society as a human being ridiculed and rejected on behalf of the kingdom of God; he has relinquished power over anyone; and he loses his life in the service of bringing good news to the world. At Gethsemane, Jesus is afraid to die, but his prayer reveals the orientation of his life: "Abba, Father . . . not what *I want* but what *you want*" (14:36). Jesus is the opposite of self-oriented. He is God-centered for others.

Living for Others Despite Loss and Persecution

In Mark, God wills that all people receive the blessings of the kingdom. And God wills for people to share the kingdom, to be agents who live so as to bring the blessings of the kingdom to others. The blessings of the kingdom are not an end in themselves, as if people are to benefit from them and the matter stops there. The kingdom calls for an orientation to a life lived for others. Living by this kingdom is nothing less than a Copernican-like revolution from being self-centered to being other-centered for the gospel.

Yet God also wills for people to take risks for the kingdom, to endure loss and persecution when necessary and unavoidable for the mission of the kingdom. This Markan view of "suffering" calls for clarification. First, Mark does not value suffering or loss for its own sake.[8] Rather, Jesus tells his disciples to pray that persecution not come (14:36). Second, in Mark's narrative, God does not will for people to suffer due to illness, disability, demonic possession, or the destructive forces of nature. The extensive Markan healings,

exorcisms, and nature miracles demonstrate that God wills to overcome these. Therefore, when Jesus tells people to "take up your cross
and follow me," he is not referring to suffering that comes from nonhuman forces, such as demons, illness, or nature.

Finally, God does not call people to suffer on behalf of people in a
position of power over them. Jesus does not tell slaves that enforced
service is among the standards of the rule of God. Hence, Jesus
would not call for a wife to endure abuse to serve the needs of her
husband or for a child to endure abuse to serve the needs of the par-
ent. On the contrary, God wills to relieve all oppression by humans
over other humans. In Mark, Jesus confronts and condemns such
human oppression wherever he encounters it. In fact, it is precisely
his opposition to human oppression that results in the oppressors'
persecution of him.

The Markan Jesus calls disciples to "lose their lives for me and the
good news." This involves two steps: "deny yourself" and "take up
your cross." "Denying oneself" refers to what one gives up in order to
live for others. "Taking up one's cross" refers to the ordeals one will
face as a result of living for others.

First, those who have status and power are called to deny themselves by relinquishing these on behalf of others. For Mark, God is
calling people to give up the self-serving values of the dominant culture and to live by true status and power in the service of God's realm.
Because of the nature of the good news and because of the way the
world is, people who live by the good news will risk the loss of these
things in the course of living their commitments.

Second, people are to take up their cross. The "cross" of suffering
that God calls people to endure is the unavoidable persecution that
comes to followers in the course of proclaiming the good news of
God's realm of salvation. Proclaiming the good news often leads followers to challenge oppression. In Mark, God does not give agents of
the kingdom the right to use force to stop those who oppress; otherwise, they would become like those whom they condemn. As a result,
those who confront oppression may suffer persecution at the hands
of the oppressors they condemn, just as Jesus did. In Mark, this suf-

fering by persecution in the course of proclaiming the good news is the "cross" that God calls people to bear for the sake of the world, a cross people take up because they have chosen to live by the good news of the kingdom of God. Hence, in Mark, Jesus does not call people to suffer, as if this were some virtue in itself. Rather, the Markan Jesus calls people to proclaim the good news—*in spite of* the suffering they may encounter because of this commitment.

Followers who are not prepared for such risks will shrink in fear and avoidance. A contemporary parallel to Mark's situation may help to clarify:

In the late 1980s, a volunteer approached a leader of the Sanctuary Movement in the United States serving refugees from Central America, and she asked to join in the work of the movement. The leader said to her, "Before you say whether you really wish to join us, let me pose some questions: Are you ready to have your telephone tapped by the government? Are you prepared to have your neighbors shun you? Are you strong enough to have your children ridiculed and harassed at school? Are you ready to be arrested and tried, with full media coverage? If you are not prepared for these things, you may not be ready to join the movement. For when push comes to shove, if you fear these things, you will not be ready to do what needs to be done for the refugees." The woman decided to think it over.

Similarly, if followers of Jesus are not ready to risk their status and their power or are not prepared for persecution, then they will not be ready to proclaim the good news. The rhetoric of Mark's Gospel leads hearers to confront their fear and to accept the persecution that may come in the course of following Jesus. Mark's Gospel calls people to celebrate the life of the kingdom and to oppose oppression in spite of the risks.

Faith

For Mark, living the standards of the kingdom is possible by faith, by trusting God.[9] The total response to the arrival of the kingdom, rightly understood, is to "put faith in the good news" of the kingdom

(1:13). The arrival of the power of the kingdom in the person of Jesus makes such faith possible. Faith is trust in the God for whom all is possible—the God who heals, drives out demons, calms storms, provides bread in the desert, and raises one to life and salvation in the new age. This faith gives courage. When one ultimately counts on God for life, one can dare to risk life for others (10:21). Thus, faith is the opposite of fear (4:40; 5:36; 6:50). In Mark, the faith that one's future salvation is in God's care gives one neither complacency nor passive security but the courage to risk even persecution—to live a life of abandon for the good news (10:29-30; 14:36).

The narrative calls followers of Jesus to have faith in God as Jesus had faith in God, the faith that enabled Jesus to live for the kingdom even though it led to his execution (8:34). By telling his story of Jesus, Mark seeks to evoke such faith and, in so doing, to turn the culture around from a society that is destructive to a society that promotes life. The ultimate consequence of living the standards of the kingdom is resurrection and eternal life in the age to come (10:30).

The Transition:
New Life, New Sight, Empowerment

How do we reverse oppression and create a world of mutual service? Such a transition from "thinking the things of humans" to "thinking the things of God" is perhaps the most difficult change human beings ever make. How do people change in such profoundly fundamental ways? How is it possible to break the tenacious grip of anxious self-preservation so as to be radically committed to the well-being of others? How do self-oriented people become God-centered in service to others? How are people enabled and empowered to relinquish the values of the world and embrace the standards of the kingdom? How do people come to a place where they are willing to face persecution and death for these convictions?

For Mark, the first step in this journey is to *receive* the gift of God's kingdom with all its blessings, then to *see* how to live life in a new way, and finally to *be empowered* to live for the good news in spite of fear. Through the rhetoric of his narrative, Mark seeks to lead people to this place.

Blessings of the Kingdom

First, like the characters in the story, the hearers of Mark are invited to receive the kingdom, for "unless you receive the rule of God as a little child [receives], you definitely will not enter into it" (10:15). Mark's story, especially the first half, offers a kingdom that brings liberation from all forms of oppression. Jesus heals the sick, drives out demons, pardons sins, cleanses lepers, restores the disabled, delivers from the threats of nature, welcomes the outcast, challenges inhumane laws, calls the wealthy to give to the poor, confronts fraud and extortion in the Temple, and challenges the leaders of Israel to produce the fruits of the vineyard. Out of compassion, the Markan Jesus offers the power of the kingdom to restore people to physical and moral wholeness. Receiving and entering this realm of God is a matter of having faith that life, now and in the future, comes from God. The blessings of the kingdom awaken such faith and make faith possible. The kingdom offers a vision to live for, a vision large enough to encompass the transformation of the world.

Seeing the World Upside Down

Second, beginning with the second half of the Gospel, Mark's narrative leads hearers to experience a fundamental change of perception— to see that this vision of the kingdom is large enough to live and to die for—that is, to understand that, in the face of all our human resistance, God wants people to risk status, power, and even life to bring the liberating life of the kingdom to others. How does Jesus try to get the disciples to see and understand these standards? He teaches them, corrects their inappropriate behavior, tells them about his own death, and gives them models—children, slaves, servants, women—to show them what they are to be like. He explains to them what they are not to be like—kings who lord it over their subjects, the wealthy who refuse to give up their wealth, and those who want to acquire the world.

Yet, in the end, Jesus' greatest witness to new sight is his own life. Can the disciples *see* this man as the Son of God, the agent who represents and reflects the very kingdom of God?[10] He exercised the power of the kingdom on behalf of others to the point where he was rejected by society's leaders, abandoned by the crowds, betrayed by friends, relinquishing his power over others, misunderstood by all, and dying as a result of opposing the oppressive authorities. If the disciples can see revealed in the faithfulness of this executed man the embodiment of God's idea of true greatness (15:2, 18, 26), then they will have seen the world upside down. They will see that God wants people to bring life to others even when they end up being persecuted, shamed, and killed for doing it. Thus, at the crucifixion, God's full standards of judgment for humans are revealed. There, the full commitment of Jesus to the values of God's rule is revealed, even in the face of death. And the resurrection of Jesus is God's affirmation that the way Jesus lived and his willingness to die for the kingdom is the way for all humans to live.

Empowerment by Example

Third, Mark's narrative empowers hearers to follow Jesus. As presented by Mark, Jesus' courage is more than example and revelation. Jesus' commitment in the face of execution empowers people to live for the good news in the face of rejection and loss. The narrative empowers hearers by leading them to identify with Jesus.[11] The narrative distances hearers from identification with the Jewish and the Gentile leaders, because these leaders will kill others to save themselves. The narrative initially leads hearers to identify with the disciples. However, when the disciples betray or abandon Jesus to save themselves, hearers distance themselves from the disciples. In the end, hearers identify with Jesus, because he is the one figure left in the story who embodies the values of the rule of God. In this regard, Jesus is not a *heroic* figure (he dies in humiliation and weakness), but a *faithful* figure.

Jesus is afraid and does not want to die, yet he is willing to do what God wills, namely, to remain faithful to the good news despite the cost (14:39). Hearers identify with the courage of Jesus and come away from the story saying, "I, too, want to be faithful in the face of death." Through the rhetoric of this story, Mark leads hearers not so much to believe something *about* Jesus as to *be like* Jesus.

Empowerment by the Purging of Fear

The narrative also empowers by purging hearers of fear. Through identification with Jesus, hearers face the experience of abandonment, rejection, mockery, physical suffering, and death. By going *vicariously* through the abandonment, rejection, mockery, physical suffering, and death of Jesus in their experience of the narrative, hearers face with courage the fears that might otherwise paralyze them. So when the Gospel ends with the women running away from the empty grave, terrified and telling no one (16:8), it is the hearers who are left to tell this story. It is the hearers who are led to say, "I will not be paralyzed into silence as the disciples and the women were. I will do what God wants, not what I want. I will tell, even if it means persecution and death." At the end, when all the characters in the story have failed to proclaim the good news about Jesus, the hearers themselves will complete the Gospel by proclaiming with courage. In Jesus' absence, they will live as Jesus lived, with faith and courage, until Jesus returns.

The Power of Example

How can a life and a death effect such empowerment? I can best illustrate it with a story about a concentration camp for prisoners in east Asia during World War II.

> In a concentration camp of American prisoners, the guards had so intimidated the prisoners and so violated every code of civilized treatment that conditions were horrible. The prisoners had tried to cope by a dog-eat-dog existence. To survive, each man was out for himself. Prisoners stole food and medical supplies

for themselves, robbed each other, ratted on other prisoners in order to get favors from the guards, and isolated new prisoners who came into the camp.

One day as they were coming in from work detail and putting away the tools, the guards discovered that a shovel was missing. The guards were irate and lined the prisoners up and threatened them.

Finally the guards said, "If the person who stole this shovel does not come forward in ten seconds, we are going to shoot all of you."

After a long silence, the guards cocked their guns and prepared to shoot. Finally, one of the prisoners stepped forward. The guards pounced on him, beat him with their gun butts, and shot him to death.

When the guards told the prisoners to finish putting away the tools, a strange thing happened. All the shovels were there. No shovel had been missing after all. In shock and silence the prisoners went back to the barracks.

It took a while for it to sink in that one of the prisoners had voluntarily given his life so that the rest would not be shot. Gradually, the attitudes of the prisoners began to change in the camp. Other acts of sacrifice began to take place. Prisoners began to share medical supplies with each other. They formed teams to attend to each other's wounds and illnesses. Some created make-shift artificial limbs for those who had lost an arm or a leg in the war. Some sick prisoners actually gave their food to weak prisoners who had a better chance for survival. Others risked death by sneaking outside the camp to procure food for the sick. They established a secret system of communication to give each other information and support. They welcomed new prisoners and quickly incorporated them into their network. The generosity was contagious.

In the midst of the most horrible conditions, there emerged a remarkably humane society of prisoners, all made possible because of the effect of this one fellow prisoner who gave his life for them to live.

And just as the example of one man empowered the other prisoners to take risks for each other, just so the telling of the story about him enables those who hear it to experience that empowerment in their own lives.[12]

Just so, for Mark, the example of Jesus and the story about him empowers those who hear it to change and to transform their society. Thus, in Mark's portrayal, Jesus does not die so that sins might be forgiven (Jesus offers forgiveness apart from his death; 2:5); rather, his faithfulness in the face of execution liberates others from the grip of self-preservation so that they too might live for others, even in the face of loss and persecution. Thus, Jesus' whole life, his faithfulness in death, and his resurrection liberate hearers from the self-oriented fear of death and empower them to live faithfully for others, resulting in humane communities of mutual service. And even if the hearers have themselves stumbled before in the face of persecution, they see new hope in the story, for Jesus remains loyal to his own frightened and stumbling disciples. Even after the disciples have failed to be faithful, Jesus promises to go ahead of them—including Peter, who denied him—in order to begin the mission anew from Galilee (16:7). The narrative thus encourages hearers to recommit themselves to proclaiming the good news and to bringing the kingdom *now*, despite past failures and ongoing persecution.

Contemporary Markan Christians

In order to grasp Mark's standards of judgment more clearly, it might be helpful to identify some contemporary figures whose lives bear the stamp of Markan Christianity. Down through history, the standards of judgment in the Gospel of Mark have been reflected in many people who have lived faithful and courageous lives of service for others. Markan Christians are represented by the orders of the church that called people to give up their livelihood and security to preach the gospel or care for the poor and the ill. Countless missionaries who have left home and country to bring the gospel to remote parts of the world belong in the Markan trajectory. In modern times, their numbers will include those who risked their lives to rescue Jews in Nazi Germany. Mother Teresa and all who have been inspired to be like her are to be counted among Christians who live out Mark's vision. And we might point to all who joined Martin Luther King Jr. in the struggle for civil rights in the United States. In all nations where people have struggled in nonviolent ways to free themselves from oppression—in Latin America, in South Africa, in the former Soviet Union, and in Asia—people have turned to Mark for courage to take risks in the fight against injustice.

Especially for Mark, with his positive portrayal of minor characters, the kingdom belongs to ordinary folks, unnamed and unrecognized, who have quietly made great sacrifices to serve their families or neighbors or someone in need. These are people who in very common situations courageously stand up for justice, speak up when others are silent, or who advocate on behalf of others—even when their actions result in misunderstanding and rejection. These are people who have an active sense of God's liberating presence in daily life. They carry out their occupations as vocations of caring service, sometimes at great risk.

Perhaps because Mark was written from a peasant perspective and portrays Jesus as a marginalized figure, many groups of poor and oppressed people have turned to Mark for empowerment that comes from knowing that they are not alone in their struggle. Many people who face discrimination and deprivation—such as Hispanic and African American women and men—have turned to Mark, where they find Jesus to be a very human figure who is in radical solidarity with them and who struggles with them in their plight. Also, many communities of women have found encouragement from Mark's challenge to men to relinquish their power over women, from Mark's portrayal of faithful female followers, and from Mark's call for mutual service in a "discipleship of equals."[13]

Such examples may get us in touch not only with the characters within Mark's narrative who embody Markan standards, they may also help us to identify with the first hearers of Mark who struggled for the courage to be faithful in the face of very difficult circumstances.[14]

The Purpose of Mark
in Its Historical Context

The purpose of Mark's Gospel as inferred from a study of the standards of judgment fits well the generally accepted historical context of Mark's Gospel. The Gospel of Mark was probably written during, or just after, the Roman-Jewish War of 66–70 C.E.[15] In that war, the Jewish nation revolted against the Roman overlords. The Romans defeated the Jews, conquering Jerusalem and destroying the Temple. Mark wrote about Jesus to show that any attempt to dominate others by force—either by Rome or by Israel—was contrary to the values God calls forth from people in the rule of God.[16]

Mark's Gospel announces that Jesus inaugurated God's rule, a realm that brings life rather than destruction, a realm that fosters service rather than domination. Jesus calls the disciples to announce this realm of God to the world. Mark's goal was nothing less than fostering this new world among all who would hear his Gospel. Mark also believed that Jesus' return and the final establishment of God's kingdom were imminent. Mark therefore enjoined urgency and alertness in the mission of spreading the news of God's kingdom to all people and all the nations before the end came.

It is generally accepted that Mark wrote to followers who risked persecution in their mission to be good news and to bring good news to the world. The time of the war was difficult for followers of Jesus. On the one hand, they were the target of persecution from other Jews, because they opposed the war. On the other hand, they were suspected by the Romans, because their leader had been executed as a revolutionary. They faced ridicule, rejection, ostracism from family and community, betrayal, arrests, trials, floggings, and death (13:5-23). It was a difficult time even to admit an association with Jesus, let alone proclaim the good news (14:66-72). Although followers of Jesus undoubtedly knew courage, they must often have failed to speak and act because of fear. Clearly this was a time of threat when people tend to resort to any means of self-preservation. Mark addressed this situation of persecution and fear, and he sought to reverse the drive to self-preservation. Mark's narrative led hearers to face the fear of loss and persecution, and it empowered them, in spite of oppression and destructiveness, to announce the good news and to spread the blessings of the kingdom of God faithfully and courageously.[17]

4

Jesus and the Syrophoenician Woman

Narrative criticism analyzes the formal features of biblical narratives: point of view, plot, character, setting, style, standards of judgment, and rhetoric.[1] Analyses of the formal features of the Gospel of Mark have shown this narrative to be of remarkably whole cloth: the narrator maintains a unifying point of view; the standards of judgment are uniform; the plot is coherent; the characters are introduced and developed with consistency; stylistic patterns persist through the story; and there is a satisfying overall rhetorical effect. Recurring designs, overlapping patterns, and interwoven motifs produce a rich texture of narrative.[2] Joanna Dewey's description of the Gospel of Mark as an "interwoven tapestry" is quite apt.[3]

Most Markan studies employing narrative criticism have dealt with the Gospel as a whole or with some feature that ranges across the entire narrative, such as Mark's technique of foreshadowing. Yet it is also important to provide narrative studies of individual episodes, studies that show how integral each episode is in the overall design of the Gospel. The episode of the Syrophoenician woman lends itself well to such a study. Our purpose, then, is to interpret the episode of the Syrophoenician woman as an integral part of the whole narrative. In light of current directions in narrative-critical studies, this analysis will keep before us the overall rhetorical effect of the narrative on a hearer or reader.[4]

The Episode

Now arising from there
he went off to the territory of Tyre.
And entering into a house
    he wanted no one to know,
but he could not escape notice.
Instead immediately hearing about him
    a woman whose little daughter had an unclean spirit
    came and fell at his feet.

Now the woman was Greek
    a Syrophoenician by birth,   } A
and she asked him
    to drive out the demon from her daughter.   } B

And he told her,
    "Let first the children be satisfied
    for it is not good to take the bread of the children   a
    and throw it to the little dogs."   b
But she answers and tells him,   } A′
    "Lord,
    even the little pups under the table   b′
    eat [some] of the crumbs of the little ones."   a′

And he told her,
    "Because of this word—go on off!   a
    [The demon] has gone from your daughter   b
    the demon."   c
And going away to her house   a′   } B′
    she found the little one thrown on the bed   b′
    and the little demon gone out.   c′

The Episode in the Larger Story-World: Manifestations of the Kingdom

In order to grasp how this episode fits into the overall narrative, we must remember that the original hearers of Mark encountered this Gentile woman after a period (a half-hour or so) of narration. The hearer has already entered the story-world, heard Jesus of Nazareth announce the kingdom of God, followed this Jewish rabbi around the Galilean countryside, seen his healings and exorcisms, experienced debates with the Jewish leaders, met Jesus' dense disciples, made evaluations about what/who is good and bad in this story, been in the dark about the mysteries of the kingdom, experienced the suspense of knowing who Jesus is while the characters in the story do not know, and much more. Only when we view the episode of the Syrophoenician woman in light of the full weight of the narrative leading up to it and indeed following it, have we begun to comprehend the episode itself.

The episode of the Syrophoenician woman fits tightly into the overall story, particularly in relation to the presentation of the kingdom of God. The establishment of God's rule over the world is the force that drives the whole plot of the narrative. Here are four ways in which this episode relates to the kingdom of God in Mark.

Display of the Kingdom

Jesus announces early in the narrative: "the kingdom of God has arrived." The Markan story that follows this programmatic announcement displays that kingdom. All subsequent healings, exorcisms, and miracles are expressions of the kingdom of God. These works of power by Jesus are a string of incredible happenings in which each event appears to the hearer to be different and more astounding in its own way—healing by touch, healing by word only, exorcising a legion of demons, calming a storm, healing someone by her touch of him, raising a child from the dead, providing bread in the desert, and so on. In our episode, Jesus exorcises a demon when the demoniac is not even present. Thus, the healing/exorcism stories are a major vehicle for conveying the activity of the rule of God as it comes in and through Jesus and his disciples. Each healing reinforces, enriches, and expands our understanding of the power of the kingdom.

Display of Faith

After Jesus announces the arrival of the kingdom, he says, "Repent, and put faith in the good news." Faith is the correlate to the power of the kingdom. It is the proper human response to the governance of God now available through Jesus.[5] Because "everything is possible to God" (10:27), therefore "everything is possible to one who has faith" in God (9:23; 11:22-24). Faith is access to the power of God. As such, the narrative that follows this initial announcement of Jesus displays the responses of faith. Those who come to Jesus in faith represent a major vehicle in the story to express this human response to the kingdom. The appearance of each new suppliant with faith expands and deepens our understanding of faith in Mark's narrative. The Syrophoenician woman, for example, reveals the faith of a Gentile and shows how cleverness can express the persistence of faith.

The Kingdom Hidden and Revealed

The healing stories in Mark convey the hidden/revealed dimensions of the kingdom. For while the suppliants respond with faith to the kingdom, they do not know the identity of Jesus as Messiah. In the first line of the Gospel, the narrator tells the hearer that Jesus is the Messiah, the son of God (1:1), but this knowledge is not available to the characters in the story, not even to the disciples.[6] Much of the suspense in this story results from this difference between what the hearers know and what the characters in the story (do not) know. Thus, while the suppliants are reliable in their faith that Jesus will grant their requests, they are unreliable in their knowledge/beliefs about Jesus. While the Syrophoenician woman has faith that Jesus will answer her request, she does not know that Jesus is the Messiah. It is not even clear that she believes in the Jewish God. Thus, some aspects of the kingdom are revealed and others are hidden.

The Plot Line of the Suppliants

In the display of the kingdom, the plot line of the suppliants intersects the plot lines of other characters. There are three main plot lines in Mark: Jesus in conflict with suppliants and demons; Jesus in conflict with the authorities; and Jesus in conflict with his disciples. The plot line with suppliants functions mainly to display the kingdom and faith, and it involves little suspenseful conflict with Jesus.

At the same time, the suppliant plot line interweaves with the other plot lines, sometimes together in the same episode and at other times providing a contrast by the juxtaposition of stories (2:1-12; 3:1-6). For example, the faith of the suppliants contrasts with the rigid resistance of the authorities. In our episode, the insistence of the Syrophoenician woman that her daughter be healed despite the uncleanness of her condition contrasts with the concern of the Jewish authorities to guard purity rules, as is evident from the episode that precedes this one.

The plot line with the suppliants also intersects with that of the disciples. The suppliants are foils for the disciples. They carry out functions, such as proclamation, that are otherwise expected of the disciples, despite Jesus' commands to the contrary: Jesus tells the leper to tell no one, but he proclaims freely (1:43-45); Jesus tells the demoniac to tell his family, but he proclaims throughout the Decapolis (5:19-20); Jesus tells Bartimaeus to go off, but he follows him to Jerusalem (10:52); and so on. This intersection complicates the story in light of the observation that the disciples themselves often do not carry out the proper functions of their role, nor do they behave as Jesus expects they should. The story of the Syrophoenician woman intersects with that of the disciples. On the one hand, the disciples have failed to understand a riddle of Jesus (as narrated in the preceding episode). On the other hand, the Syrophoenician woman understands Jesus' riddle and even responds with a riddle of her own.

Thus, the hearers experience the story of the Syrophoenician woman at a certain point in a larger narrative, in the context of a developing plot, in interaction with characters who have been introduced and revealed, and in light of the larger designs of the kingdom.

The Immediate Context in the Plot

One might think that it makes no difference where a particular healing episode occurs in the overall narrative. Because there is no developing conflict between Jesus and the suppliants, one might think that their individual stories are interchangeable. On the contrary, despite the general similarities of the suppliants and the overall role of the healing stories in the framework of Mark, each of these suppliants is integral to a particular place in the plot development. No suppliant is interchangeable with any other, because each one plays a unique role in the precise context in which she or he appears in the plot. The particular importance of each episode may be provided by the setting or by the type of ailment or by the character of the suppliant or by Jesus' manner of healing or by the reaction of the crowd or by any combination of these. For example, the exorcism in Capernaum follows shortly after Jesus has encountered Satan in the desert (1:12-27). The blind man touched twice follows the manifestation of the disciples' blindness and precedes Peter's insight that Jesus is the Messiah (8:14-30). Bartimaeus's cry to Jesus as son of David sets up the entrance to Jerusalem (10:46—11:11).

So too is the episode of the Syrophoenician woman integral to its immediate context in the plot. The episodes before and after are in the following sequence:[7]

A   Jesus feeds 5,000 Jews in a desert in Jewish territory and walks on water,

B   then heals those who come to him,

C   after which he has a controversy with Pharisees over eating food with defiled hands

D   and teaches his disciples privately, *declaring all foods clean*.

C'   Then he immediately goes off to the unclean Gentile territory of Tyre where he grants the request of an unclean Gentile woman by driving out an unclean spirit,

B'   after which he goes to other Gentile territory of the Decapolis where he heals a deaf and tongue-tied man

A'   and subsequently feeds 4,000 Gentiles in a desert in Gentile territory.

The central episode here—the declaration that all foods are clean—provides the conditions for a transition in the plot from a feeding in Jewish territory to a feeding in Gentile territory. As we shall see, the following episode of the Syrophoenician woman is the point at which the breakthrough to a mission among Gentiles occurs. As such, our episode, with its particular details, is not a generic healing that could occur anywhere else in the story. Rather, it is the turning point in an important subplot of the Gospel.

The Type-Scene of Healing: "Suppliants with Faith"

The narrator develops the plot lines of the Gospel by means of recurring type-scenes. A type-scene is an episode with certain characters and interactions that is repeated throughout the narrative.[8] The type-scene sets up a convention, thus providing familiar patterns of expectation for the hearer. There are many type-scenes in Mark: healings, exorcisms, nature miracles, conflicts with authorities, call scenes, and so on. The episode of the Syrophoenician woman is one instance of a type-scene. When the narrator tells us that the Syrophoenician woman hears about Jesus, comes to him, falls at his feet, requests an exorcism on behalf of her daughter, overcomes Jesus' resistance to her request, and receives the healing, the hearer is already very familiar with the basic pattern of these events. The hearer has encountered similar scenes featuring a leper, four men who lower a paralytic through a roof, a woman with a hemorrhage, a synagogue ruler named Jairus, among others.

The Healing Type-Scene

We might call the healing type-scene in Mark "A Suppliant with Faith."[9] There are eleven examples of this type-scene in Mark: Simon's mother-in-law (1:29-31); the leper (1:40-45); the paralytic (2:1-12); the man with the withered hand (3:1-6); Jairus's daughter (5:21; 35-43); the woman with the hemorrhage (5:24-34); the Syrophoenician woman (7:24-30); a deaf and mute man (7:31-37); the blind man at Bethsaida (8:21-26); the father who brings a boy with an unclean spirit (9:14-29); and Bartimaeus (10:46-52). Sometimes the crowd as a whole functions as suppliant with faith: in Capernaum (1:31-34); at the seaside (3:7-12); and at Gennesaret (6:53-56).

Such a type-scene differs from the type-scene "A Demoniac who Confronts" (1:21-28; 5:1-20; 9:14-27 are hybrids). In the Markan story-world, people possessed by demons cannot have faith. Therefore, in the exorcism type-scene, the demon itself confronts Jesus in fear and hostility, and Jesus drives it out. The story of the Syrophoenician woman does not belong to the exorcism type-scene, even though the malady of the child is demon possession. When a surrogate with faith pleads with Jesus on behalf of a possessed child, the story belongs to the type-scene "A Suppliant with Faith." As such, the exorcism of the daughter is embedded (implied) within the healing type-scene.

What follows are the basic Markan features of the healing type-scene of a suppliant with faith.

1. Setting of place and/or time: in a house (2:12), in the synagogue (3:1), or by the sea (5:21)

2. The suppliant has heard about Jesus (2:1; 3:8). Sometimes this is simply implicit.

3. The narrator introduces the suppliant and the malady: a leper (1:40); a synagogue ruler, Jairus (5:22); the son of Timaeus, Barti-maeus, a blind beggar (10:46)

4. The suppliant comes to Jesus for healing.

- Often the suppliant with faith is a surrogate for someone who cannot act in faith for themselves: the four men carry the paralytic (2:3); Jairus comes for a daughter near death (5:23); people bring a blind man (8:22).
- Only on the Sabbath does Jesus himself take responsibility for initiating an act of healing (3:1-6).

5. The suppliant kneels before Jesus, as the leper did (1:40), or falls at his feet, like Jairus (5:22).

6. The suppliant makes a request.

- The request may be in direct speech: the leper (1:40); Jairus (5:23); and Bartimaeus (10:47, 48).

- The request may be in indirect speech: those who request on behalf of the deaf and mute man (7:32) and the blind man (8:22).
- Other requests are unspoken. In one case, the request is an inside view of a suppliant's thinking, as with the woman who had the internal hemorrhage (5:28). In another case, the request is simply implicit in the act of getting to Jesus through a roof (2:5).

7. The suppliant overcomes an obstacle to get the request met:[10] the leper overcomes Jesus' possible unwillingness to touch him (1:40); the people who bring the paralytic dig through a roof because of the crowd (2:4); Jairus overcomes the news that his daughter has died (5:35-36); the woman with the hemorrhage gets to Jesus through the crowd despite her condition of uncleanness (5:27); the man who brings his demoniac son has faith despite the initial failure of the disciples (9:18); and Bartimaeus gets Jesus' attention despite the efforts of the crowd to silence his pleas (10:48). Thus, the suppliants embody *persistence* of faith.

8. Jesus fulfills the request: a healing or an exorcism or a restoration. He does so either by touching the person (1:41) or by laying on hands (8:23) or by grasping the hand (5:41) or by speaking a command (2:11; 3:5) or by giving a word of affirmation after the healing takes place (5:34).

9. The healing occurs. The narrator usually describes the healing in words that mirror the words of Jesus' command or the request of the suppliant. The verbal repetition affirms that the request was met precisely as it was made and precisely as Jesus commanded it.

10. Jesus gives a further command. Jesus commands people to go off (10:52) or to go to their house (5:19) or to be quiet (1:43) or to tell no one (7:36) or not to go into the village (8:26). These commands to go away and to be silent stand in contrast to Jesus' commands to his disciples to follow him and to proclaim. In Mark, Jesus never asks anyone whom he has healed to follow him, thus distinguishing those whom he calls to be disciples from those whom he heals or restores.

11. The suppliant ignores Jesus' commands. Instead of going home or keeping quiet, some suppliants go out and proclaim broadly (e.g.,

1:45). In so doing, the suppliants carry out actions otherwise expected of the twelve disciples. For example, in the episode when Jesus heals the deaf and tongue-tied man, Jesus' futile commands to silence people only make them more determined to proclaim (7:36).

12. The reaction of observers: observers express amazement (5:42); they glorify God and say, "We never saw anything like this" (2:12); the opponents go off to plot Jesus' destruction (3:6).[11]

These elements comprise the type-scene of the "Suppliant With Faith." The type-scene functions in two ways. On the one hand, the type-scene sets up a pattern of repetition for the reader. On the other hand, variation in a type-scene introduces new elements into the story. "Repetition with variation" is a predominant stylistic feature and rhetorical strategy of Mark's narrative.[12] In each familiar recurrence of the type-scene, the basic pattern remains the same but the details of the episode—time, place, characters, malady, manner of healing, and so on—differ markedly. In addition to variations in the details, there are variations in the form and features of the type-scene: the emphasis falls on different features; the order of the features varies; some features do not appear; or the functions of the features differ.

The Syrophoenician Episode as a Healing Type-Scene

In regard to the episode of the Syrophoenician woman, here are the variations introduced into the type-scene, correlated with the features set out above.

1. The setting is Tyre, Gentile territory, and Jesus goes into a house seeking to be unnoticed.

2. The story implies that the woman has heard about Jesus from the crowds who flocked to him from the regions of Tyre and Sidon earlier in the story (3:7). She hears of Jesus' presence in Tyre despite his efforts to hide.

3. The suppliant is a Gentile—a Greek, a Syrophoenician by birth. The repetition places emphasis on this feature. The absence of her name adds to the focus on her depiction as a Gentile. This feature occurs after the report that she comes and kneels.

4. 5. 6. She comes, kneels, and begs. The posture of the woman in begging for a healing is integral to Jesus' depiction of her as a scavenger dog.

7. After she succeeds in getting to Jesus, her main obstacle is to overcome his refusal to heal her, which is here couched in the form of a riddle. This is the centerpiece of the story, and great emphasis falls here. As a result of the woman's clever persistence, Jesus changes his mind, and there is a shift in the plot.

8. Jesus announces the exorcism of a person who is not present.

9. The exorcism itself is not narrated, but the demon is gone and the child is thrown on the bed, evidence of the struggle and exit of the unclean spirit.

10. 11. Jesus commands the woman to "go off." Here, however, the suppliant does not disregard this command. In this case, the command to "go off" relates to the woman's concern for her daughter. The disregard of commands in the Markan type-scene usually results in the suppliant's carrying out activity that is a foil to the disciples. Here, however, the activity that contrasts with the activity of the disciples takes place earlier in the episode, when the woman comprehends the riddle.

12. There is no reaction from observers, because the setting is private. Also, the narrator is not seeking to show an increase in popular support for Jesus in Tyre. Rather, the narrator develops this popular response in subsequent episodes in the Decapolis, which is also Gentile territory.

Thus, the story of the Syrophoenician woman reflects typical features of the Markan narrative, both in terms of the repetition of the type-scene and in regard to the introduction of variations. The fresh details stand out for the hearer because the narrator introduces them into a type-scene with which the reader is already familiar.

Rhetorical/Stylistic Techniques

We may now focus on the episode itself. I turn first to matters of style. In the Gospel of Mark, there are some stylistic devices that recur throughout the narrative. An indication of the embeddedness of this episode in the Markan narrative is the presence of these recurring stylistic patterns. I will deal here with four stylistic features: two-step progressions, suspense, parallelism, and allegorical riddles.

Two-Step Progressions

Two-step progressions are examples of repetition with variation. When Mark introduces the Syrophoenician woman, he refers to her as "a Greek, a Syrophoenician by birth." This repetition is a two-step progression in which Mark repeats something in order to get the hearers to notice it. The first step gives a generality, while the second step, the repetition, gives more specific detail and usually contains a crucial element.[13] A single instance of the two-step progression can be significant, but the accumulative impact of many occurrences leads the hearer to be attentive for a repetition. For example, "when it was evening, when the sun set," appears to be needless repetition (1:32). The first step is general. However, the second element, "when the sun set," leads the reader to pay attention to the precise moment when the Sabbath ended and people could bring the sick and possessed to Jesus for healing. Compare also "everywhere, throughout the whole countryside of Galilee" (1:28), "outside, in deserted places" (1:45), "to the other side, to Gennesaret" (6:53) and "in Bethany, at the house of Simon the leper" (14:3). Such two-step progressions pervade every level of the narrative.[14] So here too, in our episode, the narrative leads the hearer to notice that the suppliant was not only Greek-speaking, but more specifically a Gentile by birth—unquestionably not a Jew, but an outsider.[15] This specific information, so emphasized, sets the stage for the scene to follow. Again, the hearer has no problem with this two-step progression, because it is already familiar.

Parallelism

Parallelism is another form of repetition in Mark. Such repetition occurs in phrases, in sentences, and in the structure of episodes. In setting out the episode at the beginning, I charted the parallelism of lines.[16] Note how the two lines by which the narrator introduces the woman are subsequently dealt with in turn in the remaining two parts of the episode—that she was a Gentile and that she asked Jesus to drive the demon from her daughter. This repetition follows an A B A′ B′ pattern. Then note that Jesus' rejection of her request is subsequently paralleled by the woman's answer to Jesus riddle, but this time it is in a chiastic a b b′ a′ pattern. Finally, there is the parallelism between Jesus' final words to the woman and the subsequent report of the results in a pattern of a b c a′ b′ c′. In regard to this last parallelism, the command to "go off" corresponds to the phrase "and going away to her house." Then the two parts of Jesus' announcement of the exorcism, referring in turn to "your daughter" and to "the demon," correspond to the two parts of the narrator's report that "from the little one" the "demon" had gone out. Such intricate parallelism is present in virtually every episode of Mark's Gospel.[17] Repetition is a common trait of oral storytelling, and it is so carefully developed in Mark's work as to be one of the main webs that hold together this tightly woven narrative.[18]

Suspense

The introduction of the woman as "a Greek, a Syrophoenician by birth" provides for hearers information that enables the next statement to be a surprise: "And [but] she asked Jesus [a Jew!] to drive the demon from her little daughter." Both the introduction and the request create suspense, leaving the hearer to wonder how Jesus will respond. The tension is intensified by the detail previously given that when Jesus had entered a house he did not want anyone to know where he was. Jesus is trying to hide, and a Gentile requests healing. What will happen? The conflict is initially resolved when Jesus refuses her request. He views her request as illegitimate because she is outside certain spatial and temporal boundaries. She is outside the spatial boundary, because she is a Gentile and not a Jew. Therefore she is not entitled to the benefits he offers, at least not now. And she is outside the temporal boundary, for this is the time for Jews to be satisfied

"first." The time for Gentiles has not yet come. However, while Jesus'
refusal resolves the tension, it also increases the tension, because it is
unexpected and uncharacteristic of what we know so far in the narrative about Jesus as healer. The suspense is further intensified when
the woman does not accept his refusal. Again, the rhetorical devices
so carefully developed in this episode to create suspense are present
in many Markan episodes and are typical of the narrative as a whole.[19]
Here again, the whole narrative prepares the reader to expect twists
and turns, suspense and surprise—culminating, of course, in the
shocking ending of Mark's Gospel as a whole.

Allegorical Riddles

When Jesus responds to the woman, he does not reject her request in
direct manner. Rather, he answers indirectly in the form of a parable.
In Mark, the parables are consistently allegories that, like riddles,
have to be deciphered in order to be understood.[20] In every case, the
Markan parables are allegories by which Jesus is explaining to other
characters what is going on around them in the story-world: the
undivided kingdom explains Jesus' exorcisms (3:23-27); the sowing
riddles tell about Jesus' preaching and the responses to it (4:1-20); the
clean-unclean riddle explains why Jesus does not walk according to
the traditions of the elders (7:14-15); the vineyard riddle explains to
the high priests Jesus' identity, mission, and fate (12:1-11); and so on.
We infer this interpretation of the Markan parables from the explanations given in the narrative itself for some of the riddles, such as
the sower riddle and the clean-unclean riddle. We can understand the
rest of the riddles, those that have no explanations, by using the same
principles of interpretation. The characters hearing them (and the
hearers of Mark's story) must decipher the allegorical riddles in order
to understand them. For those characters who hear and understand,
the riddles clarify further; for those who do not understand, the riddles further obscure (4:10-12).

In this episode, Jesus' riddle is a carefully crafted allegory explaining to the woman why he will not heal her daughter. The following

scheme represents the elements of the allegory. In the left column is the riddle itself. The middle column displays the allegorical application as it pertains to the characters and events in this episode. On the right is the application of the allegory to the larger dynamics of Mark's whole story.

Jesus' Riddle (the Allegory)	Applied to the Episode	Applied to the Whole
First	At this time	While Jesus is alive (?)
let the children	let the Jews (not this Gentile woman)	let the Jews
be satisfied,	have the benefits from God available,	have the benefits of the kingdom,
for it is not good to take	for it is not good to take	for it is not good to take
the bread	the benefits (here an exorcism)	healings, exorcisms, restorations, resurrections, miracles—benefits of the kingdom
for the children	for the Jews	for the Jews—
and throw (it)	and carelessly give them (it)	and carelessly give them
to the little dogs.	to the Syrophoenician woman and her daughter.	to Gentiles.

We can see how the riddle relates to the story. The allegory is an extended comparison of one scene with another. The primary scene is the peasant-house setting in which children are being fed. There are dogs nearby waiting to get scraps from the food. These dogs are not pets. In ancient Israel, dogs ran in packs scavenging for food.[21] Jews considered dogs to be unclean, because dogs did not fit the category of clean animals and because dogs had contact with and ate things that were unclean. It is for this impurity that Jews referred to Gentiles as dogs. Clearly this was meant as an insult.[22] In addition to referring indirectly to the uncleanness of this Gentile woman, Jesus also appears to be playing on the depiction of the dog as a scavenger, because this is precisely the role that the woman is playing in asking for what does not properly belong to her. She is begging for food like a scavenger dog might do. Jesus says it is not good to take the bread for the children and throw it to the little dogs.

The narrator may be depicting Jesus as being playful with her by referring to Gentiles not as "dogs" but as "little dogs." In the Greek language, the diminutive often carries with it a note of endearment. Some translations attempt to capture this nuance of endearment by rendering the diminutive as "pup." Such a diminutive might have played down the unpleasant and unclean dimensions of this insult by referring to Gentiles as young dogs. Her response shows that she has not only understood the riddle but that she is also clever enough to play upon that small element of compassion suggested by this note of endearment.

However, one should be cautious about softening the harshness of Jesus' rejection. After all, this woman had not asked for a healing for herself but for a little child, and Jesus has denied her request on behalf of "God's" children. His rejection forces her to beg. The Markan Jesus may have referred to "little dogs" simply as a parallel to the woman's "little daughter." The fact that Jesus has referred to her as a little dog rather than a dog may not be any less of an insult.[23]

In any case, it is this last phrase of Jesus, "the little dogs," that the woman picks up in her response. Here is the allegorical interpretation of the woman's reply.

The Woman's Riddle (the Allegory)	Applied to the Episode	Applied to the Whole
Even	Even now	At this time
the pups	I and my daughter	Gentiles

down under the table	at the margins	who live in/near Israel
eat	(should) benefit from	(should) benefit from
some	just one exorcism	some of the works of power
of the little crumbs	from among the many benefits	from the benefits of the kingdom
of the children	for the Jews	for the Jews

In her response, the Syrophoenician woman extends Jesus' riddle. She does not oppose what Jesus has said. Rather, she develops the scenario of Jesus' allegory so that she and her daughter have a place in it. The scene now focuses not on scavenger dogs but on puppies, which (though no less scavengers) were permitted, apparently because of their dearness, to be near the children and to eat whatever crumbs inadvertently fell from the sloppy eating of the small children. Thus, the woman accepts Jesus' (diminutive) reference to Gentiles as "little dogs." In addition, she uses a different Greek word to refer to the children. This different Greek word is a diminutive that refers to "little children" and connotes fondness, here rendered as "the little ones." Thus, in her response, the Syrophoenician woman not only stays within the Jewish perspective of Jesus' riddle but she even refers to the Jewish children of God with a term of endearment.

This interchange is a repetition of the type of allegorical riddles that Jesus has spoken to this point in the narrative. The narrative has already shown the hearers how to interpret them. Hearers are to decipher the allegorical riddles as "stories within a story" that explain the story-world. The innovation in this particular episode is that the woman shows she has understood the riddle and responds with a riddle of her own. At the same time, this novel interchange occurs as a feature of the Markan type-scene "A Suppliant with Faith," for the riddle to which the woman responds is the obstacle that she as a suppliant with (persistent) faith overcomes to receive her request.

The Conflict in the Episodic Plot

We are now in a position to see clearly the nature of the conflict that drives the plot of this brief episode. Conflict analysis considers the circumstances of the conflict, what or who initiates the conflict, how it escalates, what the complications are, and what the resolution is.

Jesus goes to Gentile territory to retreat, not to heal.[24] The occasion for the conflict is that a Gentile woman requests from Jesus an exorcism for her daughter. Jesus rejects her request because it is not yet the time for Gentiles to benefit from the kingdom. He does so in the form of an allegorical riddle. This complicates the conflict. The woman then counters his denial with an amplification of his riddle. This response of the woman is a classic example from the ancient Near East of the clever request by an inferior to a superior in which there is an exchange of proverbial sayings.[25] The woman clearly treats Jesus as a superior, for he is a healer and a male. She came, fell at his feet, and made a request. He rejected her with a proverb: "It's not good to give the children's bread to dogs." As an inferior, the woman's response honors all that he says in his rejection and says nothing to contradict or shame him. She calls him "lord," recognizing his right to accept or reject her request. She responds with a proverb of her own that does not contradict but extends and qualifies his proverb: "Even little dogs get crumbs." The cleverness of her response is that she honored his rejection and still found a place for her request. Thus, not only has this woman been clever in gaining access to Jesus despite his efforts to hide, but she has also cleverly made use of the dynamics of honor and shame in order to get her request granted.[26] The conflict is resolved when Jesus grants her request and the daughter is restored.

As we have seen, the plot of the episode of the Syrophoenician woman is typical of the plots in most healing stories in Mark; that is, there is an obstacle to be overcome. In the case of the Syrophoenician woman, the obstacle is Jesus' initial refusal of her request. When the obstacle has been overcome, the conflict is resolved: the request of the suppliant is granted, and the episode comes to an end. What is left unresolved, as we shall see, has to do with the implications of this exorcism for Jesus' subsequent activity among Gentiles in general.

Characterization

Characterization is another way in which this episode is integral to the Markan story. There are basically two characters in this episode, Jesus and the woman. We infer their character traits from what they say, what they do, and what others say about them or how others react to them. It is rather amazing how many traits of each character are revealed in these brief depictions.

The Syrophoenician Woman: A Stock Character

We may distinguish among types of characters.[27] Stock characters have basically one trait. Flat characters have several consistent traits and are predictable. Round characters have many complex and/or conflicting traits and often are unpredictable. In Mark, Jesus and the disciples are round characters. The authorities are flat characters. And the minor figures are stock characters.

Within the type-scene of the suppliant who requests, there appears a stock character of the Markan narrative, "the suppliant with faith."[28] The narrator does not announce that the suppliant has faith. Rather, the narrator shows the faith to the hearers through the actions and the dialogue of the characters. For example, when the four men lower the paralytic through the roof, the narrator tells us that Jesus "saw their faith" (2:5). In another case, Jesus admonishes the suppliant, "Only have faith" (5:36). At another time, Jesus says, "Everything is possible to one who has faith" (9:23).

In Mark, faith is embodied in action. When Jesus "saw the faith" of those who brought the paralytic, it was not because he had some spiritual insight into the hearts of the four. Rather, he observed them digging through a roof to get to him for healing, and he perceived that action as faith. Embedded in the actions of the characters—coming, kneeling, asking, persisting—is the implicit trust that healing will take place. Also, Markan faith has little to do with beliefs about Jesus. For example, none of the suppliants knows that Jesus is the Messiah. Many in the crowds think he is John the Baptist or Elijah or one of the prophets (6:14). Bartimaeus inappropriately calls him "son of David" (10:47-48). In regard to the Syrophoenician woman, it is irrelevant to the narrative whether she believes in the Jewish God. The focus of faith in Mark is "trust that a request will be granted." Such trust is embodied in action, so that the coming, the kneeling, the asking, and the persisting *are* the faith. That is why, in response to the "touch" of the hemorrhaging woman (5:34) and later in response to the "begging" of Bartimaeus (10:52), Jesus says, "Your faith has restored you."

Given the expectations established by the familiar trait of the stock suppliants in the type-scene, the hearers know that a major trait of the Syrophoenician woman is her faith—even though the word "faith" does not occur in this episode. She comes to him, falls at his feet, and asks him to drive the demon from her daughter. These are all actions of faith in the Markan scheme. Also, Jesus' response to the Syrophoenician woman—"For this word, go off. The demon has gone from your daughter"—is similar to his response to the woman with the hemorrhage, "Your faith has restored you. Go off in peace, and remain free of your ailment" (5:34). We infer that Jesus interprets the request and the persistence of the Syrophoenician woman as faith.

Yet the woman's persistence really goes beyond faith. We might expect Jesus to say, "Because of your faith. . . ," but he says, "Because of this word. . . ." Jesus acknowledges, with the suggestion of surprise on his part, the insightfulness of the woman's answer. Jesus recognizes in her response the "word," a term that has been used throughout Mark to refer to the good news (e.g., 2:2; 4:33). Again, the narrator uses repetition with variation. The hearer knows from previous suppliants with faith that also this woman has faith. Yet that faith is manifest by the woman's intelligence and wit in the service of getting her daughter healed. And, as we shall see, she also succeeds in changing Jesus' mind.

Despite the cameo appearance of the woman as a suppliant with faith, her characterization is remarkably developed. We have seen that she is intelligent and clever. She has persistence in her actions on behalf of her daughter. Furthermore, in coming on behalf of her daughter, she reveals her loyalty and compassion. And her willingness to humiliate herself on behalf of the daughter shows her willingness to serve as one of the least on behalf of another. The Markan Jesus even suggests that she bears God's word to him (2:2; 4:33). All these factors contribute to making this unnamed character quite remarkable and memorable. She is a rather complex stock character!

Jesus: A Round Character

In a sense, the Syrophoenician woman "steals the scene" in this Markan episode. However, Jesus is also central to this story, and the narrator reveals much here about the character of Jesus. Jesus' initial refusal to heal the woman seems somewhat out of character. The Jesus of Mark has consistently responded favorably to requests for healing. Some commentators deal with Jesus' refusal by arguing that his initial response to the woman is merely a put-on statement by which Jesus is testing the woman's faith. I would argue instead that Jesus is portrayed here as having a genuine change of mind. He begins the scene by assuming that the kingdom is for the Jews now and only later is it for the Gentiles. He ends the scene with a willingness for Gentiles to benefit significantly from the kingdom even now.

We can perhaps see the narrative roots of Jesus' initial refusal to heal this Gentile woman by looking at his single earlier encounter with Gentiles in Mark. He had crossed the lake in a storm after teaching a huge crowd by the sea (4:15-41). Upon arriving in the Gentile territory of the Decapolis, he was confronted by a demoniac from whom he exorcised a legion of demons (5:1-20). All the people there were frightened of Jesus and responded by pleading with Jesus to go away from their territory. In other words, Jesus was not welcome among Gentiles. He then left Gentile territory, following his own later advice to his disciples: "Whatever place does not receive you or hear you, go away from there . . ." (6:11). At the beginning of our episode, then, the Markan Jesus appears to have the view that Gentiles will not receive the benefits of the kingdom until the Jews (the children) have been fed "first."

Such an attitude may explain why the Markan Jesus, when he retreated to Gentile territory, went into a house in order to escape notice. In Mark's portrayal, he has had no reception among Gentiles and does not therefore make himself available to them. This is the point of view Jesus expresses in his riddle. Yet, after the Syrophoenician woman shows faith by answering in such a way as to lead Jesus to see things differently, he immediately goes back to the Decapolis. This immediate return "up the middle of the territory of the Decapolis" clearly shows to the hearer the connection between our episode and Jesus' previous unsuccessful foray into Gentile territory of the Decapolis.[29] Upon returning to the Decapolis, Jesus is immediately approached by characters who want a deaf and mute man healed. By implication, the people bringing the deaf and mute man have heard of Jesus from the man freed from the Legion of demons, because the healed demoniac had gone throughout the Decapolis telling everyone what Jesus had done for him (5:20). The proclaiming (sowing) that this man did was now bearing fruit.

At this point, a pattern of crowd response recurs in Gentile territory similar to that which occurred earlier among Jews:[30] Jesus heals someone (a deaf and mute man), Jesus commands people to tell no one, they nevertheless spread the word, people thereby hear about him and a huge crowd gathers, and Jesus feeds the crowd. The repetition of this pattern of crowd response shows the Markan Jesus engaging in a major ministry among Gentiles similar to that which he had done among Jews. Hence, as a result of the encounter with the woman in Tyre, Jesus now makes the benefits of the kingdom widely available in nearby Gentile territory. Note that, in Mark's portrayal, the result of Jesus' change of mind was not merely a granting of an exception for this woman (contrast Matt. 15:21-28). Rather, his return to the Decapolis to heal and to feed four thousand Gentiles shows that his change of mind resulted in a major change of strategy in mission.

This change of attitude on Jesus' part is confirmed by the verbal threads that run through three related episodes: (1) the first feeding (in Jewish territory), (2) the story of the Syrophoenician woman, and (3) the second feeding (in Gentile territory). The key verbal threads are "take," "bread," "be satisfied," and "eat." (1) In the feeding in Jewish territory (6:30-44), Jesus "took" "bread," and the crowds "ate" and were "satisfied." (2) Then, in our episode (7:24-30), Jesus tells the Syrophoenician woman that the children are to be "satisfied" first and that it is not right to "take" the "bread" for the children and throw it to the dogs. The woman replies that even the pups "eat" the children's crumbs. (3) In the subsequent feeding in Gentile territory (8:1-13), Jesus "took" "bread" and people "ate" and were "satisfied." This last episode shows Jesus doing what he initially had said to the Syrophoenician woman that he would not do, before he changed his mind. Verbal threads are a major means by which Mark weaves the tapestry of his narrative.[31] The threads running through these three episodes confirm the role of the Syrophoenician woman in leading Jesus to make this major shift to a mission in Gentile territory.

As Mark portrays it, Jesus does not completely abandon the larger eschatological framework. He still considers in general that Jews should be satisfied. Yet Jesus has changed his mind and even now allows Gentiles to share the benefits of the kingdom. These episodes clearly foreshadow a later Gentile mission projected into the future of the story-world. For before Jesus dies, he will tell his disciples, with a key verbal echo of our episode, that before the end comes "the good news must *first* be proclaimed to all the Gentile nations" (13:10).

Settings:
The Crossing of Boundaries

We are now in a position to see the most important focus of this narrative in the larger plot of Mark's story. This episode is fundamentally about crossing boundaries. We have already mentioned the settings in this episode. Jesus goes to Gentile territory, and he heals the daughter of a Gentile woman. Both in terms of the physical settings and the attendant social relationships, Jesus crosses boundaries.

Purity and Defilement

One of the major conflicts across the Gospel of Mark is the conflict between the differing attitudes toward physical and social boundaries by Jesus and the leaders of Israel.[32] In Mark's portrayal, the leaders of Israel see boundaries as lines to be guarded in order to protect the holiness of God's people against the pernicious influence of impurity. They refuse to eat with sinners, wash hands before eating, prohibit unclean foods, keep Gentiles from the Temple, and so on. By contrast, Jesus makes an onslaught upon boundaries, because he sees holiness as a reality that *spreads* purity. Jesus touches a leper, eats with tax collectors, pardons sinners, drives out "unclean" spirits, heals on the Sabbath, is touched by a woman with a flow of blood, grasps the hands of a corpse, goes to a cemetery in Gentile territory where he drives out a legion of unclean spirits into a herd of pigs. The climax of this development in the plot comes with the series of episodes I have been considering—in which Jesus declares all foods clean, heals Gentiles, and feeds a Gentile crowd in the desert. All these boundary-crossing events began with Jesus' baptism in the Jordan, when God crossed the boundary between heaven and earth by sending the Holy Spirit to empower Jesus to spread the kingdom.

The narrative presents Jesus with an understanding of God and impurity that is different from that of the leaders of Israel. As depicted in the narrative, the leaders of Israel believe God and God's holy people will be protected from defilement by withdrawing from what is unclean. By contrast, Jesus does not act as if God or God's people will be defiled by what is unclean. Instead of seeing God as one who withdraws from impurity, Jesus sees God as an active force that renders clean that which was unclean. The *Holy* Spirit spreads wholeness and purity. Thus, instead of avoiding contact, Jesus makes contact and brings wholeness.[33] So when Jesus touches the leper, instead of being rendered unclean by the contact, Jesus cleanses the leper.

When Jesus is touched by the woman with the flow of blood, instead of being rendered impure, Jesus makes the woman whole. When Jesus touches the corpse, instead of being defiled, Jesus makes alive.

Jew and Gentile

In the narrative, Jesus crosses many culturally established boundaries internal to Israel. However, the external geographical and social boundary separating Israel from the Gentiles is the boundary against which all internal boundaries are hedges.[34] Once Jesus has abrogated the food laws, the door to contact with Gentiles is wide open. Immediately after Jesus declares all foods clean, he goes to (unclean) Gentile territory and encounters the Syrophoenician woman. We see the same sequence in the Acts of the Apostles, where immediately after Peter has a vision in which all foods are declared clean, he goes to the (unclean) house of Cornelius and inaugurates the mission among Gentiles (Acts 10:1-48). Just as the Cornelius episode is the breakthrough in the Acts of the Apostles, so Jesus' contact with the Syrophoenician woman in Mark is the point at which the fundamental social boundary is crossed. The subsequent feeding of 4,000 Gentiles in the Decapolis is the outcome of this breakthrough.

Rhetorically, the episode has great force with the hearers, for Jesus' own reluctance to heal a Gentile may represent the resistance to Gentiles that Mark expected the hearers of his Gospel to entertain. When Jesus the Jewish protagonist changes his mind in response to the woman's faith, heals her, and then retraces his steps to the Decapolis, heals a man there, and feeds a crowd in the desert, the hearers are led to follow. At the point in the narrative when this feeding of bread to Gentiles takes place, all of the boundary-crossings preparatory to a world mission have been resolved. Immediately after this second foray into the Decapolis, Jesus returns to Jewish territory to resume his mission there and to begin the journey to Jerusalem. Later, it comes as no surprise to the hearer when Jesus tells his disciples that between the time of his death and his return in glory, "the good news must first be proclaimed to all the Gentile nations" (13:10). Our episode thus represents a major shift of strategy within the narrated plot and foreshadows the future of the narrative world when the disciples are to proclaim to all the Gentile nations.

The Standards of Judgment

Standards of judgment are those values embedded in a narrative by which the hearer is led to judge the goodness or badness of the characters and their actions.[35] The standards of judgment represent the moral fabric of a narrative.

Two Ways

Mark has woven his narrative tightly in this regard, for the whole Gospel reflects a moral dualism in which there are two ways, each of which mirrors the other as its opposite. These two ways are identified in the story as "thinking the things of God" and "thinking the things of people" (8:33). These two ways represent "what God wants of people" as a contrast to "what people want for themselves." The key features of each way of life can be set out as follows.

The Things of God	The Things of Humans
faith	lack of faith
courage	fear
losing one's life for the good news	saving one's life
being least	being great
being servant	lording over people
doing good	doing harm

When we look at the Markan characters, we see that they embody one choice or the other. Jesus embodies the things of God, while the authorities embody the things of people. The disciples vacillate between the two ways, for they want to follow Jesus but they do not want to give up their cultural values. The minor characters—the little ones who have faith—share with Jesus the positive values of the rule of God, for example, the faith of the woman with the flow of blood

(5:25-34), the persistence of Bartimaeus (10:46-52), the willingness of the widow to contribute "her whole living" (12:41-44), the service of the woman who anoints Jesus (14:3-9), the courage of Joseph of Arimathea (15:44-47), and so on. The Syrophoenician woman embodies the things of God in several ways. She exemplifies faith. In coming on behalf of her daughter, she is serving and bringing life. In her willingness to be identified as a little dog, she is "least" on behalf of her daughter. When we thus see her behavior in the context of this larger moral fabric of Mark's narrative world, we see even more clearly how fully integrated this episode is within Mark's Gospel.

Least of All

Particularly significant to this story is the portrayal of the Syrophoenician woman measuring up to the Markan standard of being "least." Later in the story, Jesus tells the disciples that if they wish to be great they are to be "least of all and everyone's servant." For Mark, being least is never an end itself, much less an expression of humility for its own sake. Rather, it is always a means of elevating others of lower status or serving others with less power. Here the woman humbles herself to serve the needs of her daughter.

There are eight diminutives in our episode, a signal of the narrator's development of this motif of least-ness: "little daughter" occurs once, "little dogs" twice, "crumbs" once, and "little ones" twice. In addition, the regular word for demon, used twice here, is itself a diminutive, thus depicting an unclean spirit as "a little demon." This is an extraordinary number of diminutives in such a brief episode.

We can now see how the woman is "least" on behalf of her daughter. In her approach to Jesus, the woman was kneeling, begging, and giving honor as an inferior. The diminutives in her response to his rejection reinforce the picture of the woman humbling herself on behalf of her daughter: "Even the little dogs down under the table eat some of the crumbs of the little ones." Thus, she diminishes herself by being willing to be identified as a little scavenger dog, down under the table, eating some of the little children's crumbs—in order to get her daughter healed. In so doing, the Syrophoenician woman antici-pates Jesus' teaching about the greatness of being least. Later in the narration, when hearing Jesus' teaching about greatness, the hearer may recall the Syrophoenician woman and her daughter and include them among the "the little ones who have faith" (9:42). In fact, at the end of our episode, the narrator picks up on her depiction of the Jews as the "little ones" and refers in turn to the woman's Gentile daugh-ter as the "little one," thereby including her as one of the "children" of God.

Gender and the Subversion of Dominance

I have kept the issue of the gender of the suppliant until the end of our analysis. I have done this because the femaleness of the suppliant is not essential for the story to work as a crossing into Gentile terri-tory. Gender is not essential to this episode, as it is, for example, in the episodes with the woman having a flow of blood and with the poor widow. The story would have worked if a Gentile male had come on behalf of his daughter or son. Yet this observation makes the pres-ence of a woman here all the more remarkable, and it changes every-thing. It is a woman who finds Jesus, a woman who approaches Jesus in a house, a woman who challenges Jesus' words, a woman who gives "the word," a woman who gets Jesus to change his mind, a woman who paves the way for the whole mission to the Gentiles.

The role of women in Mark is a complex matter.[36] On the one hand, Mark's narrative is clearly androcentric: male-preference lan-guage refers to people in general, male pronouns represent the many, and masculine language depicts God and Satan. The author often identifies women by their relationship to a male: Simon's mother-in-law, Mary the mother of Jesus, Jesus' sisters (who, unlike the brothers, are not named), the wife of Herod, Mary the mother of James and Joses. There are a limited number of women. They approach Jesus mainly in houses. Most are not followers of Jesus but are recipients of healing. Few women have speaking parts. In fact, women sometimes appear as people about whom males talk, such as in the cases of the woman who anoints Jesus and of the poor widow. In these cases, women are held up by the male Jesus as models for male behavior.[37]

Yet many aspects of the Markan narrative may be somewhat uncustomary for the times. Jesus has public contact with women. He heals women. The narrator does not depict all women by their relationship to males: the woman with the flow of blood, the Syrophoenician woman, the one who anoints him, the widow, Mary the Magdalene. The narrator tells us that the disciples leave sisters and mothers as well as brothers and fathers in order to follow Jesus. In turn, those who do the will of God are mothers and sisters as well as brothers to Jesus. Although there are none among the twelve, women "follow" Jesus, "serve" him throughout Galilee, and "come up with him" to Jerusalem—language that is used to depict discipleship (15:40-41). When the twelve have fled, women are present at the crucifixion and then go to anoint his body after the Sabbath. In the end, the burden of proclaiming the good news is laid on the women when the twelve male disciples were nowhere to be found.

Also, Mark is anti-patriarchal. Jesus teaches that the disciples are not to lord it over anyone, not to exert authority over anyone. Jesus makes no provision for communal roles that would authorize some to exercise authority over others. The narrator never mentions Jesus' own father (6:3). His followers leave fathers, but they do not receive fathers (10:29-30). This paves the way for women, slaves, and children to be the models for all followers. Women are models of faith (the woman with the flow of blood), serving (Simon's mother-in-law, the woman who anoints, the women at the grave), being least (the poor widow), and giving their lives (the poor widow). The few women who respond negatively to John and Jesus in Mark are connected with the wealthy upper classes: Herodias, her daughter, and the maid of the high priest. Apart from these exceptions, the women in Mark exemplify what the lower classes in general also exemplify in Mark. As such, the women play a similar role to other minor characters, the Markan "little people."

By depicting minor characters, particularly women, in such positive roles, Mark subverts any presumption to dominance by the other group characters. In contrast to the destructiveness of the leaders, Mark shows the service of the minor characters. In contrast to the failures of the disciples, Mark depicts the minor characters performing the responsibilities of disciples. In contrast to the Jewish people as a whole, Mark shows some Gentiles just as eager with faith as some Jews are to receive the benefits of the kingdom. Finally, in contrast to the patriarchy of males, Mark displays women as models for discipleship. In a sense, the story of the Syrophoenician woman is so significant because it subverts pretensions of all these groups. Here is a model for leaders about how to serve. Here is a non-disciple who understands Jesus' riddles. Here is a non-Jew who has persistent faith. Here is a Gentile "dog" who is least in the esteem of Jewish culture, but who in the eyes of God and of God's agent Jesus (and the narrator) is truly great. Here is a woman who models the values of the kingdom.

Complexity of the Episode

The episode of the Syrophoenician woman is an integral part of the fabric that constitutes Mark's narrative. In order to explain this one passage it becomes necessary, in a sense, to repeat the whole narrative of Mark from beginning to end. In terms of what precedes this story in Mark's narrative, the hearers come to this episode after a period of experiencing type-scenes, character revelations, plot developments, thematic interweaving, stylistic devices, and rhetorical strategies. In terms of what follows, the episode of the Syrophoenician woman continues to provide echoes in the hearing of the audience throughout the rest of the (hour and a half of) narration. When the whole narrative is completed (or repeated), the hearer recalls this single episode as an integral part of the interwoven tapestry of Mark's Gospel.

Much of what contributes to the complexity of this episode is that so many Markan motifs and patterns run through the episode. In light of this complexity, we can see how reductionistic it is to offer one title to this episode (as provided by some translations) when any number of titles could be given: Another Healing of the Kingdom; Exorcism from a Distance!; A Gentile with Faith; A Clever Foreigner; Finally, A Riddle Understood; A Foil for the Disciples; Jesus Changes His Mind; The Kingdom Shared with Gentiles; An Outsider Becomes an Insider; Crossing the Final Boundary; The Beginning of a Mission to Gentiles; Foreshadowing the Mission to the World; The Least Are the Greatest; The Family of God's Children is Extended; The Syrophoenician Woman.

Rhetorical Impact in Historical Context

When we interpret this episode in light of the themes of the whole story, we are also able to see more clearly the rhetorical impact this story may have had on an ancient audience as a boundary-crossing narrative. If the Gospel of Mark was written in Galilee from a peasant perspective,[38] this passage may well reflect realistically the hostility between Galileans and Tyrians, especially during or just after the Roman Jewish War of 66–70 C.E., the time when Mark was most likely written.[39] At the opening of the war, Tyrians assaulted Jews in the city of Tyre and in the villages under their aegis. These actions may have reflected the hostility between Jews and Gentiles of Tyre already present at that time and probably represented the Tyrian fear of Jewish aggression against them for long standing oppression.[40] Galilee would have been affected by these animosities. Galilee served as the breadbasket for Tyre. Tyrians were able to eat well because wealthy Tyrians could afford food from Galilee, when the poor Jewish peasants of the villages in Galilee may not have had enough to eat for themselves.[41]

In this context, Jesus' proverb might have expressed the actual views of the Galileans toward the Tyrians at the time Mark was written: "Let our children be satisfied first. It isn't good to throw away our children's bread to the dogs." Ironically, the woman's proverb may well have expressed the despair of the Galileans themselves, that (unlike we Galileans), "Even dogs get crumbs." The followers of Jesus in Mark's audience may have shared a Galilean hostility toward Tyre implied by these proverbial sayings.[42]

In such a context, Mark's story of the Syrophoenician woman functioned much like the story of the Ninevites who repented in response to Jonah's reluctant preaching or like the parable about the (oxymoronic) good Samaritan. The story challenges the audience not to set limits on the universality of the good news of the kingdom of God. The entire first part of Mark's story prepares the hearers to go with Jesus across this final boundary to Gentile territory. To portray Jesus himself expressing the hostility that Mark's audience may have had toward Tyrians and then changing his mind in response to the cleverness and faith of this Gentile woman from Tyre enables Mark to make the point in a most graphic way. In the narrative, the Syrophoenician woman defuses the initial rejection of Jesus by accepting the epithet of "little dog" and by referring to the Jewish children with the endearing term of "the little ones." In this way, a story set in Jesus' time defuses and disarms the hostility of hearers in Mark's time.

Conclusion

This extraordinary little story attacks presumptions and limits on many fronts: this is a Gentile who gets her daughter healed; this is a woman who disdains status more than the men do; this is an insightful suppliant who understands better than the disciples do; this is an impure person who has greater access to God than the "pure" (narrative) leaders of Israel; this is a woman whose story leads hearers to overcome a presumption and a hostility that would limit the kingdom to the Jewish children of God. In this episode, Mark seeks to attack the very heart of human resistance to the universality of the gospel and in so doing calls his hearers to sow the seeds of the kingdom everywhere.

5

Network for Mission:
The Social System of the Jesus Movement
in Mark

Models from the social sciences are valuable tools for the study of early Christianity.[1] Social-scientific models deal with such matters as the nature of sects, attitudes toward boundaries, rituals of social change, the dynamics of purity systems, the uses of power and authority, and the relationship between social group and cosmology. Such models enable New Testament scholars to pose fresh questions that draw attention to social dynamics hitherto unnoticed. We can apply models from the social sciences not only to the historical world of early Christianity but also to the narrative world of a biblical text. The narrative world referred to here is neither that of the historical events referred to by the narrative nor that of the historical situation of the audience to which the narrative was written but rather the social world presented in the narrative itself. As such, I propose here to apply models from the social sciences to the narrative world of the Gospel of Mark.

This chapter therefore is an anthropological analysis of the narrative world created by the writer of Mark's Gospel. The narrative world of the Gospel of Mark is an interpretation of reality, a version of the historical world of the author's past. The author was obviously describing and interpreting historical events of the past. Nevertheless, the resulting version of those events presented in the narrative has a conceptual autonomy independent of the events described—much as a painting such as Leonardo's *Mona Lisa* offers a vision of reality independent of the accuracy or inaccuracy of its representation.[2] Narrative worlds are "literary constructions represented in stories"—all that the narrative implies or expresses about its actors and their actions in time and space.[3] In the narrative, the author has portrayed three key elements that constitute a world: *settings*, such as deserts, villages, Jerusalem; *characters*, such as Jesus, the disciples, the authorities in Israel; and *events*, such as healings, conflicts, exorcisms, and a crucifixion. In addition, the narrative world has its own geographical space, temporal world of past and future, a moral framework of good and evil, and a cosmology of heaven and earth, God and Satan, angels and demons. The focus of this chapter, then, is the story-world of the Gospel of Mark, not the actual events of the historical Jesus or the historical situation of the author.[4]

Traditionally, biblical scholars have treated the Gospel narrative as a "window" through which to view the historical Jesus or the author's historical community. In that approach, the meaning lies behind the text, in the reconstruction of historical events. Recently, however, contemporary literary critics have provided us with tools to treat the Gospel narrative as a "mirror" that reflects a story-world. In this approach, the meaning lies in front of the text, in the relationship between the narrative and the reader.[5] We study each Gospel in the same way we would study a short story or novel.[6] And a literary text such as a short story or novel has a frame around it, such that if a typical narrative is not in fact a closed system, it is in some sense a limited world with a relatively coherent symbol system. As such, we can interpret the social world portrayed in the story in the same way that a social scientist studies the social world of a culture. In fact, anthropologist Clifford Geertz has compared the analysis of a small tightly knit society having a somewhat unified symbol system with the exegesis of a text.[7] In this chapter I collapse Geertz's comparison and offer an anthropological analysis of the social world presented by an author in a narrative.[8]

The social-scientific study of a narrative world proceeds, then, as might an analysis of the social dynamics of a culture. I look at the social interactions depicted in the narrative and the social meanings embedded in the text that sustain those interactions.[9] In regard to social arrangements, our focus is on the Jesus movement as portrayed in the narrative of Mark's Gospel. My purpose is to give a social description of this movement. I examine its configuration, formation, boundary definition, boundary mechanisms, rituals of affiliation, boundary maintenance procedures, internal roles, and attitudes toward power and authority. In regard to social meanings, I analyze the larger symbolic world in the story that reinforces and sustains the particular social configuration of the Jesus movement: the view of the kingdom of God, the understanding of time and space, and the cultural norms and moral values. Also, there are conflicts within the narrative between Jesus and the authorities and between Jesus and the disciples that help to sharpen our understanding of the distinctiveness of the Jesus movement in relation to the dominant culture as depicted in the story.

My thesis is that the Jesus movement depicted in Mark is a renewal faction in the configuration of a network centered around the holy man Jesus and oriented to mission and that the overarching symbolic world in the narrative—its moral and cosmological framework—mandates and supports such a social movement.

The Cosmological Framework

The larger symbolic framework of the narrative is that God is establishing rulership over the world. This takes place in two stages; part of the first stage is narrated (the narration from John to the women at the grave), while the remainder of the first stage as well as the second stage are forecast into the future within the narrative world by the characters.[10] The first stage extends from the appearance of John the Baptist to the inauguration of the second stage (the end—13:7, 13), which will occur within a generation. At the onset of the first stage,

God sends John to prepare the way (1:1-8). Then the heavens are opened and God declares Jesus to be the Messiah-Son and anoints him with the Holy Spirit to carry out the task of announcing and ushering in God's kingdom (1:9-11). Jesus in turn appoints twelve disciples to be with him and to expand his work during his lifetime. And they are to carry on after his death (3:13-19). In this first stage, the agents of God (Jesus and his core group of followers) display the nearness of the kingdom by exercising authority over nonhuman forces that oppress or destroy people—demons, illness, and nature. The agents go first to Israel and then to the Gentile nations, proclaiming and showing the good news of the kingdom in order to give people of all nations an opportunity to repent before the end comes (13:10). The spreading of the good news in the first stage of the kingdom of God is urgent, for, before the generation has ended (projected into the future of the narrative world), God will inaugurate the second stage by establishing the kingdom finally and fully on earth (9:1; 13:30). In the second stage (also projected into the imminent future within the narrative world), the risen Jesus will return from heaven at God's right hand and gather the chosen ones who have spread out to proclaim to the four corners of the earth (13:26-27). When the end comes, there will be no further opportunity to repent, for the kingdom will have come openly and in power and judgment over people.

The Jesus Network

Within this larger symbolic framework of the narrative, Jesus establishes neither a stationary community nor a tightly knit sect, but a prophetic, holy-person movement in the configuration of a network.[11]

Much work has been done by social scientists on the dynamics of networks.[12] In one sense, all social relations of a person can be viewed as a web of interrelated networks. Yet our concern here is with a social movement, the establishment of a network by means of recruitment. Networks can be simple or complex. Social scientists can chart the dynamics of the relationships between leader and followers and among followers. They can distinguish the first order, second order, or third order zones of influence and interaction. They can analyze the nature of the transactions in the network, what is exchanged and in what ways participants benefit. They can explore the way in which allegiance to one network overlaps and conflicts with allegiances to other networks that might be based on kinship, place of origin, or occupation. Other facets for analysis include the methods of recruitment,[13] the social makeup and size of the network, the centrality of the leader, the development of clusters among participants, the role of sympathizers in distinction to participants, and the ideology that gives coherence to the network as a movement. All of these issues guide our subsequent discussion of the Jesus network depicted in Mark.

As portrayed in Mark's narrative, Jesus recruits people to participate in a network the goal of which is to renew Israel by ushering in the kingdom of God and as preparation for the end.[14] To accomplish this goal, Jesus establishes a network in which others relate to him like branches and twigs on a tree. Jesus chooses twelve so they might be with him (3:13-19), and he sends them out in pairs to proclaim and heal (6:6-13). When they go out, people receive them in their houses. Jesus, the holy person who proclaims and heals, is the center of the network; the disciples who receive authority from Jesus to proclaim and to drive out demons represent a second order zone of interaction; and those who receive Jesus or the disciples, put faith in their proclamation, and offer them hospitality are a third order zone of interaction. From the originating end of the network, Jesus sends out disciples to proclaim and to heal. At the receiving end of the network, sympathizers or supporters give hospitality by receiving the disciples in houses (6:10) or giving them a cup of water (9:41).

Such a network is typical of peasant relationships in collectivist cultures by which people are bound to each other in reciprocal transactions.[15] In this case, the reciprocity is rooted, on the one hand, in preaching and healing and, on the other hand, in hospitality: Jesus and the disciples proclaim and heal, while sympathizers "receive" them—listen, show faith, and provide hospitality.[16] In the ancient world, such hospitality was a significant means to generate loyalty and express solidarity.[17] When Jesus tells the disciples that those who have left everything for him and the good news will receive a hundred times as many houses and brothers and sisters and children and fields (10:29-30), he is referring, I would suggest, neither to a communal sharing of property (as in Acts 2:42-47) nor to a communal experience marked by household roles (as in 1 Peter) but to solidarity through hospitality as the disciples journey from place to place.[18] This network of solidarity through hospitality reaches to the furthest connection with Jesus' name—an unknown exorcist acts in Jesus' name (9:38), someone receives a child in Jesus' name (9:37), or a person gives a cup of water to someone who comes in Jesus' name (9:41). As depicted in Mark's narrative world, such a network serves well the mission to proclaim the good news to the edges of the earth before the end comes (13:10).

The whole thrust of the narrative reinforces this portrait of a network with core participants constantly on the move. Jesus goes from place to place throughout Galilee and then travels to Jerusalem. When his disciples want him to remain in one place, Jesus tells them "Let's go on to the next towns, so I might proclaim there too, for that's why I came out" (1:38). The action in this Gospel is quick and the movement is continuous; Jesus heals a person or encounters opponents and then moves on. It is taken for granted that Jesus will receive hospitality in houses as he goes here and there: Capernaum (1:29; 2:1; 9:33); Tyre (7:24); Bethany (11:11, 19; 14:3); Jerusalem (14:15); and other houses (e.g., 3:20). At Nazareth, however, he is not received (6:1-6). So too the disciples receive hospitality while they are in the locales that receive them (6:10). When the crowds are too large, Jesus meets the people by the lake (2:13; 3:7; 4:1) or in a deserted place between villages (1:45; 6:32). In addition, the motif of being "on the way" is a resonating metaphor depicting the itinerant lifestyle of Jesus and the core disciples who follow him.[19]

Network Formation:
Recruitment and Reinforcement

In the narrative, Jesus' first step in network formation is recruitment. Jesus calls and appoints the group of twelve disciples.[20] Early in the story, he recruits the four fishermen (1:16-20) and Levi (2:13-14). Then he calls those of his choosing to a mountain and appoints the twelve in order that they might be with him, proclaim, and drive out demons (3:13-19). Later, he sends out this core group in pairs to proclaim and heal (6:6-13), to be "fishers for people." The core group of disciples is comprised of Jewish males from the peasant classes in various villages. The only occupation stated is that of fishing. Levi the tax collector is called, but he is not included among the twelve. Otherwise, the narrator tells little about the disciples.

In order to carry out the mandate of the kingdom to spread the good news, Jesus and the disciples whom he has recruited must be mobile. Horizontal mobility is a distinguishing mark of network members in the first stage of the kingdom. To become mobile, Jesus and the disciples must separate from the things that render them stationary—family, property, work, and village (e.g., 1:16-20; 2:14; 10:28). As such, Jesus calls certain people to make a break with these things by inviting them to "come after me" or to "follow me"—a call to become a disciple. Later, Jesus instructs them to travel lightly (6:8), suggesting that he is eager for members of the network to spread out as quickly and as widely as possible. Jesus admonishes the disciples to "take nothing on the way except a walking stick only—no bread, no beggar's bag, no coins in the belt—but to strap on sandals and not wear two tunics" (6:8-9). These prohibitions against taking coins or bread or an extra tunic on the way serve to deny the disciples domestic independence and to render the disciples completely dependent upon the hospitality of other households. If the disciples are to eat and to have a place to stay, they must continue to proclaim. The instructions for mission ensure, therefore, that the disciples will remain mobile and will continue to proclaim from place to place.

In addition to recruitment, the Markan Jesus performs other acts of network formation that strengthen the network and assure its continuation. For example, in Mark's narrative, Jesus takes the disciples with him much of the time as he moves from place to place, and he gives them instructions to care for his needs: keep a boat ready (3:9), get a donkey (11:1-7), and prepare the Passover meal (14:12-16). He also teaches them, often privately; for example, he explains the riddles to them in private (e.g., 4:10, 34) and takes them aside to tell them about his death (9:30; 10:32). These actions have the dual function of keeping the network centered around Jesus and at the same time of preparing the disciples to carry out their own part in the network. Jesus also makes great efforts to prepare the disciples for his absence from them after his death—expecting them to perform exorcisms on their own (9:16-19), explaining to them the meaning of his death (8:31-37; 9:33-35; 10:32-45), teaching them to have faith and to pray (9:28-29; 11:22-25), forewarning them about what will happen after his death (13:1-37), and preparing them for their own suffering by persecution (e.g., 9:34; 10:38-40; 13:9-13). Although the Markan Jesus is impatient with the disciples, he does not give up on them. He has promised to make them fishers of people, and he does so.[21] He also tells them that they will receive eternal life for their sacrificial faith in leaving family and vocation and risking death for him and the good news (10:30). All these additional elements of network formation serve the primary network activity of proclaiming and healing. That is, in order for the disciples to proclaim and heal, they must have faith, understand the rule of God, comprehend the meaning of Jesus' death, be prepared to accept and face the persecution they may encounter, and be ready to carry on in his absence. Thus, once Jesus initiates the network, the training of core participants serves to sustain the network and to prepare for its continuation after his death.

Regarding the extent of the network that Jesus forms, we should observe that other characters beyond the twelve disciples also engage in core network activity—proclaiming, going from place to place, following Jesus. For example, Jesus invites the crowd to "come after him"

(8:34). He calls the rich man to follow him (10:17-21). The women who are mentioned for the first time in the scenes of Jesus' death had been following him and serving him when he was in Galilee (15:40-31). An unnamed exorcist performs in Jesus' name (9:38). Also to be included are those characters whom Jesus heals, whom Mark often depicts as spreading the word. This creates a fourth order zone to the network. The presence of such people in zone four subverts any claim to dominance and privilege by the twelve disciples as a separate group. However, people who have been healed and then proclaim often do so against Jesus' wishes. For, as depicted in Mark's narrative, Jesus never asks those whom he heals or exorcises of a demon to "follow" him, that is, to assume the roles of the core group of disciples. Rather, Jesus tells these people to tell no one (1:44) or to go off (10:52) or to return to their houses (2:11; 5:19).[22] The implication is that they are to return to their families and their everyday lives. Later, as renewed Israelites who are sympathizers of the movement, they may provide hospitality to those who proclaim from place to place (compare, by implication, Simon the leper, 14:3).

In Mark's depiction, Jesus sets up a network by which he extends his proclamation quickly and widely. The social interactions of the Jesus network as depicted in Mark's narrative are thus oriented toward mission and mobility. This mission orientation is achieved by the formation of a network that facilitates mobility so that core disciples reach as many people as possible. Yet Jesus also sets up the network in such a way as to keep himself at the center. His core group is small; Jesus limits the number of disciples to twelve. And Jesus makes them dependent upon him. They are to "be with him," and he is the one who will give them authority and send them out. Jesus does not appoint the twelve until the extent of the crowds require it (3:7-14), and he does not send out the twelve until he encounters opposition in his hometown (6:1-13). His instructions to the disciples serve to keep followers from breaking away and beginning their own faction. And he discourages (though he does not prevent) sympathizers outside the core group from carrying out the role of disciples. Such dependency formation of the core group leaves Jesus as the central node of the network—even during his absence after his death when the disciples are to carry on "in Jesus' name."[23]

Lack of Communal Formation

In Mark's narrative world there is no explicit formation of ongoing, stationary "communities." The Gospels of Matthew and John depict Jesus giving directions for Christian communal life after his death (e.g., Matt. 18:16-20; John 13:12-17; 15:9-17). The author of the Gospel of Luke presents the picture of the early Christian community in the Acts of the Apostles (e.g., 2:42-47). So too, the Didache provides for Christian leadership and organization at the village level.[24] The Markan Jesus, however, does not make any provision for clusters of adherents in the Jesus movement to form stationary communities.[25]

Consider, for example, communal formation at the second order zone of the network, relations among the twelve. The narrator describes the disciples as a group, and they act as a group. Nevertheless, their relationship to each other is depicted primarily as a secondary relation based on their primary relation to Jesus: Jesus sends them out by twos (6:6-13); he often includes only Peter, James, and John in his actions (5:37; 9:2; 13:3; 14:33); Peter and "James and John" have separate encounters with Jesus (8:32-33; 10:35-40); and when the disciples argue with each other about who is greatest, it is not primarily an argument about their relation to each other but about the separate status of each in relation to Jesus, as shown by the request of James and John (for whom blood relationship was yet stronger than fictive kinship in relation to the other disciples) to sit on the right or left of Jesus in his glory. Nor does Jesus offer the disciples as a group any promise of authority together at the end, as, for example, Matthew and Luke portray Jesus promising the disciples that they will sit on twelve thrones (Matt. 19:28; Luke 22:29-30). The Markan Jesus sets the twelve apart for their role in the network, but he does not establish them as a separate community or as leaders of a separate community.

Also, the disciples may continue their relationships in other kinship and village networks. Peter and Andrew are brothers; Peter's mother-in-law lives in their house (1:29-31); James and John are brothers and their father is still living (1:20). These four disciples are also dwellers in the same village of Capernaum, and they participate in the occupation of fishing. After they break with these relations to join the Jesus movement, their kinship and village relations may continue as they return home from time to time (9:33; 16:7), although it appears that they no longer engage in fishing. Loyalty to the Jesus network takes precedence over all other loyalties. Yet the interactions of the other network relations may continue, because, again, Jesus does not make a separate community of the disciples.[26]

And after Jesus' death, it is not communal relations among the twelve that are to continue but rather their participation in the network. The primary post-resurrection picture of the future within the narrative is one in which the disciples continue to go out to villages and cities where they will be handed over to sanhedrins, beaten in synagogues, and brought before governors and kings (13:9).[27] Their relations with each other are relations that support network activity. Jesus tells the disciples not to harm one of the "little ones who have faith," referring to others in the network who proclaim or give hospitality, such as the unnamed exorcist (9:37-38) and the little children (10:13-16). Jesus also tells the disciples not to argue among themselves about who is greatest, but to be "servants of all" and "be at peace with each other" (9:33-50). Again, these admonitions provide the support needed to maintain the network, and no provisions are made for community structure, leadership, or discipline. The major thrust of the narrative is not formation of communities but the preparation of participants in the network to be faithful despite the potential abandonment by friends (14:50), betrayal by family (13:12), and the hatred of all (13:13). Thus, while Jesus makes provision for the core group to continue as a network, he does little to provide for ongoing communal relations among the twelve.

In the same way, Mark's Jesus does not provide for relations between and among those at the third order zone of the network, the sympathizers who receive the disciples by hospitality. In the larger sense, everyone who does the will of God is mother, sister, or brother, but this kinship language in Mark does not appear to refer to roles that followers are to play in relation to each other (3:34-35). Rather, references to fictive kinship relations primarily identify people as being on God's side by virtue of their favorable response to Jesus. Thus, familial language refers to the *solidarity* of those who give a favorable reception to Jesus and his renewal movement, not to communal relations among them. In Mark's narrative, the houses where people gather are depicted not as house churches but as places where hospitality is offered to Jesus and the disciples at the times and in the locations where they proclaim and heal.[28] The houses are places where Jesus and/or his disciples stay and eat and where, in addition to the marketplace and deserted places between villages, people will gather to hear them during their stay in that locale. While people may spread the word about Jesus in the local region where they live, there is no indication that the people in the villages will gather at times when a traveling disciple is not present. Unlike the other Gospels, Jesus does not give instructions about ongoing communal relations for those who hear him or give him hospitality (contrast Matt. 18:15-20; Luke 22:19; John 13:14, 35). On the contrary, as we have seen, Jesus even discourages an ongoing relation between himself and those outside the group of the twelve—except perhaps with those who arrange for him to have a donkey available (11:3) or a room ready (14:14) or with Simon the leper, who gives Jesus hospitality near Jerusalem (14:3). These exceptions reinforce the notion that the primary relations in the Jesus movement in Mark are not those of stationary communities, but of reciprocity in a network based on proclaiming and hospitality.

Also, it is striking that the narrative does not establish communal rites to be repeated, either of Baptism or of the Lord's Supper. Mark presents John's baptism as a preparation that preceded the arrival of the "stronger one." John is the only one who baptizes in water (1:4). When Jesus comes, he will baptize in the Holy Spirit (1:8). After John is arrested, Jesus and the disciples continue to call for repentance (6:12) and Jesus offers forgiveness (2:5; 4:12), but, in Mark's narrative, neither repentance nor forgiveness are any longer connected with a baptism in water. Jesus' later commission to the disciples involves only proclamation, not baptism (13:10; contrast Matt. 28:19).[29] Also, Jesus does not institute an ongoing communal meal. The Passover meal is simply the last meal Jesus has with his disciples before his death (14:12-26; contrast, for example, Luke 22:19). It is portrayed as a dramatic moment in Jesus' last hours related to the meaning of his impending death, and there is no indication in the narrative that it is to be repeated later without Jesus.[30]

Hence, in Mark, there is no establishment of stationary communities with ongoing gatherings for ritual either by the core group of disciples or by clusters of sympathizers in the villages. There is only the establishment of a network. And those who are on the receiving end of the network relate to each other through those proclaimers and healers to whom they give hospitality. This narrative portrayal of the Jesus renewal movement as a network of proclaiming and hospitality is reinforced by the observation that, in the Gospel of Mark, ethical instructions are not about how people should treat each other in Christian communities. Rather, Markan ethical instructions are either about the reciprocity in the network (proclaiming and receiving) or about ordinary family and village life (such as marriage, Sabbath, and food).

The major insight that emerges from this analysis is this: the Jesus network depicted in Mark functions as a renewal movement. Through his own activity and that of his core of disciples, Jesus is seeking not to create a separate community or sect but to revitalize or transform existing communal relations. Thus, Jesus employs the network not to gain members for a new, separate community but to spread the effects of a revitalization process.[31] His goal is to call for renewed allegiance to the God of Israel, in response to the presence of God's kingdom and in preparation for the end—which calls for a revitalization or transformation of existing relations. Hence, as people are renewed—repent, put faith in the good news, are taught by Jesus, become healed or exorcised of a demon, or freed from a handicap—they return revitalized to the relationships in their families and villages. As such, Mark does not depict Jesus and the disciples as figures who establish communities or clusters but as "change agents" who spread renewal at a local level and then move on to the next village.[32] The role of the core group members is to be on the road, and the sympathizers who give hospitality to them are sedentary, renewed Israelites. The future projected within Mark's narrative world appears to be that the core disciples are to continue the same interactions of renewal as they spread the proclamation of the good news into the wider geographical arena of the Gentile nations before the end comes.

Definition of the Network Boundary

The participants and sympathizers in the Jesus network share a common point of view, common values and commitments, expressed minimally in a favorable response to Jesus and a willingness to associate with the Jesus network. In this regard, it is helpful to clarify what distinguishes people who affiliate with the Jesus network from those who do not, to identify the line that separates insiders from outsiders, and to show how the boundary is defined.[33]

Jesus is the character in the narrative who defines the boundary of the network. This boundary distinguishes those who are on the inside from those who are on the outside, those who are for Jesus from those who are against him. Jesus is with God (in terms of the new thing God is doing in establishing the kingdom), and those who are for Jesus align themselves with the renewal of Israel in light of the presence of God's kingdom. Jesus defines this boundary in his opening words: "The time is fulfilled, and the kingdom of God has arrived. Repent, and put faith in the good news" (1:15). People who repent and have renewed faith are *for* Jesus; they are on the inside. The disciples show faith by leaving everything to follow Jesus (1:15-20). Others show faith by coming to Jesus for their own or someone else's healing (e.g., 2:3-5). Still others show faith by hospitality; they receive in houses, provide a meal, give a cup of water, or anoint with oil (e.g., 9:41-42). Others are simply with Jesus as part of the crowds who flock to him or follow him in the desert. Jesus does not assume that all those in the crowd will give favorable responses (4:11) or that all who respond will remain loyal (4:16-19). But, in general, those who respond favorably are on the inside. By contrast, people who react against Jesus are on the outside. Some question him in order to indict him (e.g., 2:7). Others accuse him outright in order to discredit him (3:22). Yet others plot to destroy him (3:1-6). Those who respond negatively and reject Jesus are on the outside—those who do not repent, whose hearts are hardened, who oppose and accuse Jesus, who do not "hear" Jesus, or who refuse hospitality to Jesus or his disciples.

As the story progresses, Jesus explains more fully to adherents the norms of the movement. It is typical of recruitment movements that people initially join because of a specific desire (for example, to become fishers of people) or need (for example, to be healed) and only later do they learn the full ideology of the movement.[34] As Mark's story develops, Jesus sharpens the distinction between those with him and those against him in terms of the contrast between those who think "the things of God" and those who think "the things of people" (8:33). Thinking the things of God represents what God wills for people—to lose one's life for the good news of the kingdom of God, to be least, and to be a slave to others (8:35; 9:35; 10:43-35). Thinking the things of people represents what people want for themselves—to save their lives, to be great, and to have power over others. These additional ideal norms define the external boundary more stringently and take into account the possibility of people falling away in the face of persecution or due to the lure of the things of this age (4:1-20).

Yet these standards also open the boundary encompassing God's people to include people outside the network. For example, there is the widow who puts the coins into the Temple treasury (12:41-44). This character is actually outside the network established by Jesus. In the narrative, she has had no contact with Jesus or his disciples but is simply observed by Jesus; yet Jesus refers to her as an exemplary figure. Presumably, she does the will of God according to Markan standards—she is least, and by putting into the treasury out of her need she loses her life ("her whole living"). The implication is that it is not necessary for a person to be linked to the Jesus network in order for that person to be within the bounds of those who think the things of God. Thus, there are two boundaries: the network boundary as defined by association with Jesus or Jesus' name, and the boundary of the kingdom. Because Jesus is not establishing a substitute community for Israel, he affirms kingdom activity when he sees it whether it is due to his network activity or not.

This last observation fits with the Markan depiction of Jesus' preaching as sowing, whereby the type of soil that is already there when the word is proclaimed shapes the responses of the hearers (4:1-20). The proclamation provides an occasion for the hearers to reveal if they are on "God's side" or not. Because the behavior of the widow is consonant with "doing the things of God," Jesus knows without proclaiming to her that her behavior is within the bounds of God's people. In this way, the figure of the widow, as well as Joseph of Arimathea, the centurion, and other minor characters in the Markan narrative world serve to undermine an assumption that the boundary of the network is the same as the boundary of God's people. Such an assumption is also subverted by the depiction of some inside the Jesus network who behave contrary to "the things of God." For example, the disciples often behave according to "the things of people": they argue about who is greatest (9:34), dominate others (9:38; 10:13-15), and flee to save their lives (14:50). Thus, Mark's narrative shows that, while the definition of the boundary of God's people is clear, it is not easy to determine who is inside and who is outside the boundary. Some people outside the Jesus network may be among God's people and some inside the network may not. The network has deliberately porous boundaries. As such, Mark depicts the Jesus movement existing not to guard boundaries for its own preservation but to be wide open in service to the community of Israel. In this way, the teaching of the Markan Jesus discourages adherents from thinking of their faction in exclusivistic ways.

In the narrative, the boundary definition of the Jesus network effectively cuts across all other boundaries for identifying God's people, especially those set by the authorities of Israelite society. The

authorities as portrayed in Mark's story have set different boundaries, according to their interpretation of God's will, as the means to
determine who is with God and who is against God: clean/unclean;
Jew/Gentile; those who follow the traditions of the elders/those who
do not; God's land/Gentile land; the "righteous" according to the
Law/the "sinners." The Jesus network cuts across all these traditional
boundary lines: village of origin, ties of ancestry, family, class, nation-
ality, religious belief and practice, and ascribed power roles. Because
the boundary definition of the Jesus network contains no prejudgments about who may be in or out, the limit of the Jesus movement
in Mark is potentially the whole world—"from the extremities of
earth to the extremities of heaven" (13:27). The people inside the network have defined the boundary and provide boundary mechanisms,
but they do not predetermine or set limits on who associates with the
network and who does not. As we shall see, only those outside the network who reject the network determine its limits.

Extent of the Network

We may clarify the nonexclusivistic thrust of the Jesus movement in
Mark by comparing within the narrative world the operational space
of the network with geographical space. Geographical space refers to
the larger organization of the perceived space of the cosmos, while
operational space refers to the parameters in which a given group will
permit its participants to be active. In some groups, such as the
Essenes at Qumran, a sect will permit its members to operate only in
a severely limited area within the full extent of cosmological space.[35]
In other groups, operational space equals potentially the full extent
of geographical space in the cosmos.

In the Markan narrative, Jesus' opponents observe a major geographical distinction between Israel and the nations, and their operational space is within Israel. Within that boundary, the Pharisees
further set themselves apart from those who are unclean. For the
Pharisees, the boundaries of separation were thus socioreligious as

well as geographical—observed at the Temple, on the Sabbath (3:1-6), at meals (2:15-17), in the exclusion of lepers and unclean women, in terms of unclean food (7:1-23), and with regard to other instances of defilement, such as corpses or demons or blood or illnesses. Thus, the operational space of Jesus' opponents in the narrative is determined by the geographical lines they set at the national boundary and by the social boundaries they set within the nation.

By contrast, the Jesus network, as depicted in the narrative, recognizes only one operational limit, the full extent of geographical or cosmic space, the outer ends of the flat earth.[36] There are only a few clues in the story that reveal the depiction of the cosmos—perhaps as being quite limited in scope, with Gentile nations surrounding Israel, and with reachable "ends of the earth." In any case, the disciples are to proclaim the good news to all the Gentile nations (13:10). As such, the operational space equals the full extent of geographical space, however that was imagined.

Nor does the network observe social boundaries. In the narrative, the only limiting boundary in some doubt is the social and geographical boundaries between Jews and Gentiles. On the first occasion when Jesus goes to Gentile territory, to the Decapolis, and drives out the demons, he soon leaves because Gentiles do not want him there (5:1-20). On the second occasion when Jesus goes to Gentile territory, to the region of Tyre, he seeks to remain in seclusion but is discovered. He even refuses to exorcise a demon from the daughter of a Syrophoenician woman (7:24-30), telling her that the children (Jews) should be satisfied first before the dogs (Gentiles) receive the benefits of the kingdom. Yet her insight and persistence serve to change Jesus' mind (heart), and he goes directly back to the Decapolis, where he heals a deaf-mute and feeds a large crowd in the desert (7:31—8:13). From this point in the narrative, Jesus no longer treats the Jew/Gentile distinction as a boundary either for separation or for delay. This event removes the last social boundary that might inhibit proclamation in any way. After Jesus' death, after Israel and Jerusalem have been confronted with the good news, the disciples will proclaim to synagogues and sanhedrins (Jews in Palestine and in the Diaspora) and before governors and kings (among Gentiles, 13:9). It seems that the mandate given to the disciples in the narrative is to proclaim the good news to the ends of the (flat) earth.[37] The Jesus network that is projected into the future of the narrative world after Jesus' death aims at being a cosmic renewal movement before the end comes.

Thus, in the Markan narrative, the Jesus network disregards all social and geographical boundaries as means to determine insiders from outsiders, who is with the kingdom and who is against it. In addition to entering Gentile territory, Jesus crosses every social boundary of uncleanness. He touches a leper (1:40-45), eats with tax collectors (2:15-17), has contact with a woman having a flow of blood, places hands on a corpse (5:21-43), and drives out "unclean" spirits in a graveyard in Gentile territory (5:1-20).[38] Consequently, for the Jesus network, boundaries that limit contact with people are ignored. Even God is depicted as abandoning the spatial confines of the Temple in order to be accessible wherever people pray in faith (15:38; 11:22-25). The only remaining boundary is the ends of the earth—the four winds, the extremity of earth and the extremity of heaven—where the son of humanity will send his angels to gather the chosen ones at the establishment of the rule of God in power (13:27). A cosmology imagined in this way, with no limiting internal boundaries, best serves the spreading influence of the core participants of the Jesus network. In turn, the network, with its refusal to guard boundaries serves to maintain the open cosmology.

This Markan portrait of the spreading proclamation of the kingdom by a core group of disciples in a network is reinforced in the narrative by the implied ideology of holiness embraced by the Jesus network in contrast to that of the authorities as they are depicted in the narrative.[39] For the Markan authorities, holiness seems to be a force that must be protected from the pernicious influence of uncleanness. As such, the Jewish leaders, based on their allegiance to God's commands, erect barriers against contact with "sinners," unclean people, and Gentiles, so that the holy people and the holy God are not polluted. By contrast, for the Jesus network in Mark, the flow of power is reversed, such that holiness seems to be a power that overcomes uncleanness. The paradigm is this: when Jesus touches a leper, instead of Jesus being rendered unclean, Jesus cleanses the leper (1:40-45). Jesus spreads wholeness (holiness) everywhere, making the maimed whole, cleansing the leper, and overpowering unclean spirits. In the narrative, the appearance of the spreading power of holiness through the Holy Spirit (1:8-12), bringing healing and wholeness, is one of the important dimensions of Jesus' announcement: "The kingdom of God has arrived" (1:15). For God has ripped open the heavens, crossed the boundary from heaven to earth, anointed Jesus with the *Holy Spirit*, which in turn drives Jesus to confront Satan and plunder Satan's goods. In the narrative depiction, this spreading holiness is the impelling cosmic force behind the expanding social network of Jesus' renewal movement.

Boundary Mechanisms of the Network

Boundary mechanisms are devices or triggers that test people and reveal by their response whether they are sympathizers of a group or not, that is, whether they are inside a boundary of influence or not. Boundary mechanisms are thus words or actions that trigger a response from people. By their response, people identify whether they are for or against that particular movement.

We can infer from the parable of the sower and the explanation of it how the boundary mechanisms work in Mark's narrative world (4:1-20). Jesus (the sower) sows the word (seed), and different types of people (soils) respond in different ways. In a sense, some people are already with God or at least predisposed to be with God's kingdom, and the boundary mechanisms give these characters occasions to show the kind of people they are and to produce fruit. Yet in another sense, the response may be a real boundary-crossing from opposition to active affiliation, a meaningful change or choice on the part of the person, since what the word seeks to elicit is repentance in faith leading to forgiveness (1:15; 4:12). Others may reject the network because they find the boundary mechanism offensive. Thus, boundary mechanisms either situate people on the inside or effect a rejection.

In the Jesus movement in Mark, there are several boundary mechanisms. For example, the words of proclamation by Jesus and the disciples are boundary mechanisms. As such, the parable itself is a boundary mechanism.[40] The response that the parable elicits is, on the one hand, an understanding that leads to repentance and renewed faith in God or, on the other hand, a greater blindness and hardness of heart (4:3, 9, 11-12). Thus, the parable divides the hearers by virtue of their responses into those who understand and those who do not, those who have the secret about the presence of the rule of God in Jesus' activity and those for whom the parable only obscures further, those who are inside the boundary and those who are not. In a similar way, the actions of Jesus, particularly the healings and the exorcisms, function as boundary mechanisms (not that this is their only or even primary function). Most who observe the healings respond favorably; they praise God or spread the word or come for further healing. Others, however, respond negatively; they accuse Jesus of healing on the Sabbath (3:2) or of being possessed by Satan (3:22) and thus go off to plot against him (3:6). Furthermore, Jesus himself is a boundary mechanism. And for those who hear the disciples who are sent out, Jesus' "name" is a boundary mechanism (9:41; 13:9, 13). A favorable acceptance of Jesus identifies one as a sympathizer to Jesus' renewal movement, while an unfavorable response places one on the outside. Jesus, his words, and his actions, represent the presence of the rule of God. Those who side with him will be in the rule of God when it comes in power; those who reject him will be shunned or excluded (8:38).

The key event in the Gospel that serves as a boundary mechanism is the death of Jesus. Parables and healings are not entirely adequate as boundary mechanisms, because a reaction to them does not take into account whether a person will persist in association with Jesus' name in the face of oppression and persecution—the loss of status or power and the threat of death. Trouble and persecution as well as the anxieties of the age and the lure of wealth can lead a person to fall away from the commitment to proclaim the good news or can lead a person to refuse any longer to associate with those who do proclaim

(4:16-17). A follower can have a hardened heart (6:52; 8:17). Relevant also is whether a follower either seeks to be restored from failure (cf. 16:7) or turns against Jesus (14:21). Thus, a favorable reaction to Jesus at the beginning of his activity is not an adequate indication that people will be loyal when difficulties arise or when sacrifices are called for. Jesus' death is therefore a key boundary mechanism, because the reaction to it reveals whether people understand Jesus fully, will support Jesus' cause when Jesus is rejected, and will accept their own suffering for Jesus' name. For those who are ashamed of Jesus as one who will be rejected and killed, of them also the son of humanity will be ashamed when he comes in glory (8:38). By implication, each testing or persecution for Jesus' name is a boundary mechanism for those already in the movement.[41]

In the narrative world, Jesus and the disciples provide boundary mechanisms by their proclamation first within Israel and then to all nations, to as many people as possible before the end comes. By proclaiming and healing in Jesus' name, the disciples give the people of all nations the opportunity to reveal their true character and repent before the final judgment comes. The disciples are to sow seeds everywhere, then "sleep and arise," leaving the responses up to people and to God (4:26-27). When the Jesus network reaches "the extremity of earth," the end will come and the rule of God will be established in judgment and salvation (19:27). In a sense then, the Jesus network functions not only as a renewal movement, but also as an "identification" and "opportunity" movement in preparation for the imminent end, whereby people, in response to boundary mechanisms, are identified as being with God (as defined by Jesus) or not, and they are given an opportunity to repent.

Rituals of Network Affiliation

Rituals of affiliation refer to those patterns of behavior, however minimal or extensive, that represent the crossing of the boundary from outside to inside.[42] For the core disciples, the ritual is that they leave those things that represent stability and security in order to go off with Jesus in response to a call to discipleship: Simon and Andrew drop their nets (1:17-18); James and John leave their father with the hired hands in the boat (1:19-20); Levi leaves the tax office (2:13-14); and the twelve go off to the mountain (3:13-19). The wealthy man aborts this ritual by refusing to give up his property (10:17-31). The Markan Jesus summarizes the ritual when he says that those who follow him have "left houses or brothers or sisters or a father or a mother or children or fields" (10:29). Jesus and the disciples thus leave behind those things that would compete with their allegiance to the network and that would inhibit their movement from place to place. Jesus states the heart of the ritual when he says that those who want to follow him are to take up their cross (8:34); that is, they are to be prepared to make any sacrifice and to take any risk necessary in the service of the good news. Thus, for the disciples, the ritual of affiliation involves sacrifice and risk and is thereby consistent with their mission role, which in turn requires sacrifice and risk.

For those sympathizers who come for healing or who "receive" Jesus and his disciples, there are other patterns of behavior that comprise the rituals of affiliation. For example, those who are healed frequently express common patterns of behavior: they come to Jesus, persist in overcoming obstacles, kneel before him, and plead with him (e.g., 1:40-45; 2:1-12; 7:24-30). Others offer hospitality, receiving Jesus and his disciples into their houses, offering a meal, or giving a cup of water. In the narrative, the most widespread ritual of affiliation is the simple act of coming to Jesus as part of a crowd that greets him or follows him around or expresses amazement at a healing. All these behaviors identify a favorable response to Jesus.

All of the rituals of affiliation are actions that, within the standards of the story, are expressions of faith in God. The rituals of affiliation are thus in line with Jesus' opening invitation to respond to the presence of the kingdom of God by repenting and putting faith in the good news (1:15). As the story progresses, the requirements of continued affiliation, as we have seen, become more stringent. The disciples are to separate not only from the structures of their family and village life, they are also to separate from some of the norms and structures of the society. In the story, both Jesus and the leaders of Israel share the core value of the culture: obedience to God, primarily as expressed in the Jewish Law (Torah). Yet each group has a different interpretation of the Law and a contrasting view of the structures necessary to carrying out God's will. In the narrative, the authorities represent the dominant interpretation of the Law in the society as portrayed in the story: they believe that people were made for laws (2:27); they judge the new movement by the old categories (2:21-22); and they do not eat with sinners (2:16) or heal on the Sabbath (3:2) or allow someone who has made the "corban" vow any longer to help parents (7:9-13). In the narrative, Jesus is unable to effect a transformation of these structures, and so it becomes necessary to break with such practices. This break does not represent a break with the Jewish Law as such, but with practices based on a Pharisaic interpretation of the Law.[43] In the narrative, the Pharisees appear to interpret the Law in light of the importance of holiness as separation (cf. Exod. 19:5-6; Lev. 19:2). By contrast, Jesus interprets the Law in light of the commandments to "love God" and to "love the neighbor as oneself" (12:28-34; compare Deut. 6:4).

Furthermore, the people in the network are to break with cultural-political practices and structures that are oppressive and self-serving. The authorities want to save their lives, be great, and exert authority over people. As such, they employ laws to accuse and dominate (e.g., 3:1-6); they destroy others to save themselves (11:18); and they neglect or take advantage of those in need (12:40). Jesus tells the disciples to refuse to participate in such relationships: "It is not to be like this among you" (10:42-45). The disciples are not to identify with these structures, because these structures are contrary to God's will for people as Jesus interprets it and contrary to the structures of the kingdom of God as Jesus proclaims it. Besides, the narrative leaders over Israel who embrace these structures will be destroyed and the vineyard given to others (12:1-12). The Temple will be destroyed (13:2), and the whole system will give way to the coming kingdom of God. In contrast to the national leaders and the Gentile "great ones," the disciples are to serve, be least, and lose life for others, so as to be prepared to participate in the imminent coming of the kingdom of God in its second and final stage.

Nonmaintenance of the Network Boundary

Boundary maintenance refers to actions taken by people inside a group to guard the external boundary of the group.[44] In social groups, the possibilities for boundary maintenance are to exclude certain individuals or categories of people from crossing inside the boundary, to expel people already inside the boundary, and to break off from another part of the group by fission or schism. In the Jesus network depicted in Mark, there is no provision given for any of these options. As we have seen, Jesus *defines* the boundary line that identifies whether a person is part of Jesus' renewal movement or against it, but Jesus does *not maintain* the boundary or establish means to guard the boundary. This is so because the Markan Jesus is not creating an alternate community, the boundaries of which need to be guarded against certain groups from without or certain apostates from within. The Jesus network is in an expansive rather than a defensive posture. In any case, it is illuminating to observe the absence of, indeed the prohibition against, procedures for boundary maintenance in the Markan narrative world.

Nonexclusion or Self-Exclusion

In Mark, as we have seen, there is every effort given not to exclude people or to prevent them by any prejudgment from the opportunity to sympathize with the renewal movement and affiliate with the network. Those who sow the seeds are to proclaim everywhere without regard to the kinds of people (soil) being addressed. Jesus welcomes all who come to him and crosses every barrier to reach people. Jesus receives little children, the people with the least social status and power (9:36-37), and he rebukes the disciples when they try to prevent children from coming to him (10:13-16). He condemns the high priests because they have not provided for Gentiles to worship in the Temple (11:15-19). No prejudgments about people are to prevent affiliation with the network.

While the leader of the network has defined the external boundary, those on the inside do not set the location of that boundary in terms of who enters and who does not. Rather, only the people outside who come in contact with the network decide if they will be in or out. Thus, there is self-exclusion only. We see this when Jesus goes to Gentile territory and exorcises a demon but then leaves when people plead with him to go away from their territory (5:16-18). Likewise, the disciples go to all villages until people do not receive them, at which point they go away and shake off the dust under their feet (6:11). Such an act simply testifies to a decision already made by other people to exclude themselves by rejecting the Jesus movement.[45] The key line is, "Whoever is not against us is for us" (9:40). Jesus does *not* say, "Whoever is not for us is against us." The emphasis is on outsiders who reject. Thus, the limits of the network are set not by those within, but by those outside who reject the proclamation. That is, the role of those inside is to provide boundary mechanisms everywhere: those who encounter the network and reject it set the outer limits of the network, and those who encounter the network and do not reject it are included on the inside.

Nonexpulsion

In Mark's narrative, we see the same prohibitions against expulsion that we have seen in regard to exclusion. When the disciples attempt to stop an exorcist from driving out demons in Jesus' name, Jesus tells them not to stop that person or prevent him from exorcising (9:38-41). Here is someone who is an affiliate of the larger network simply by virtue of using Jesus' name (zone four), but who is unacceptable to the disciples because he was "not following us." Jesus strictly warns the disciples against causing to stumble such "little ones who have faith" (9:42).

Similarly, Jesus himself continues to be loyal to the disciples and does not disown or expel them despite their lack of faith and understanding, their fear and failure, their flight and denial. Even after his death, the message to his disciples that Jesus will go ahead of them to Galilee includes "even Peter" (16:7). In this regard, note especially Jesus' treatment of Judas. Jesus knows at the beginning of the Passover meal that one of the twelve disciples will betray him, and he says that "it would be better for this man if he had not been born" (14:17-21). Yet he shares the bread as well as the cup with his disciples, and they "all" drink from it (14:23).[46] This is an extraordinary gesture, especially in light of the significance of meals as a cultural expression among ancient Jews of inclusiveness/exclusiveness. Judas turned "against" Jesus, just as Peter had become a direct adversary ("Satan") to Jesus and as the disciples had had hearts that were hardened. Yet Jesus makes no move to expel or dissociate from any of them. He continues to be loyal to them, while they disqualify themselves. Likewise, in the narrative world, followers are prohibited from expelling others in the movement.

Non-schism

Nor is any schism anticipated for this group. In the future projected for the Jesus network within the world of Mark's narrative, there is no indication that one part of the Jesus movement will break from another part. The only exception might be Jesus' warning to his disciples not to be misled in the future by people coming in his name, saying "I am" (13:6). The Markan Jesus may be predicting here that figures outside the network, rival messianic claimants to Jesus, will come in the name of "messiah." These are false prophets and false messiahs to whom others point, saying, "Look, here is the messiah, there he is" (13:21-22). The disciples should not be misled by them.[47] If this interpretation is correct, then there is no fission or separation from others within the movement; rather, Jesus' words are a warning to those inside the network not to be misled by other factions outside the network who, by signs and wonders, might lead them astray. On the other hand, the Markan Jesus may be predicting that his later followers will emerge in his name prophesying falsely and claiming to be Jesus returning.[48] In this case, Jesus' warnings to the disciples serve to guard the disciples against others within the larger Jesus network who have formed their own factions and placed themselves at the center. As such, the Markan Jesus is warning the disciples to keep him at the center of the movement even after his death. Yet even here, the disciples are not to stop these people or to expel them (cf. 9:39) but only to avoid being misled by them.

Warnings

The major boundary maintenance in the narrative world is Jesus warning people. He warns people on the inside to avoid behavior that would later place them outside. Sometimes he does this in the form of commands in the imperative. For example, he warns the disciples to beware of the leaven of the Pharisees and the Herodians—in order to keep their hearts from being hardened (8:15, 17). More often, however, he warns people of the consequences to occur in the future as a result of their present behavior. He warns them that they will lose their lives (8:35), that the son of humanity will be ashamed of them (8:38), that they will be thrown to Gehenna (9:43-49), that they will be least (10:31), that they might not enter the kingdom of God (10:15), that it would be better if the betrayer had not been born (14:21), and that it would be better if a person who caused others to sin would have a millstone tied around the neck and be thrown into the sea (9:42). None of these sanctions serves to expel anyone in the present; rather, the expulsion and punishment will be in the near future at the end, when the kingdom will finally be established in glory and power. As such, the warnings are usually made in the form of a conditional statement: "Whoever does certain behavior . . . the following conse-quences will take place for that person in the future." Although the projected consequences will involve future shunning and severe pun-ishments by God, the warning of these future consequences by Jesus, like so much else in Mark, has the effect of being a noncoercive form of boundary maintenance in the present. The warnings encourage followers to repent and be restored.[49] Even here, the warnings serve not to keep people within a new "community" established by Jesus, but to encourage people to continue to identify with and participate in a renewal movement in preparation for the coming kingdom of God.

The Markan Jesus makes another kind of statement to those who have already chosen to reject the movement or whose behavior is clearly outside the limits of doing the will of God: those who call the Holy Spirit a demon will never be pardoned (3:29); those who devour the houses of widows will get a more severe sentence (12:40); those in the vineyard who fail to bear fruit will be destroyed (12:9); and the Powerful One will judge those who consider Jesus' claim of messiahship to be blasphemy (14:62). These statements clearly are not warnings, as if meant to lead these people to repentance. Nor are they pronouncements effecting a judgment. That is left up to God. Rather, these statements are made subsequent to the offending behavior, and they identify what in the future will be the consequences from God for their behavior.

Thus, there is almost no boundary maintenance in the Gospel of Mark—no exclusion (people exclude themselves), no expulsion (only warnings to the effect that the future will bring expulsion), and no fission (only warnings not to be misled by others). As we have seen, these features are consonant with the general portrayal of Jesus' movement as a renewal movement in Israel. Jesus does not guard boundaries, because he is not seeking to create an alternative community but to spread revitalization in light of his announcement about the kingdom of God. The core participants continue to spread the good news, while the renewed sympathizers return home. As we shall see, the prohibition against guarding boundaries (that is, exercising discipline) is consonant with the larger norms in the world of the story, represented by the admonitions to be servants to all and not to lord over or exert authority over others. The prohibition against guarding boundaries is also consonant with the attitude expressed in the narrative toward bodily boundaries, namely that "there is nothing outside people that by going into them is able to defile them" (7:1-23). Followers are to guard neither the group boundary nor the bodily boundary. Thus, there is a coherent system in the narrative world of Mark that reflects a consistent refusal to guard boundaries at all levels—the cosmological, the social, and the bodily.[50]

Roles within the Network

An analysis of roles reveals the internal organization of a group. The Jesus network as depicted in Mark is a loosely organized core group with supporters in the various villages and towns. As we have seen, the Markan Jesus does not establish organized communities with some people in charge and others not. Rather, the Jesus movement is a network based on proclaiming and giving hospitality marked by a willingness to associate with the name of Jesus. These roles are typical of renewal factions: a leader sets the goals; a core group of the network has some benefit to offer; and supporters receive the benefit and give hospitality, acclamation, and loyalty in return.

In the narrative world, Jesus makes a sharp distinction between the two roles of proclaiming and receiving. The first role is set out most clearly in relation to the twelve disciples: they are to be with Jesus (3:14); they are to go from village to village (6:7-13); and they are to proclaim, heal, and drive out demons (3:15). By choosing twelve, Jesus sets a definite limit to those who will be fulfilling the role of proclaimers. Early in the story, there are many disciples following Jesus (2:13-15), but he chooses twelve from among them (3:12-19). From this point on, the term "disciples" refers to the twelve. While other people may follow Jesus or proclaim, only these twelve are called disciples. This limited use of the word is consistent with their functional role in a teacher-disciple relationship, whereby the twelve are with him as disciples, learn from him, do his bidding, and seek to be like him.[51]

Sometimes, there is a larger group of people who gather around the twelve but who are not called disciples: "those around him" when Jesus explains the parable of the sower (4:10), the crowd with the disciples when Jesus tells them to take up their cross (8:34), and those who follow along going up to Jerusalem (10:32). In this category are perhaps also Levi (2:14), the exorcist who drives out demons in Jesus' name (9:38), and the rich man who would have followed Jesus had he accepted Jesus' invitation (10:17-22). These are people who may "follow" Jesus and do things similar to the disciples but who are not part of the twelve and are not called "disciples." The Markan Jesus clearly distinguishes the discipleship roles from the roles of those who receive healing. Jesus never asks anyone he heals to follow him or to become a disciple. As we have seen, Jesus tells those who are healed or exorcised of a demon not to proclaim, not to spread the word (e.g., 1:44). He tells them to go home (2:11) or to tell their family (5:19-20) or to go away (10:52) or to stay away from the village (8:26). These people are to play their role throughout the Gospel by coming to Jesus for healing or by offering hospitality to Jesus and the disciples as they go from place to place.[52]

Despite a Markan portrayal of Jesus as one who distinguishes these roles, the narrative as a whole consistently blurs and subverts the distinction between the two roles. The people who are healed act like disciples. They ignore Jesus' instructions and proceed to proclaim (7:37), spread the word (1:45), follow (10:52), go from village to village telling about Jesus (5:20), and show an understanding of Jesus' riddles (7:28-29). The distinctiveness of the discipleship role is further subverted in the story when people other than the disciples perform functions that are associated with discipleship—burying Jesus (15:42-47; cf. John's disciples in 6:29) and going to the grave to anoint his body (12:1-2; cf. 14:3-9; see John 19:39-42). The subversion is reinforced by the types of characters who carry out these roles in contrast to the Jewish males who make up the core group: a former leper (1:45), a Gentile who was exorcised of a demon (5:20), a Gentile woman (7:24-30), a former beggar (10:52), and the women at the grave (15:40-41; 16:1-8).[53] At the end of the Gospel, the women who had been "following" Jesus and "serving" him in Galilee were even told by the young man at the grave to "go, tell. . . ." This blurring of roles is reinforced by the consistent depiction of the disciples as failing to carry out their role. Not only do the disciples fail to anoint Jesus or to bury him but they also fail to listen (8:14-21), understand (4:13; 7:18), follow instructions (13:35; cf. 14:37), show faith (4:40; 9:19), and support Jesus faithfully in his hour of ordeal (14:32-42).

This narrative blurring of the roles set out by Jesus has two very important effects on the hearers of the Gospel.[54] In the first place, the subversion of roles leaves the hearers confused about role definitions in the network and about who is to carry out those roles, thereby encouraging ordinary folk among the hearers to assume discipleship roles. In the second place, the subversion of roles leaves hearers reluctant to think that the disciples are to be considered in any higher rank and authority than others, for the disciples often fail where others succeed. There are to be no pretensions to status or privilege based on leadership roles. These effects are consonant with the explicit statements in the Gospel that discourage people from seeking status and authority for themselves.

Internal Relationships: Collateral Solidarity and Nonhierarchical Roles

The relationships of the Jesus' movement in Mark are collateral; that is, they are relationships spread out horizontally without hierarchy and without regard for endurance through time. Collateral relationships stand in contrast to lineal relationships in which there is a concern for endurance through time and the need for hierarchical structures in order to guarantee succession of leadership.[55] Because the Markan Jesus is the center of the network and is to remain so even after his death and because the time is short before Jesus will return to power, there is no concern with succession and therefore no need for hierarchy. As such, the relationships in the network are collateral rather than lineal.

In regard to the relationships among those in the network, Jesus discourages a hierarchy of status and power. He condemns the disciples when they argue with each other about who is greatest (9:33-37). He denies the request of James and John for places to sit on the right and left in his glory (10:35-40). The disciples expect to have power and status as a result of being with Jesus, but this expectation is completely overturned by the narrative. Jesus tells the disciples to emulate the status of a child (10:14) and to renounce power over people in favor of the posture of a servant or a slave (10:41-45). "Child" and "servant" are household terms, which, if their use in Mark's Gospel is to be properly understood, must be placed in the larger context of fictive kinship relationships in the Gospel.

Fictive or metaphorical kinship refers to those familial-like relationships that develop among people who are not necessarily related by birth and who are held together by commitments and roles that are similar to those within households of birth families. When we look at the larger framework of fictive kinship or household-like relationships in the Gospel of Mark, we see two different uses of household terms: one set of terms establishes collateral solidarity, and the other set of terms establishes the types of roles people are to play in relation to each other.

First, the network established by Jesus as depicted in Mark's Gospel is described in terms of nonhierarchical kinship relations. Jesus says, "Whoever does the will of God is my brother and sister and mother" (3:35). Later, he observes that the disciples who have left their blood relatives receive "houses and brothers and sisters and mothers and (adult) children" (10:30). I have pointed out that the language used in these passages does not refer to communal roles people are to play in relation to each other but to the solidarity among those who do the will of God by responding favorably to Jesus. This solidarity is to be stronger than natural kinship ties, as evidenced by Jesus' break with his family and the fact that the disciples leave theirs (1:20; 10:28). The mothers, sisters, brothers, and adult children whom the core group of disciples receive as a result of leaving their blood relatives represent the familial-like solidarity that comes not from separate, organized communities, but from the hospitality offered in the relationships between the disciples sent out and those who receive them in their houses. Disciples also have solidarity with each other for the same reasons, even when they are related by birth, as is the case with the brothers Peter and Andrew and the brothers James and John.

Second, the roles within this collateral solidarity are depicted as horizontal and collateral. Again the key is the choice of language. Note that the household roles that are missing in the two passages cited above are fathers, servants, and little children. The term "fathers" is absent, because there are to be no fathers in the network.[56] God is the only Father (11:25; 14:36). The disciples are to leave their birth fathers (10:29), but they do not receive fathers in the new fictive kinship relations (10:30). There are to be no authority figures in the network, for no one is to dominate another. "Servants" and "little children" are absent from the passages cited above, because these are the roles everyone in the network is to take in relation to everyone else. The roles that people assume for themselves are to have the status of little children (9:37; 10:15) and the authority of servants and slaves (9:35; 10:43-45). In terms of status, the roles of servants, slaves, and little children were the lowest among household roles. In terms of power and authority, the servant and the slave roles are functionally oriented toward others. That is, there was no one under the slave over whom the slave could exercise any authority. Everything a slave did was, by definition, for the benefit of others. Thus, the roles in the network are not, strictly speaking, egalitarian, either in terms of power or in terms of status. Rather, the roles are contra-hierarchical.[57] The roles prescribed for the network are a reaction against the oppressive use of power over people in the larger society. Followers are not to be like the Gentile "great ones" who lord it over others and exert authority over people (10:42-45). Followers are to be slaves of each other, some proclaiming and healing, others offering hospitality.

Thus, those who do the will of God are to see themselves in solidarity as brothers, sisters, mothers, and (adult) children in contrast to the outsiders (3:34-35; 10:29-30), but in relation to each other and in relation to all, they are to see themselves as slaves and servants and children with respect to status and power (9:35; 10:43). Jesus is the prime exemplar of these roles. It is compatible with this concern for humility and service that followers of Jesus are to welcome small children (9:36-37; 10:13-16) and are not to divorce wives or husbands (10:1-12). Followers are to leave and, if necessary, to break with fathers, mothers, sisters, brothers, and (older) children, but they are not to abandon responsibility for wives or little children.[58]

These admonitions of Jesus to be as servants and children function to subvert any community organization, just as his admonitions not to exclude or to expel serve to subvert boundary maintenance. There simply are no means given in the narrative world for participants in the network to make decisions about leaders, organization, discipline, or boundary maintenance. The Jesus of Mark subverts the organizational means to establish and maintain separate ongoing communities, for, as we have seen, the Jesus network as depicted in Mark is a renewal movement in mission. Again, Jesus' opposition to boundary maintenance and hierarchy is consonant with the larger cosmic values of the narrative, for the roles of the network express Jesus' teaching of love for God and neighbor, values that Jesus promulgates for the revitalization of Israel.

Power and Authority
in the Kingdom of God

I now look more closely at the larger moral framework in Mark's narrative world that supports and sustains these social dynamics of the network. I do this in terms of Mark's understanding of the dynamics of authority and power in the kingdom of God.

The concept of authority is difficult to delineate.[59] I will use the concept here primarily in the sense of "authorization," the right given to someone by something (e.g., law or custom) or someone (e.g., God) to do a task, along with the resources to carry it out. Authority must be acknowledged to be effective. In the case of Mark, Jesus is authorized by God to be the Messiah and is given the power of the Spirit to carry out that task. Authority is distinct from coercion; for when coercion is employed, authorization is irrelevant. We can also distinguish authority from persuasion, for, again, when a person persuades someone by an argument, the authorization of the person is irrelevant. We identify power as a force that may be employed in coercion (e.g., killing) or in noncoercive ways as an expression of authority (e.g., healing). Likewise, influence may be exerted as an effect of authority or as the result of persuasion.

In the Markan narrative world, a contrast is developed between the authority of Jesus and the authority of the leaders of Israel. Jesus' teaching has divine authority, while the scribes' teaching has no divine authority (1:21-28). Jesus has his authorization from God, while the leaders, by implication, have their authority from people (11:27-33). Jesus does not look to the reactions of people, but truthfully teaches the way of God (12:14); the leaders of Israel speak and act in response to what the people will favor or approve, out of fear of the loss of honor or power (6:26; 11:32; 15:15). Jesus does not use his authority to gain status or a position of power; the leaders of Israel use their power in coercive ways to keep their positions, employing legal and illegal means to get rid of Jesus, whose popularity with the people they fear (11:18; 12:12). Jesus does not use his power to lord it over people or to exercise authority over people by coercing them but to serve (10:45); the leaders of Israel are destructive, seeking to dominate the crowds and to manipulate the legal process in order to put Jesus to death. These contrasting narrative portraits of "authority from God" and "authority from people" are consistently maintained throughout the story.

The distinctiveness of Jesus' authority in Mark's narrative world is that he does not—indeed cannot—use power to lord it over people. Jesus has power over all nonhuman forces that oppress people, but he has no power over people. Jesus can use power to coerce demons and nature and to get rid of illness, but he cannot use his power from God to control people. Indeed, in one breath, he can command a leper to be cleansed and get immediate results and, in the next breath, command the healed man to be quiet—only to see him go out and spread the word (1:40-45). Time after time, Jesus does powerful acts in storms and deserts and over illnesses and maladies and deformities, but he cannot make people do what they do not want to do. For example, he can heal a man of deafness and muteness but he cannot get him to stop talking about it (7:31-37). And he can heal people only when they have faith, for in his hometown he could not do works of power because of the lack of faith (6:5). Thus, the authorization that Jesus has from God does not include power to coerce people

and can be successfully exercised only when people acknowledge it
(cf. also 10:21-22).

Furthermore, the Markan Jesus teaches that it is wrong to use
power, any power, to control others. Jesus does not seek to control
people, but to reach people and to influence them. While the model
he uses for driving out demons is a violent one of plundering a house
(3:23-27), by contrast the models he uses for proclaiming to people
are those of sowing seeds (4:14) and fishing (1:17). Like the slaves and
the son in the parable of the vineyard, Jesus calls for the fruits of the
vineyard from the leadership of Israel but he does nothing to take the
fruits by force or to punish the farmers for their failure to produce
them (12:1-11). Such punishment is left to God. Only God has the
right to punish (12:9). Only in the Temple does Jesus use force (11:15-
17), and then only briefly as a symbolic prophetic action designed to
foreshadow the impending destruction of the Temple. And it is God,
not Jesus, who will destroy the Temple (13:2). Thus, in terms of the
values of the kingdom of God, humans are not to exercise power or
exert authority over other humans in coercive ways.

This prohibition is reinforced by the observation that no follower
of Jesus is to exercise discipline over another. As we have seen, there is
no exclusion or expulsion. Indeed, there is no leadership with authorization to carry out discipline. If a person has sinned against another
or caused another to sin, that person is to cut off his own hand or tear
out her own eye, in order to ensure that the offense does not happen
again (9:43-48). A follower may punish self but not another. No follower is to exert power over any other person.

Rather, God grants power for people to restore others. This power
from God restores the proper dominion of humans over creation,
for power is available to people over all nonhuman forces that
oppress or destroy people—demons, the destructive forces of nature
such as storms and desert wastes and fig trees, illnesses, and other
physical maladies. This is the power the disciples receive when Jesus
authorizes them to heal and drive out demons. This power is available through faith in God. Everything is possible to one who has
faith (9:23). Because all things are possible to *God,* therefore every-

thing is possible to one who puts faith in God (10:27). In Mark, faith has to do not with creedal belief but with access to power. Faith is trust that God will act. The prayer of faith expresses this most explicitly: "Have faith in God and I swear to you that whoever says to this mountain, 'Be taken up and thrown into the sea,' and does not doubt in their heart but has faith that what they say will happen, it will be so for them. So I tell you that whatever you ask for and pray for have faith that you have gotten it, and it will be so for you" (11:22-25). By means of faith, a person has access to God to grant an exorcism or a healing or liberation from the domination of nature for the benefit of people (cf. 4:40; 6:27). Thus, in Mark, faith is the source of access to divine power, and it is always clear that God does the work of power itself.

In Mark, those who have faith receive what they request from God, as long as the request is not made to gain status or power or to avoid persecution.[60] On the one hand, James and John are denied their request to sit on Jesus' right and left (even when they express a willingness to die for the good news, 10:40). On the other hand, Bartimaeus is granted his request (even with an incorrect view of Jesus as Son of David, 11:51), because Bartimaeus asks for a healing rather than for status for himself or power over others. This prohibition against self-aggrandizement in status and power explains why the prayer of faith in requests from God is followed by the admonition to forgive others who have offended the petitioner (11:25) and why Jesus ends his prayer at Gethsemane with the willingness to submit to God's will rather than to his own (14:36). The larger context of God's will in the kingdom is that people use power to serve others, not to dominate or to gain advantage.

Thus, in the Markan narrative world, Jesus has no power from God to coerce others. Nor does Jesus believe God wants humans to use their ordinary capacities to dominate, control, or oppress others. Jesus is left then with the influence of his authority in proclaiming and healing and with the persuasive arguments he offers in his teaching as the means to bring God's rule. Through teaching, correction, and example Jesus seeks to influence his disciples. He seeks also to defeat the authorities in debate, to get his point across and yet evade indictment—to avoid their control of him. And Jesus influences people by warning them. Jesus' sanctions against the disciples and the opponents are threats about what God will do in the future. Even then, it will not be Jesus who carries out the threats. Jesus will sit on God's right hand, but it will be God who puts the messiah's enemies down under his feet (12:36).

Thus, the Markan Jesus refuses to use power to control others. Toward the end of Mark's story, therefore, Jesus becomes the one who is controlled by others, for they do not hesitate to use their power to coerce. The opponents seize Jesus by a deception (14:1-2), hold a kangaroo court at night (14:55), suborn witnesses against him (14:56), bring many charges against him before Pilate (15:3), and stir up the crowd to request Jesus' death (15:11). Yet in a curious way their control of Jesus is ironic. For Jesus has placed himself in a position for this to happen. In fact, there is a sense in which he brings on his demise by his attack on the Temple (11:16), his humiliation of the opponents in debate (12:34), and the self-incriminating testimony he gives at the trial (14:62). By his challenge of their oppressiveness, Jesus leads the opponents to reveal themselves as people who have their authority from the crowd and who use it in destructive ways. Jesus is in charge of himself, and God will ultimately be in charge of the situation. This is expressed well when Jesus responds to the high priest's accusing question with the words, "You will see the son of humanity seated at the right hand of the Powerful One (14:62)." At the end, when the second and final stage of the kingdom of God occurs, Jesus will be at the side of God, and God will punish the high priests for their blasphemy. This is the judgment that Jesus pronounces on the high priest. Thus, while the high priests are controlling Jesus in the present, it is a control that is only temporary and that is part of God's plan. Hence, it can even be said that it is God who strikes down the shepherd (14:27). And God will have the last word, for, in Mark's narrative world, power properly belongs only to God and those to whom God delegates (limited) authority.

In the narrative world, this absolute moral aversion in the cosmological framework to humans lording it over other humans supports
the social organization of the network in which there is no maintenance of external boundaries, no hierarchy of authority, and a mandate for renewed Israelites and Gentiles to be servants of one another.
Only God has the right to use power over people, and God's judgment is yet to take place in the future. Meanwhile, the present time is
a transitional state for followers of the Jesus movement. Followers are
to use neither their own power nor God's power to gain domination
over others or even to defend themselves. They are to oppose human
oppression with words, while they wait for God's action. This situation leaves them extremely vulnerable. They cannot abandon the
movement nor can they fail, unless they want to risk being judged
when the rule of God comes in power. The only good choice for the
core group of disciples is to prepare for the end by courageously proclaiming the good news until they reach the ends of the earth when
Jesus will return at the right hand of power. Thus, the cosmological
framework of values supports the social network that is oriented
wholly toward mission and renewal.

Temporal Imminence
and Ongoing Mobility

In the Markan cosmology, the historical future is very compressed.
There is little time before the rule of God will come in power. The end
will come before the people of Jesus' time have all died (9:1), before the
end of Jesus' generation (13:30). The past time has been leading up to
this time, through prophecy and earlier attempts to get Israel to
respond to God's efforts to get fruit from the vineyard (12:1-7). The
present time is for the purpose of giving the people of Israel and of all
nations the opportunity to hear the good news before the end comes
and to take sides by their response to the good news (13:10). During
this time, there are to be open boundaries and no hierarchy. Very soon,
however, everything will change when the rule of God comes in power.

Also, during this time, as we have seen, the various aspects of structure portrayed in the story keep the disciples in a state of ongoing horizontal mobility: the mandate to proclaim to all nations before the end comes; the prohibition of hierarchical structures; the lack of boundary maintenance; the absence of internal discipline; the absence of communal rituals; and the lack of provisions to establish stationary communities. Also, as we have seen, the missionary instructions to the disciples create mobility. The disciples are not to carry bread or money or extra clothes; rather they are to depend completely upon the hospitality they receive as they move from village to village. In Mark, Jesus fosters ongoing liminality in this transitional stage and prohibits reaggregation into new social forms until the end, in order that the movement might retain maximum mobility for mission to all Gentile nations.[61] In fact, Jesus prohibits almost everything that would retard or inhibit mission. This impulse toward mission is integrally related to the shortening of the time. The narrative portrayal suggests that there is to be no retarding of the mission until all nations have heard the good news.

Then the end will come, and only then will there be reaggregation into the new community in the rule of God. The narrative envisions that, at that time, those on the outside of the boundary that Jesus has defined will be destroyed (12:7), excluded, expelled (9:43-48), judged (14:62), and shunned (8:38). By contrast, the chosen ones will be gathered (13:27), saved (8:35; 13:13), and given eternal life (10:30). The boundary defined by Jesus will be established and maintained in power. Then God will rule over people in a hierarchy of power with Jesus on the throne at God's right hand (12:38; 14:62), two others at Jesus' right and left (10:40), and many others who range from great to least (10:31). There will also be greater and lesser punishments (12:40).

In the Markan narrative world, only for a brief period is there to be an opportunity to prove oneself ready to enter the kingdom. The missionary disciples prove their readiness by proclaiming without regard for societal boundaries or the threat of persecution, while those in the villages prove their readiness by offering hospitality, showing faith, risking the persecution that comes from association with the name of Jesus, and doing other things that reflect the values of "the things of God." Just as the operational space for the group was potentially all space, so operational time for the group becomes all the time. There should be no rest. Since the end may come at any time, followers must always stay alert and be on guard against a testing (13:32-36). For the missionary disciples, all time is devoted to proclamation. Others who identify with Jesus carry on their ordinary lives, but they too must "keep watch" at all times to be prepared for a testing (13:37). Such testing will come in the form of persecution—arrests, floggings, trials, betrayals by family and friends, and the hatred of all. Persecution increases the temporal tension, because, "If the Lord had not shortened the days, no one would be saved" (13:20). However, the Lord has shortened the time before the end will come for the sake of the "chosen ones." Jesus encourages the disciples with the word that "those who endure to the end will be saved" (13:13).

In this cosmology of the kingdom, the inclusive geographical space and the compressed time combine to create great urgency. The disciples are to reach the limits of space before the limit of time is up. There is a definite limit to the geographical space, for the narrator conceives of a confined world. At the same time, there is a definite limit to present historical time. Those who proclaim are to reach the ends of the earth before the generation ends. At that time, the imminent arrival of the kingdom of God in power will bring an end to the strain of the geographical limit, for then the chosen ones will be gathered from the four winds.

Conclusions

I have analyzed the Jesus movement in Mark with the help of concepts from the social sciences. My focus has been on the Markan narrative world. I have not attempted to infer anything about the historical Jesus, the historical disciples, the historical leaders of Israel, or the nature of Mark's audience. In a sense, the author's capacity to communicate with an audience is possible because the author shares a common social system with the hearers. We can assume that the social meanings portrayed in the narrative are familiar to the hearers, and perhaps both author and first hearers participated in the Jesus renewal movement similar to the way it is portrayed in the narrative. There is, however, the uncertain question of how much the social system urged by Jesus in the narrative is actually lived out by hearers and how much it represents an ideal for which they should strive. As such, there may be a difference between the social system that the author shares in common with the audience and the social system that the author wishes to promote as a goal or a corrective to the audience. Here I wanted simply to focus on the kind of social system the narrative promotes among followers of Jesus.

I argue that Mark wrote to ensure that the missionary thrust of the Christian movement should continue until it reached the ends of the earth or the passage of "this generation." Two ideas stand in creative tension: the good news must first be preached to all the nations, and the end will come within the generation. The whole purpose of Jesus' apocalyptic discourse in Mark is to preserve this tension. On the one hand, the end is not yet, because those who say "I am" and thereby imply that the messiah has come are not correct and because the wars and famines are only the beginning of the birth pains (13:5-8). Therefore, the narrative suggests, do not stop mission, for the end has not yet come! It is necessary first for the good news to be proclaimed to all the Gentile nations. Yet, on the other hand, the end will come soon— God has shortened the time (13:20), and it will occur before Jesus' generation is over (13:30). And when that happens, the angels will gather God's people from the four winds (13:27). Therefore, do not stop mission, for the end will come soon!

Throughout the narrative, the author promotes among hearers a renewal movement with a thoroughgoing thrust toward mission by portraying a network of mobility and hospitality. Core members of the network cross all boundaries that would prevent contact with people. In addition, the author discourages roles appropriate to stationary communities. There are only two roles in the network— those who go from place to place proclaiming and those who receive them. And, as we have seen, those who receive often carry out the role of those who proclaim. As such, the narrative works against the establishment of organization and hierarchical roles, because that would retard mission, just as all excess baggage on a mission would retard movement. There is no good choice but to keep going. Furthermore, the abandonment of the Temple by God eliminates any attachment to "place," for God is now accessible to people wherever they stand praying in faith (15:38; 11:22-24). And the rhetoric of the narrative as a whole impels hearers, even those not a part of the core of disciples, to participate in the proclamation of the good news.

In Mark's narrative world, the only retarding effect on the missionary thrust of the network is the effort of Jesus, the leader, to keep himself at the center of the network: Jesus does not appoint or send out the disciples until the pressure of the crowds (3:6-19) and the presence of opposition (6:1-13) call for it; he limits the core group to twelve (3:14) and discourages sympathizers from proclaiming; he makes the disciples dependent upon him; he instructs the disciples to witness after his death in his name (9:37, 41; 13:9, 13); he calls disciples to die "for me and the good news" (8:35); he warns disciples not to be misled by others who come in his name and who may be forming their own factions (13:5-6); he discourages the disciples from forming their own factions by keeping them mobile and by prohibiting hierarchical relationships; and Jesus will return soon on God's right hand (13:26-37). Furthermore, in the narrative, the disciples are depicted as failures and hence not worthy of allegiance as leaders of factions. Also, the rhetoric at the end of the story—when the women flee in fear and silence (16:8)—leads the hearers to want to do the opposite, to be courageous and to speak out. So, for the hearers, Jesus is the only worthy figure in the narrative to emulate and follow. In all these ways, the narrative serves to keep Jesus at the center of the network, both for the core disciples as well as for others who proclaim.

Apart from these retarding factors that function to centralize the network around Jesus, the entire thrust of the network is toward mission to the ends of the earth. The only obstacle to the mission of the disciples is the fear of persecution. The narrative spends much effort getting the hearers—both core disciples and local supporters—to see that Jesus' death was no accident (8:31) and that it will be necessary for those who follow Jesus to be prepared to suffer persecution also (8:34-38). The hearers are led to see and to follow in spite of the persecution or death awaiting them. The first part of the narrative deals with the role of healing that followers are to carry out in proclaiming, while the second half deals with the persecution that followers will have to endure as a result of proclaiming. There is no opposition between the first and the second halves of the Gospel, except that without the second half, the first half is incomplete. Those who are core missionary disciples will fail in their mission, will not proclaim to the ends of the earth, unless they are prepared for the inevitable persecution that will come in the course of their proclaiming.

The argument of this chapter echoes the longstanding view that Mark's Gospel was written to help people face persecution. Yet I hope to have placed this view in the larger context of a pervasive concern for the missionary thrust of the Jesus network in the face of an imminent end. By looking at the organization of the Jesus network depicted in Mark, I have sought to uncover an interrelation between cosmology and social dynamics and tried to show how the social system of Jesus' renewal movement fosters missionary proclamation. The resulting insights get at the heart of the peculiarly Markan way of viewing the world and perhaps also enhance our understanding of Mark's purpose in writing the Gospel.

6

Crossing Boundaries:

Purity and Defilement in Mark

The purpose of this essay is to analyze the dynamics of purity and defilement in the Gospel of Mark. In order to do this, I will first summarize several approaches to the social study of the New Testament and then apply these to the narrative world of the Gospel of Mark in an effort to discern the views and behavior about purity and defilement that the author of Mark proffers for the followers of Jesus in his time.

Introduction to Social Study
of the New Testament

The New Testament is a profoundly social document. Each writing in the New Testament emerged from a community. Each writing addressed specific people with a unique message for a given time, place, and circumstance. Each writing was deeply embedded in a particular culture and history. Each writer shared a common social system with readers that enabled communication to take place. The writings of the New Testament were social acts.

Our reading of the New Testament is also a social act. Particularly for those of us in Western developed countries, reading the New Testament is a cross-cultural experience. The writers of the New Testament were first-century people; we are from the early twenty-first century in the West. Our language, customs, economy, political order, social system, values, cultural knowledge, and ethos are very different from the cultures of the first century. We tend to project our urban industrial society back onto writings that are from a pre-industrial peasant society. We read into the writings our modern Western cultural assumptions about life—our notions of individualism, progress, freedom, class structure, time, mobility, and so on. We have our twentieth-century "cognitive maps" by which we select, sort, and comprehend the material we read in the New Testament. In so doing, however, we misunderstand writings addressed to first-century people.

A text from the first century is like a door between two rooms, an opening through which to look into another culture, a different world. However, if we look at the door without going through it, we see only how the space for the door fits into the decor of the room on our side of the door—with all the cultural assumptions and social configurations of our own time and place. We see it only in the context of the world we inhabit. Instead, we need imaginatively to walk through the opening into the world on the other side of the door, into the very different cultures of first-century Palestine and the Roman Empire—and then turn and look at the space for the door (the text) in the context of the decor of the first century Mediterranean time and place. The question is: How can we understand the New Testament as a collection of writings from the eastern Mediterranean world of the first century rather than impose the meanings we bring to the text from our time and place? The social study of the New Testament addresses this question.

In recent decades, there has been an explosion of social studies of the New Testament. Seminars in scholarly societies have appeared under such titles as "The Social Description of Early Christianity," "Social Sciences and the New Testament," "The Social Facets Seminar," and "The Context Group." All these groups are devoted to sharing and promoting scholarship on the social study of the New Testament. Biblical scholars are eager to understand the society, the culture, and the communities in and behind the New Testament writings.

Four Approaches to Social Study of the New Testament

As a way to describe this emerging social study of the New Testament, we identify four approaches that have emerged: (1) social description, (2) social history, (3) the sociology of knowledge, and (4) the use of models from the social sciences, particularly cultural anthropology These approaches overlap and depend on each other.

Social Description

Social description draws upon all the information we have from the ancient world: literature, archeological excavations, art, coins, inscriptions, and so on. Scholars gather, analyze, and organize this information to describe every aspect of the social environment of the New Testament in its original setting: occupations, tools, houses, roads, means of travel, money, economic realities, architecture, villages and cities, laws, social classes, markets, clothes, foodstuffs, cooking practices, and so on. Such social description enhances our understanding of the daily cultures and customs in Palestine and in the Roman Empire at the time of Jesus and the early Christian movement.

One way to think about social description is to imagine you are the director of a film portraying scenes from the life of Jesus. For example, take the story about Jesus healing the man with the withered hand (Mark 3:1-6). What information do you need in order to make this scene authentic? What did a synagogue look like? Was it a *stoa* (porch) in a market area, a freestanding building, or a room in another structure? Who went there? What did they do? Did they read from the Torah? Was it a papyrus book or a parchment roll? How did they dress? What was the Sabbath? What were the practices and the prohibitions related to the Sabbath at that time? How did people treat a man with a "withered hand" in that culture? What Sabbath laws were at stake? How serious were penalties for violation of the Sabbath? Who were the Pharisees? How would they bring charges against Jesus? Why in the end did they not indict him? Why did they seek to meet with the Herodians? If you were a director staging such a drama, you would develop a passion for such questions as a means to comprehend fully this scene.

Understanding such a story is like understanding an anecdote or a joke from another culture. You have to know what ideas and information are being assumed before you can "get" the meaning. For example, the Pharisees were watching to indict Jesus because it was illegal to work on the Sabbath, and healing was considered to be work. Such a situation was serious, because observing the Sabbath was a solemn religious obligation and because penalties for flagrant offenses could be severe. Synagogues likely also functioned as courts of law, which is why this setting was so threatening to Jesus. And the key question is, Why did the Pharisees not indict Jesus when he healed the man? The reason is that Jesus cleverly evaded indictment by avoiding any real "work." He does not touch the man or command him to "be healed" but only tells him to "stretch out the hand!" No wonder the Pharisees went off in frustration to plot with the Herodians to destroy Jesus. They went to the Herodians because the Roman appointed king, Herod Antipas, alone had the right to carry out capital punishment in Galilee under the Romans. Such sociohistorical information is essential for readers to "get" the story in Mark's narrative.

Many fine studies describe daily life in the social worlds of the first century. In New Testament studies, Abraham J. Malherbe, John E. Stambaugh, David L. Balch, Eric M. Meyers, James Strange, K. C. Hanson, and Douglas E. Oakman, among many others describe the material and social life of the first century. In so doing, they provide vital means for us to understand people, events, and stories from that time.

Social History

Social historians seek to understand the broad sweep of change in history. This approach applies a comprehensive knowledge of social description through time to produce a social history of the period. Scholars such as Gerd Theissen, Wayne Meeks, Martin Hengel, Ekkehard Stegemann, and Wolfgang Stegemann have sought to answer critical questions of social history. For example, How did Christianity develop in the rural areas of Palestine? How did Christianity develop in the urban areas of the ancient world? How did the Greek culture and the Jewish culture interrelate in the period of Roman imperialism? What were the social causes and dynamics of the Roman-Jewish War of 66 to 70 C.E., and how did this war affect the early Christian movement? Then the question becomes: How do these developments fit into the social movements of the larger Greco-Roman world of that time. Regarding the study of biblical literature, those who take this approach might ask how the Gospel of Mark fits into the social and political history of the times, much as we might ask the place of Franklin's *Poor Richard's Almanac* in pre-industrial America or the relation of Steinbeck's *The Grapes of Wrath* to the Great Depression.

To deal with social history in relation to Mark, we might pose the following questions: What were the social forces behind the writing of the Gospel of Mark? What political conditions prevailed in that time and place? How did the Roman-Jewish War of 66 to 70 C.E. affect the writing of the Gospel? What was Mark's community like, and how did they spread the good news? How much did the expectation of an imminent end to the world impel the writing of this Gospel? Did the Gospel serve lower classes, upper classes, or both? Were the readers Jewish? If not, how much did they know of or identify with the Jewish people? What groups persecuted Mark's community? What was the fate of Mark's community in the context of the Roman Empire? Although one cannot do a broad social history based on one writing, nevertheless social historians can seek to explain the appearance of Mark's Gospel in the sweep of the social history of the time. Unfortunately, the task is difficult because Mark refers to his own time only indirectly in the story.

As an illustration, we might ask how the Roman-Jewish War of 66 to 70 C.E. affected the writing of Mark's Gospel. In 66 C.E., the Jews expelled the Roman troops from Palestine and rallied for independence. Diverse groups from all over Israel joined the war movement—lower class groups resisting economic oppression, sectarian groups fighting for the first commandment prohibition against any lord but God, and high-priestly groups seeking better terms in the Roman relationship. The war ended in disaster for the Jews. The Romans returned, defeated the nation, and, in 70 C.E., destroyed Jerusalem and razed the Temple. Writing his Gospel during or just after the war, Mark told a story about events preceding the war. The Jewish Messiah had already come in the person of Jesus, who preached to his disciples that they should be like servants and not like the leaders of the Gentile nations who lord it over people (10:42-45). The leaders of Israel rejected Jesus. Jesus in turn predicted their downfall and that of the Temple (12:9; 13:2; 14:62). At the trial scenes, the high priests stirred up the crowd to call for Jesus' execution and to choose freedom for Barabbas, a prisoner who had committed murder in an insurrection (15:6-15). When Jesus died, God split the curtain and left the Temple and Israel to destruction (15:38). We can see how Mark wrote this story in part to reveal what he considered to be the destructive attitudes in Israel and in the Roman Empire that resulted in the Roman-Jewish War. He also showed how Jesus' point of view differed from those of other Jewish groups and of the Roman colonial power.

With this approach, we can see how the sociopolitical history of the time shaped the Gospel of Mark. In turn, we can also see how this early Christian writing fits into the broader social history of the Roman period. Recently, some social historians have constructed the past from the perspective of the oppressed, seeking to unmask the dynamics of oppression and to recover the lives of the poor, outcasts, slaves, and women from all social strata of ancient cultures. The Gospels are prime sources for such social histories, as Elisabeth Schüssler Fiorenza and Ched Myers have shown in their studies of Mark.

Sociology of Knowledge: Worldviews and Social Configurations

This approach offers the insight that different worldviews support different social orders. The first aspect of this approach is to construct the worldview, the everyday assumptions, of a given culture or group. The second aspect is to see how this worldview gave legitimacy to and maintained the particular social order of the group or society from which it emerged.

First, sociology of knowledge deals with what people in a particular culture take for granted in their understanding of the world, their "social construction of reality."[1] Whereas social description focuses on the material realities of a society, sociology of knowledge deals with how that society organizes and interprets those realities. Each society interprets, organizes, and experiences life in its own way. Each society has sets of common values and customary ways in which people interact. Each society has shared beliefs about time, space, and the meaning of life. All these facets make up the common sense of a given culture. Such beliefs and understandings constitute the fabric of meaning without which a "society" does not exist. People seldom question these assumptions. People simply grow up taking the world of shared meanings for granted.

If we are to understand the first-century cultures and subcultures, we should be aware of the assumptions we make from our own cultures and subcultures. Otherwise, we will unconsciously project them onto our reading of a writing such as Mark's Gospel. To see and judge other societies by our own assumptions is cultural ethnocentrism. The first-century Mediterranean cultures would consider "the way things are" to be quite different from the dominant United States culture. For example, many people in the United States may assume that it is good for an individual to "get ahead," but some cultures, including the peasant cultures of the first century, view "getting ahead" as dishonorable and destructive of the social order. Thus, the sociology of knowledge is about the everyday understandings of the world that people in a culture take for granted, what everyone in that culture "knows" to be true. If we are to understand the cultures of the first century, we need to appreciate how their cultures are different from our own.

When children grow up enculturated into a particular society, sociologists refer to this process as "primary socialization." When people enter another society and take on the basic assumptions of this other culture, sociologists refer to this process as "resocialization at the primary level." Such resocialization in primary assumptions is also a way to understand conversion. The Christian movement arose in particular cultures and led people to redefine the way they thought about some assumptions of those cultures and to abandon other assumptions. It called them to inhabit the world in a different way, to convert.[2] Thus, from the perspective of sociology of knowledge, early Christianity offered an alternate world of meaning for those who chose to inhabit it. Reading or hearing a narrative like Mark can be a way to enter such a new symbolic universe. We could even see the hearers' experience of Mark's narrative as a process of enculturation into the values of the kingdom of God. We might ask: What assumptions about life does the author of Mark take for granted with the hearers? What assumptions does the author lead the hearers to abandon? What new views does the author want the hearers to adopt?

Consider, for example, the strange world of space and time in the narrative world of Mark's Gospel. Early in the story, the narrator tells us that Jesus saw "the heavens being torn open" and "the Spirit coming upon him" (1:9-11).[3] After this, "a voice from the heavens" addressed Jesus. Immediately, the Spirit drove Jesus to the desert to be "tested by Satan," and "angels" served him (1:12-13). Subsequently, Jesus appeared in Galilee where he "drove out many demons" (1:39). When we combine these and other clues, we see that the author holds a Hebrew conception of the cosmos. There is no notion of a universe infinite in time and space, but a limited and flat earth with a canopy over it, heavens reaching from earth up to where God dwells, and Satan dominating an earth populated by angels and demons. Many other elements of the story fill out this spatial picture of the cosmos, such as Jesus going "up onto a mountain to pray" (6:46), the promise to gather disciples "from the four winds" (13:27), and the prophecy that Jesus would "come on the clouds of heaven" (14:62). The author does not argue for this view of the cosmos but simply assumes that the audience shares the same worldview. At the same time, Mark wants to change the hearers' temporal view of the cosmos. Mark wants to convince hearers that God's kingdom began with the baptism of Jesus (1:14-15) and that the fulfillment of that kingdom would come before the end of Jesus' generation (9:1; 13:30).

To ferret out a comprehensive picture of how Mark imagines the world, we might consider his views about nature and history, past and future, laws and customs, the human condition, sin and illness, purity and pollution, death and the afterlife, and so on. By culling details from the narrative, we can put together cultural assumptions the author makes about the world. In this way, we can sort out which primary cultural assumptions the author takes for granted and which primary assumptions the author wishes to challenge or change—such as purity rules or certain ethical values or attitudes toward death.

The second facet of the sociology of knowledge correlates such worldviews with particular social organizations. Here sociologists make the argument that a mutual relationship exists between the assumptions of a given culture or group and the social organization of that group. How does the worldview of a group generate, legitimate, and maintain the particular social order of the group? In turn, how does the social order of a group influence the worldview of that group? There is no "necessary" correlation between worldview and social order, but efforts to make correlations are illuminating.[4]

For example, Wayne Meeks argues that the symbolic universe expressed in the Gospel of John supports a certain kind of social group.[5] The Gospel of John portrays Jesus as "the man from heaven" who brings knowledge of God to the world; yet only some people understand him, while most people do not accept him at all. Such a belief system about Jesus, Meeks argues, supports a small, tight-knit group of people who understand Jesus, but who are isolated and alienated from the general society of people who do not understand. As such, the belief system in the Gospel of John gave religious legitimacy to the group's isolation from the world.

Similarly, in the narrative world of Mark's Gospel, there is a correlation between the worldview held by the characters in Mark's story and the social organization of the Jesus movement depicted there. The worldview that Jesus teaches his followers involves these assumptions: God's kingdom has begun (1:15); followers are to cross boundaries to proclaim the good news to the ends of the earth (13:10, 27); and the mission is urgent, because the end of history will come soon (13:5-37). This missionary commitment to spread the good news to all nations before the end comes supports a social organization very different from that of John's Gospel. Instead of fostering a tight-knit group isolated from the world, Mark depicts a loose-knit social network based on hospitality as disciples go from place to place proclaiming the Gospel (1:17; 6:7-13; 10:29-30).[6] Thus, the sociology of knowledge helps one to see how the group's "knowledge" of the world relates to the social order of that group.

Models from Cultural Anthropology

A fourth area of social study of the New Testament involves the use of models from cultural anthropology. From the study of many cultures, anthropologists formulate models to map the dynamics of a culture and to describe certain phenomena that occur in many cultures. Models deal with such matters as kinship systems, power relations, rituals, purity-pollution rules, economies, and so on.

A model is a simplified description of like events or interactions drawn from the study of many cultures or groups. Models are not a tool to research historical information. Rather, they aid in the process of interpretation. Models help to overcome ethnocentrism by providing a framework different from our own cultural maps with which to organize and assess information. The point of using a model is not to fit facts into an abstract paradigm. Rather, a model serves as a heuristic device to probe and to question, to notice details we might have ignored, and to see connections that explain dynamics and relationships. For example, if we understand the characteristic features of demonic possession from the study of many cultures, we will know better how to investigate and understand demonic possession in first-century Israel. Biblical scholars draw upon the models of anthropologists whose work is especially helpful in the study of early Christianity. They change and adapt the models to the specific historical situations in New Testament times.

For example, Robin Scroggs drew a model from the work of Max Weber and Ernst Troeltsch on the characteristics of religious sects.[7] Scroggs applied the model to the early Christian church to show in what ways it was indeed a typical religious sect. John G. Gager drew upon the work of anthropologist Leon Festinger about religious sects that expected the end of the world.[8] Gager applied the model to the earliest Christians because they expected that Jesus would return within their own generation. Gager argued that when this did not happen the early Christians responded like other such sects: they intensified their missionary activities rather than give up their beliefs.

Bruce Malina has made the most comprehensive effort to map the framework of first-century cultures by using models drawn from the study of modern Mediterranean societies.[9] As such, he interprets the New Testament with models drawn from societies that are in historical continuity with those of the first-century Mediterranean region. He provides the following five models. (1) Honor/shame: In contrast to our social preference for economic gain, first-century Mediterranean people sought above all else to gain honor. (2) Collectivist personality: In contrast to our quest for individual freedom, people got their identity from embeddedness in and conformity to a group. (3) Limited-goods economy: In contrast to our assumption that economic acquisition can be unlimited, people held to the peasant notion that all goods are limited and in short supply. (4) Patrilinear kinship: First-century cultures had a patrilinear kinship system in which people married within their own group. (5) Purity and defilement: Society was organized according to rules for purity and pollution. Malina's work lays out the dynamics of each of these models and applies them to various New Testament writings. Other scholars have developed cross-cultural models for the study of healing, demonology, deviance, among many others.

Cultural anthropologists may take one of three approaches to analyze a society or group:[10]

1. Models may come from a structural-functionalist approach, which assumes that social forces work together to create a balance

and to harmonize society. Here the challenge is to see how different parts of a society work together and how problems are overcome by efforts to restore a harmony of integrative functions to the society. This approach tends to see society in terms of how it preserves the status quo.

2. Models may come from a conflict framework of analysis, which assumes that different parts of society are in conflict with each other. Here the challenge is to grasp the dynamics of clashes of power and to see how conflicts between societal groups are resolved. This approach tends to see society in terms of changes that take place in struggles over domination and oppression.

3. Models may come from a symbolic framework of understanding, which focuses on the meanings people assign to social interactions. Here the challenge is to discern the symbolic meanings that members of the society share and to determine how those symbols change.

Several scholars have applied models from cultural anthropology to the Gospel of Mark. Vernon K. Robbins analyzed the social roles of the teacher Jesus and his disciples.[11] John J. Pilch has studied Markan assumptions about the nature of illness, healing, and exorcism.[12] Herman Waetjen employed a model about millenarian sects to highlight the new social order that Jesus announces in his establishment of the kingdom.[13] Jerome Neyrey applied a model from the work of anthropologist Mary Douglas to display the dimensions of purity and pollution in Mark's narrative.[14] As with all methodologies, scholars differ in regard to the nature, uses, and results of the models.

Conclusion

The four approaches to the social study of the New Testament outlined above interrelate with and depend upon one another. They may be used together with great profit. In fact, John Elliott has developed a method that combines several social approaches in the service of interpreting a New Testament text, a method he calls "social-scientific criticism."[15] Such an approach draws upon social description and models from cultural anthropology to reconstruct the sociopolitical situation of the audience and the author's strategy for dealing with it. Elliott analyzes 1 Peter as a letter written to Christians who were displaced aliens in Asia Minor. This approach works especially well with letters in which the author, readers, and social situation are identified directly in the letter. There are, however, many ways to combine these methods with benefit. In the case study that follows, I draw on social description, social history, worldview (sociology of knowledge), and models from cultural anthropology to study one facet of the narrative world of the Gospel of Mark.

A Case Study: Purity and Defilement in Mark

In order to illustrate the social study of the New Testament, I will analyze the dynamics of clean and unclean in the Gospel of Mark. In this study, I am assuming that Mark was written in Galilee or rural Syria around 70 C.E. and that his audience shared a social world similar to that of Jesus' time depicted in the narrative.[16] After briefly introducing the case of Mark, I describe the social phenomenon of purity and defilement in first-century Israel and then show its relevance to the narrative world of Mark. In order to clarify the issues at stake, I then apply models from the symbolic approach to cultural anthropology.

In the case of Mark, it will be helpful to clarify certain assumptions. First, the analysis focuses on the *narrative world* of Mark's Gospel. Thus, it does not deal with the historical Jesus or with Mark's community but with the society and the Jesus movement portrayed in Mark's narrative. Second, I am helped in my analysis of the narrative world by a description of the social experience of purity and pollution in first-century Israel. This is the experience that first-century hearers brought to the encounter with Mark's Gospel and that they "knew" as the worldview and social practices into which they were enculturated. However, it is necessary for contemporary hearers to recover this information as a basis to understand the narrative world of Mark's Gospel. Finally, although I focus on one motif in Mark, it will become clear how integrally related the study of purity is with many aspects of the Markan story-world.

In the text of Mark we encounter phenomena that are strange to us. Jesus drives out "unclean spirits" (1:23; 5:2); he "cleanses a leper" (1:40-45); and Pharisees accuse Jesus' disciples of eating bread with "defiled hands" (7:1-23). These notions of clean and unclean have nothing to do with our modern ideas of sanitation. Rather, they are unseen forces capable of making things pure or polluted, holy or defiled, clean or unclean. When we investigate the Jewish society of Palestine in the first century, we realize that issues of purity and pollution pervaded the whole culture. When we apply this background material to an understanding of the narrative world of Mark, we see that the forces of purity and defilement are integral to many aspects of the story: holiness, graves, corpses, Gentiles, Sabbath, foods, hearts, and so on. The issues of purity are writ large across the pages of Mark's story.

Social Description and Worldview in First-Century Israel

In the first century, the Jewish nation was a Temple state under the imperialistic domination of the Roman Empire.[17] For Jews living there, religious, political, and economic life centered around the Temple in Jerusalem. This Temple was a huge complex that dominated the city. It housed more than two thousand priests at a time. During religious festivals, the Temple teemed with tens of thousands of Jews from all over the known world. The Jewish people believed that God dwelt on earth in the inner sanctuary of the Temple. God's presence there and proper worship in the Temple would guarantee the prosperity of the nation, the productivity of the land, and the security of the nation from foreign domination. Furthermore, Jerusalem was God's holy city, and the land was God's holy land. Israel was a theocracy, a form of government in which God is considered to be the origin and head of state. Within the nation, the high priests had the task of governing the nation (within Roman

parameters) and providing proper worship in the Temple. The San-
hedrin was the administrative and judicial council. The Pharisees
and scribes were experts in the interpretation of the Law or Torah,
the five books of Moses. As the people of God, the Jews believed they
were set apart to be holy, dedicated to the Lord, to worship God
faithfully, and to follow God's laws.

The Concept of Holiness

What gave this whole system coherence was the concept of holiness.
Holiness was a core value of the Jews, as stated (by God) in the Law:
"You shall be holy, for I the Lord your God am holy" (Lev. 19:2). God
was holy, and the people were to be holy. Because God was holy, God
would not tolerate immorality. And God wanted people to worship
rightly. The Law of Israel therefore dealt with holiness. The Law con-
tained the moral codes for holy behavior among people in the nation.
The Law included the regulations for the observance of holy times
and holy festivals to guarantee prosperous life on the land. The Law
prescribed the regulations for proper worship in the Temple. The Law
detailed the holiness codes about those animals that people were permitted to eat and those animals that would defile people, the definition of leprosy, the rituals for cleansing, and so on. Moreover, the Law
prescribed rituals and sacrifices as means to purge defilement from
the land, the Temple, and the people. Hence, Jews in Palestine were
devoted to preserving God's holiness and to preserving their own
holiness.

First, most Jews were devoted to preserving God's holiness. They
protected God's dwelling in the Temple from unclean people and
things that defile. For example, only the high priest went into the
Holy of Holies. Only priests in a state of purity could enter the Temple court to offer sacrifices, and they offered there only animals classified as pure and without blemish. All Israelites were to be in a state
of purity when they came to worship in the Temple. Otherwise, they
would defile the Temple. In turn, God might destroy the unclean person who came into God's presence in the Temple. If people defiled the

sanctuary in a flagrant way, God might withdraw from the sanctuary, thereby removing the protection and the benefits that God's presence there secured.

Second, Jews in Palestine were concerned to preserve the holiness of God's people. For example, Jews avoided contact with unclean people and things—lepers, menstruating women, corpses, and Gentiles, among others. Such contact defiled a person for a period lasting from one to seven days. Such a state of defilement prohibited people from participation in festivals, certain meals, and Temple functions. To become pure again, the defiled person was required by the Law to do ritual washings, endure a waiting period, and/or make an offering to God. In a collectivist culture, such as that of ancient Israel, the sanctions against unclean people—shunning or prescriptions for cleansing—were not meant to punish the unclean person but to protect the community.

Third, there was a distinction between ritual purity and moral purity. Ritual purity had to do with people or things that were defiled by virtue of contact with what was unclean. Such defilement threatened the community and rendered the person unqualified to participate in certain communal activities and in rituals. In addition to ritual purity, there was moral purity. Jews were to avoid immorality and idolatry. While these were not defiling by virtue of contact, they were thought to defile the community. Also, the effects of flagrant immorality committed outside the Temple could reach into the Temple and violate God's presence.

Maps of Holiness

We can see how Jews in Palestine organized their world to preserve their holiness. Jerome Neyrey has demonstrated the structures of holiness by reference to "cultural maps" of places, people, things, and times that served to organize Jewish life.[18] Although these maps of holiness come from later writings, they nevertheless reflect an earlier time and are helpful in understanding the mentality of holiness that prevailed in the first century.

Take first the map of places from the *Mishnah*, the early third-century collection of oral commentary on the Torah. It offers a geographical listing *(m. Kelim* 1.6-9), cited in ascending order of holiness:

1. The land of Israel is holier than any other land.
2. The walled cities of Israel are still more holy.
3. Within the walls of Jerusalem is still more holy.
4. The Temple Mount is still more holy.
5. The rampart is still more holy.
6. The Court of Women is still more holy.
7. The Court of the Israelites is still more holy.
8. The Court of Priests is still more holy.
9. Between the porch and altar is still more holy.
10. The sanctuary is still more holy.
11. The Holy of Holies is still more holy.

Notice that the Holy of Holies, where God resides on earth, is the holiest place. At all costs, the Jews must protect this inner sanctuary of the Temple from defilement. The degree of holiness outward from the sanctuary corresponds directly with the nearness to or distance from this sanctuary. In this listing, certain people belong in certain spaces. Each group is holy enough to attain its proper place but not pure enough to penetrate closer to the sanctuary without bringing defilement. Notice that the territory of Gentile nations is outside the map. In general, the Jews avoided contact with Gentiles because they represented immorality, idolatry, and ritual impurity. Neyrey also presents the purity map of people from the later Jewish *Tosefta* (*t. Meg.*), cited in descending order of holiness:

1. high priest
2. priests
3. Levites
4. Israelites
5. converts
6. freed slaves
7. disqualified priests
8. Temple slaves
9. bastards

10. eunuchs
11. others with physical deformities

Note how some of these people correlate with places on the geographical map. Only the high priest could enter the Holy of Holies. Only priests and Levites could enter the Court of the Priests. Only male members of groups 5 through 7 could enter the Court of the Israelites, and so on. Again, the map does not include Gentiles, because they are not holy. They could only enter the outer court of the Temple, the Court of the Gentiles. Also, the map does not include women in the scheme of holiness. Because of menstruation, women were often unclean themselves and also bore the perpetual threat of defiling Israelite males.

Neyrey presents other maps. One such list specifies who can marry whom. Another map lists the degrees of defilement attached to people and to things that will defile by contact, such as a leper, the corpse of an animal or a human, bodily fluids out of place, or persons considered defiled. Another map lists the hierarchy of holy times not to be defiled by certain prohibited behavior, such as the Sabbath days and the Passover festival.

Diversity of Approaches to Purity and Defilement

Holiness was a core value of the society. It was the major concept by which the nation-culture structured and classified everything in its world—people, places, objects, and times. All groups and sects agreed on the importance of purity. However, various Jewish sects in Palestine understood purity in different ways and applied the regulations about it in different ways.

1. The sect of the *Sadducees* included mainly chief priests and other aristocrats. They believed that proper worship in the Temple was essential to the holiness that preserved the life of the nation. As such, they applied the strict purity regulations only to life at the Temple. Lower priests and Levites needed to be pure only when they took their annual two-week stint of service in the Temple. Ordinary Israelites needed to preserve their purity only when they entered the Court of

the Israelites to offer sacrifices. Jews were to offer at the sanctuary only pure, unblemished animals. As Sadducees, the high priests guarded everything and everyone who entered the Temple in order to ensure the purity of this holy place.

2. The *Pharisees* studied the written law and also passed down oral traditions of their interpretation and application of the Law. Like the Sadducees, they applied purity regulations to the Temple. However, they went further and applied the purity regulations to all Israelites and to all times, not just when people were at the Temple. Pharisees believed that all Israel was a kingdom of priests. Just as priests kept themselves pure while doing service in the Temple, so all Jews should at all times observe the purity regulations. Just as the priests performed ritual washings before meals as a removal of defilement from contact with that which was unclean, so all Jews should wash hands and food and utensils before eating. They should do this in order to cleanse themselves from direct and indirect contact they may deliberately or inadvertently have had with unclean things or people. The Pharisees were also strict in observing purity regulations in the Law that were not directly connected to the Temple as such. The Pharisees promoted these measures as a "fence" or margin to protect people from defilement due to contact with Gentiles.

3. The sect of *Essenes* had the strictest purity regulations.[19] The Essenes had withdrawn from the life of the nation and the Temple in the second century B.C.E. and established a community at Qumran on the shores of the Dead Sea. They believed that the Maccabean high priests and their descendants were not legitimate and as such had defiled the Temple and the whole land by their presence there. In their view, God had withdrawn from the Temple because of these violations. So, too, the Essenes withdrew. At Qumran, the Essenes carried out the strictest holiness codes as if for the Temple. They did so on the conviction that their community was now the Temple, the only place holy enough for God to dwell on earth. The Essenes offered no sacrifices, but they preserved holiness for the presence of God on earth in the hope that God would soon inaugurate a new order in Israel and the world.

Most Jews in Palestine were peasants who followed the regulations when they went to the Temple for festivals. Few of them, however, had the time or the resources to carry out the ritual prescriptions the Pharisees advocated. Furthermore, many Jews ignored other laws as well, such as some of the Sabbath regulations and some requirements for tithes due the Temple. Many Jews had direct contact with Gentiles in the marketplaces of the cities and indirect contact through Jewish tax collectors. The Pharisees looked upon ordinary Jews who disregarded purity regulations as "sinners."

This system of holiness served Israel well throughout its history, preserving a minority culture from absorption into dominant cultures. At the time of Jesus, the culture and religion of the Jews were threatened with assimilation into the dominant Greek culture and the imperialism of the Roman Empire. The Jewish structures of purity protected the people from these threats of cultural domination. By keeping themselves separate from Gentiles, the Jews maintained their beliefs and practices. At the same time, they sought by their holiness to be an example of purity for the nations. The Jewish nation hoped that eventually the Gentile nations would be drawn to Jerusalem as the place of justice and true worship.

Purity and Defilement in the Narrative World of Mark

When we turn to the depiction of the Jewish nation in the Gospel of Mark, we see issues of purity and defilement throughout: the Holy Spirit, lepers, work on the Sabbath, corpses, unclean spirits, Gentiles, sinners, unclean foods, and so on. As portrayed in Mark's story, the leaders of the nation uphold the laws of ritual purity as we have outlined them. By contrast, Jesus makes an onslaught against these purity rules and regulations. In Mark's view, Jesus is indeed holy, for the "Holy Spirit" comes upon Jesus at his baptism (1:10) and he is called "the Holy One of God" (1:24). Nevertheless, Jesus counters the purity rules that preserved and protected the holiness of the nation.

- He encounters "unclean spirits" (1:21-28).
- He touches a leper (1:40-45).

- He heals Simon's mother-in-law on the Sabbath (1:29-31).
- He pardons "sinners" (2:1-12).
- He calls a tax collector to follow him (2:13-14).
- He eats with tax collectors and sinners (2:15-17).
- His disciples pluck grain on the holy Sabbath (2:23-28).
- He heals an impaired man on the Sabbath (3:1-6).
- He drives unclean spirits from a man at a graveyard in Gentile territory, and they go into a herd of swine (5:1-20).
- He heals a woman with a flow of blood (5:25-34).
- He touches the corpse of a little girl (5:35-43).
- His disciples eat bread with defiled hands (7:1-15).
- He declares that all foods are clean (7:17-23).
- He heals a Gentile woman in Tyre whom he calls a "dog" (7:24-30).
- He uses spittle in the act of healing (7:31-36; 8:22-26).
- He feeds and eats with Gentiles in a desert (8:1-10).

Instead of using purity regulations to guard and protect, the Markan Jesus transgresses the boundaries of purity. Through the agency of the Holy Spirit upon Jesus, God enters the arena of impurity without regard to the risk of defilement.

In Mark's portrayal, the leaders of the nation protect the boundaries of ritual purity that Jesus violates.

- They accuse Jesus of blasphemy for claiming the right to pardon sins (2:1-12).
- They challenge his eating with tax collectors and sinners (2:15-17).
- They challenge the disciples' plucking grain on the Sabbath (2:23-28).
- They seek charges against Jesus for healing on the Sabbath and they plot to destroy him (3:1-6).
- They say Jesus is possessed by Satan, not the Holy Spirit (3:22-30).
- They accuse Jesus because his disciples violate the traditions of the elders by eating bread with unwashed (defiled) hands (7:1-15).
- They condemn him to death for blasphemy against God (14:53-65).

Models from Cultural Anthropology

How can we make sense of these issues of purity? How do the notions of purity and pollution work? What is the difference in the two approaches to purity between Jesus and the Jewish leaders? How can we unpack the dynamics of Mark's story? To deal with these questions, we can turn to explanations, insights, and models from cultural anthropology.

Model for Purity and Pollution

For example, we can understand better the concepts of purity and pollution by making use of a model from the British cultural anthropologist Mary Douglas.[20] In her view, purity represents the notion of order, that there are places for things and things are in their place. By contrast, pollution represents the notion of disorder, that some things have no place or that things are out of their place. Purity and pollution imply, therefore, an ordered classification of things and people with corresponding boundaries. Thus, if we observe what a culture considers to be pure and polluted, we can see how that culture gives order to the world.

As Douglas points out, dirt or that which pollutes is "matter out of place." Soil belongs in a garden, but soil does not belong in a house. When soil is in a house, we consider it to be "dirt" because it is out of place. This is an analogy for the whole purity-pollution system. The assumption is that there are "places" for things and people and animals and behaviors—a place for everything and everything in its place. We have already seen how thoroughly Israel had classified people, places, objects, and times in terms of holiness. Purity occurs when something or someone has a place and is properly in place. Pollution occurs when something or someone is out of place or when something or someone has no place in the system. Purity rules of avoidance and cleansing are ways of dealing with things and people that are out of place or do not belong. Such regulations serve to make the world conform to the structure of ideas. By keeping the purity rules, people impose order on experience and achieve harmony or consonance between worldview and behavior.

Douglas's analysis of the ancient Hebrew system of purity-pollution illustrates the model clearly. The ancient Hebrew culture as reflected in Leviticus is a purity-pollution system based on "holiness." The notion of holiness is rooted in two concepts: wholeness and set-apartness. First, holiness has to do with what is whole. That which is pure and holy is that which conforms wholly to its classification. Now we can see why human beings with "deformities" were considered marginal and unclean and why animals with blemishes were considered unclean and were not to be offered at the Temple. They were not considered to be whole and therefore did not fit wholly within their class. Also, we can see why fish (sea creatures) and cattle (land creatures) and doves (air creatures) are clean animals and do not defile people who eat them. These animals fit the Israelite definition of "normal" animals. Conversely, eels (no fins) and pigs (no cloven hoof) and ostriches (do not fly) do not fit the Hebrew classification of normal or whole animals. These animals are therefore not clean and will defile those who eat them. In light of these explanations, we can now understand the list of holy places cited previously and the list of those people who belong in each place. Gentiles are unclean because there is no place for them in the system.

Second, holiness has to do with things and people that are set apart, things that by virtue of being in their place are kept away from certain other things; that is, things are holy when they are in their place, when they are not where they do not belong. As such, blood, spit, and semen can be unclean and can render others unclean. They belong inside the body. When they come out of their place, such as when blood comes out in a menstrual flow, they render the person unclean and will in turn defile others. Lepers are unclean because they have boils or breaks in the skin where pus or fluid comes out. Also, it was important for certain people to stay apart from certain places. No one can enter the Holy of Holies except the high priest. Women who go beyond their place into the Court of the Priests will defile it. Gentiles were prohibited from entering the inner court of the

Temple on penalty of death. Thus, in the Hebrew culture, there was an ordered classification of the world with proper places for people and things. Things or people that did not fit the classification or that were out of place were considered to be unclean and capable of making other things and people unclean.

In Mark's depiction of the Jewish nation, the authorities support this system. But in Mark's portrayal Jesus has a different Jewish approach. Jesus does not reinforce the purity system of the authorities. He crosses boundaries, redraws them, redefines them, or eliminates them. As a result, he has contact with all types of unclean people and objects; he goes to places that are out of bounds, and he violates holy times. What is the key to this clash between the authorities and Jesus? How can we explain these two very different approaches to purity?

Model for Boundaries

We can get insight into the different approaches of the leaders and Jesus by delineating their differing attitudes toward boundaries. We have already seen the connection between purity and boundaries. In his work on boundaries, Jonathan Smith helps us to see the fundamental difference between these two approaches to purity depicted in Mark's Gospel.[21] Smith argues that the difference between the authorities and Jesus is so dramatic as to represent polar opposites. One approach erects boundaries and preserves holiness by guarding against that which would defile. The other approach crosses boundaries and risks defilement to make what is unclean pure.

The one choice is "the affirmation of one's place" within the order of certain boundaries. Here, "each person is called to dwell in a limited world in which everything has its given place and role to fulfill. To be sacred is to remain in place. To break out, to cross boundaries, is to open the world to the threat of chaos, to commit transgression."[22] In this approach, the hero is one who discerns order and helps people fulfill their roles within that order. We can see that the leaders of Israel in Mark embrace this stance.

The other choice expresses a desire "to be unbounded, to be liberated." In this view, boundaries have become oppressive and restrictive or are simply limiting. Here people do not define themselves "by the degree to which they harmonize themselves and their society to the cosmic patterns of order, but rather to the degree to which they can escape that order."[23] Here, "positive sacred power is to be gained from the violation of the given boundaries of the world, from the transcendence of the way things ordinarily are."[24] In this approach, the heroic figure is the one who enables people to escape the bounds. We can see that Jesus and his followers in Mark embrace this stance not in order to attain their own personal freedom but to bring the reign of God to those who are outcasts.

These stances, Smith argues, are "the two basic existential options" open to human beings. A total worldview is implied in each of these stances. Smith resists giving a higher value to one stance or the other. Order can be creative or oppressive. The transgression of order can be creative or destructive. Yet the two options represent such fundamentally different worldviews that "to change stance is to totally alter one's symbols and to inhabit a different world."[25]

Model Connecting Purity and Boundaries

How can we bring these two different worldviews into sharper focus? To help us, we can now turn to another model from the work of Mary Douglas. She argues that a given culture or group tends to have a uniform approach toward all boundaries. She shows how people in the same culture have a similar attitude toward boundaries at several levels of experience. One can see this "unity of experience" in the attitude toward boundaries at three levels:

1. the cosmological boundaries that the people project through their belief systems about God and the world
2. the bodily boundaries of individuals within the culture
3. the social boundaries of the group or culture

Douglas argues that the attitude toward boundaries tends to be the same at each of these levels. For example, if a society is anxious about what goes in and out of the orifices of the bodily boundary, then this society will probably also guard the social boundary carefully to protect who comes in and who goes out of their social group. In such a society, in regard to beliefs at the cosmological level, one would expect to find a dualism with a distinct boundary separating the good from the evil, the holy from the unclean. "Conversely," Douglas says, "if [in a different kind of society] there is no concern to preserve social boundaries, I would not expect to find concern with bodily boundaries."[26] And in such a society, with little concern to guard social boundaries or bodily boundaries, the beliefs about God and the world will show ambiguity and interaction on the boundary between good and evil.

Guarding Boundaries: The Authorities

We can see how the system works when we notice how the view of boundaries in the Jewish culture of the first century is the same at the cosmological, bodily, and social levels.

Cosmological Boundaries

At the cosmological level, the dominant motif is the pursuit of holiness by separation from what is unclean. There is a boundary around God to protect God's holiness and to separate God from all that would defile. People are to guard this boundary in order to keep God from withdrawing. On earth, God is located in the holiest place in the Temple. As we have seen, many boundaries surround this place. The cosmic order also includes boundaries for people and animals. Cosmological lines separate Israel from the Gentile nations. Other lines separate animals into clean and unclean. Thus the boundaries in the cosmology separate the clean from the unclean. As we have seen, people are to guard these boundaries in order to keep what is holy separated from that which defiles.

Bodily boundaries

Similarly, the skin of the body is a boundary to be guarded. The skin makes a person a bounded system. The skin keeps certain things in place inside the body, such as spit, blood, and semen. When out of place, these things will make a person unclean. Similarly, people can guard the skin from unclean things going in from outside the body, for example, by refusing to eat the meat of an unclean animal. Such unclean food taken in from the outside will defile a person. Hence, people guard the boundary of the body to avoid contact with what is unclean, because what comes out and certain things that go in will pollute people.

Social Boundaries

The boundary of Israel distinguishes Jews from Gentiles. Only male Jews who are circumcised and without blemish are considered pure. Jews who have contact with Gentiles become unclean, and intermarriage is strictly prohibited. At the same time, Gentiles who come among Jews are generally considered to be "out of place" in the Jewish community and, as we have seen, are prohibited from entering the sanctuary on penalty of death. Generally speaking, Jews guarded the social boundary to keep Jews in and Gentiles out. People also avoided those within the nation who are considered unclean, such as lepers, menstruating women, and corpses.

In the whole scheme, the most important level is that of the social group. The bodily boundaries and the cosmological order protect and maintain the social boundaries of the group or society. Thus, Douglas notes, "Israel is the boundary that all other boundaries celebrate and that gives them their historic load of meaning."[27] The whole classification system existed in order to protect and sustain the group. The avoidance of unclean food and of unclean people within the nation was a hedge against the outer boundary that separated Jew from Gentile. Thus, according to Douglas's model, there was a coherence of attitude and behavior in relation to boundaries at several levels, and the coherence served to reinforce the group's experience of its social boundary.

As we have seen, this system is also represented by the depiction of the authorities in Mark's story. They separate from the unclean in Israel (2:15-17), guard the holy Sabbath from defilement (2:23—3:6), guard God from blasphemy (2:1-12; 14:53-65), guard the Temple from unclean people (11:15-18) and blemished sacrifices (12:32-33), and guard the body from impure food (7:1-23).

Crossing Boundaries: The Jesus Movement in Mark

The Jewish movement of Jesus in Mark illustrates a contrasting attitude toward boundaries, the effort to be "unbounded" in order to overcome obstacles in the service of the kingdom of God. Here we see what happens when people abrogate purity rules, cross boundaries, or redraw them. Whereas the authorities in Mark's story guarded boundaries, Jesus and his followers transgressed boundaries. Whereas the leaders saw boundaries as means of protection, the Jesus movement saw boundaries as oppressive and limiting. Whereas the leaders withdrew from uncleanness, the Jesus movement attacked or ignored uncleanness. Whereas the Pharisees avoided contact with that which defiled, Jesus and his followers sought contact. The leaders had power by staying within the ordered boundaries, whereas the Jesus movement expressed power by crossing boundaries. In short, the Jesus movement, as depicted by Mark, treated boundaries as lines to cross, redraw, or eliminate.

In Mark's depiction of the Jesus movement, we see again a consonance, albeit of a very different character, in the attitude toward boundaries at the cosmological, the bodily, and the social levels.

Cosmological Boundaries

Mark's narrative shares the core value of the Jewish society in depicting God as holy. The empowering force behind the activity in the kingdom of God is the "Holy Spirit" (1:8-10), and Jesus is the "Holy One of God" (1:24). However, in contrast to the view that people are to attain holiness by separation from the threatening, pernicious force of impurity, Mark presents the view that people are to overcome uncleanness by spreading wholeness. Here God does not withdraw because of the threat of defilement by contact with the unclean. Rather, God's holiness is an active force that expands and invades in order to remove and to overcome uncleanness. Thus, in contrast to the view that God is to be protected within the confines of the Temple, the Markan God spreads the life-giving power of the kingdom through Jesus and his followers into the world wherever people are receptive to it.

In Mark, God's holiness spreads even into the territory of Satan. Satan is the adversary of God, and Mark refers to the demons under Satan's authority as "unclean spirits." Before the kingdom arrived, the world was Satan's house (3:23-29). Now, however, God breaks out of the confines of heaven, rips apart the boundary between heaven and earth, and invades Satan's territory (1:9-13). To establish rulership over the world, God crosses into Satan's arena. God sends down the *Holy* Spirit upon Jesus at his baptism (1:10-11). Immediately, the Spirit drives Jesus to confront Satan in the desert. Through the agency of Jesus, God binds Satan and plunders Satan's house (3:22-30). As such, God reclaims people from the destructiveness of the "unclean spirits" (1:12-13; 5:1-20; 9:14-19). The "holy" work of God is that which brings life and overcomes the destructive work of Satan (3:4; 9:42-49).

Also, in Mark, God breaks out of the confines of the Temple to be available everywhere. The Jewish leaders know that God resides on earth in the Temple, and they protect God from what is unclean. Jesus condemns the Temple as holy space because the leaders use it to set boundaries and prohibit the Gentile nations from worshiping there (11:17). God therefore leaves the Temple in order to spread out over the earth. At the death of Jesus, God rips apart the curtain of the sanctuary and breaks out of the confines of the sanctuary (15:38). God leaves the Temple and becomes available anywhere on earth to grant blessings and to pardon sins. The Temple is no longer needed for rituals and sacrifices, because God is now accessible wherever people offer prayers of faith and forgiveness (11:20-25).

Furthermore, Mark eliminates the cosmological boundaries that would identify people or things as unclean in and of themselves. For example, Mark eliminates the notion that animals might be unclean in and of themselves, for the Markan Jesus declares all foods clean (7:19). Also, Mark eliminates the notion that Gentiles are unclean in and of themselves. Mark rejects the boundary line distinguishing pure Jews from impure Gentiles. In Mark's view, any Jew or Gentile may be *with* God's kingdom or *against* God, based on faith and moral behavior rather than on ritual purity (3:29; 7:29). Also, Gentile territory is not unclean in and of itself (4:1-20; 7:24—8:10).

Mark's Jesus does not eliminate the line distinguishing God's people from others. He redraws the boundary line in terms of moral behavior rather than ritual impurity.[28] He eliminates dietary boundaries and "ritual defilements" that come by external contact with unclean things, but he does not abrogate purity notions altogether. Rather, he redefines purity of people and times in terms of faith in the rule of God and moral behavior enjoined by the Law and the Prophets, as interpreted by Jesus (7:14-23; 12:28-34). Those who respond favorably to Jesus and his teaching are on the inside; those who reject him and his teaching are on the outside (3:31-35; 4:10-13). Those who do the will of God are Jesus' "brother and sister and mother," whereas those who do not do the will of God are in opposition to Jesus and are on the outside (3:31-35). In order to give all people an opportunity to be on the inside, the followers of Jesus are to proclaim to all people, Jew and Gentile alike, without respect to ritual purity or impurity (13:10, 27). Thus Jesus redraws the line distinguishing God's people without respect to "ritual" purity or impurity.

As portrayed in the narrative, God is spreading holiness throughout the earth. Followers are also to spread out in order to tell others the good news. They are not to avoid people or animals or things that are considered unclean by society.

Bodily Boundaries

In consonance with this approach to cosmic boundaries, the followers of Jesus do not guard the body against things going in from the outside. The Markan Jesus says, "'There is nothing from outside that by entering people is able to defile them, because it does not enter into the heart, but goes into the stomach and on out into the latrine'—thus he declared all foods clean" (7:17-19). Therefore, there is no need to wash the hands before eating or to protect the body from taking in certain foods or to be concerned about the waste that goes out into the latrine, because Jesus declared all foods to be clean (7:1-23). This attitude toward the bodily boundary replicates the attitude toward the social boundary. As anyone may enter the network without making the group unclean, so anything may go into the body without making it unclean. There is no need to guard the boundaries from what is outside the person or the group.

There are two exceptions to the prohibition against guarding the boundary of the body. First, in Mark, demons are "unclean spirits" who enter and possess people. Unlike foods, they do not enter the stomach and go on out. Rather, they affect the whole person, including the heart, making faith and morality impossible. To drive out an unclean spirit by the power of the "Holy" Spirit is thereby to render a person clean. Second, people are to guard the bodily boundary against fornication and adultery. Here the focus is not so much on guarding physical boundaries but on ensuring that immoral and destructive behavior will not come out from the heart (10:1-12).

In Mark, what renders one clean or unclean is the moral behavior that comes out of the heart. As God spreads the kingdom and as the Jesus movement spreads holiness, so the individual spreads love for God and neighbor outward from the whole heart (12:29-31). However, immoral behavior that goes out from the heart can make that person unclean (7:20-23). Jesus says, "For from inside, from the hearts of people come the evil designs: fornications, thefts, murders, adulteries, acts of greed, acts of malice, deceit, licentiousness, envious eye, blasphemy, arrogance, reckless folly. All these wicked things come out from within and defile the person" (7:21-23). Thus, Mark eliminates ritual purity or defilement as a demarcation. In its place, he draws a line between moral and immoral behavior as that which determines purity or defilement. Mark honors moral behavior coming from the inside rather than guarding against unclean things from the outside.

In the same way, the Markan Jesus gives place to moral behavior over against physical wholeness. Mark shows through the many healings that it is God's will to make people physically whole. Yet, rather than cause someone else to sin, it is better to cut off one's own hand [or foot or eye] and to enter the rule of God maimed than to have two hands and be thrown into Gehenna (9:42-49). Thus, physical wholeness is not a criterion for being acceptable to God; rather, it is what comes out of the heart that makes one acceptable. This concern for morality over ritual purity and physical wholeness is evident in the "wise" statement of the scribe that loving God and the neighbor with the "whole" heart is more important than all the "whole" burnt offerings and sacrifices (pure animals without blemish, 12:32-33).

As such, the only maintenance Jesus recommends for the bodily boundary is for followers to do whatever they must do in order not to let harmful actions come out from the heart. One guards not the body but the heart so that what comes out of the heart is life-giving for others rather than destructive (3:1-6).

Social Boundaries

The attitude toward social boundaries in Mark's narrative world reveals the same expansiveness as we find at the cosmic level and the same openness we find in relation to the bodily boundaries. The Jesus movement described in the narrative of Mark is not a stationary community that seeks to protect its boundaries but a network going out from Jesus like branches on a tree: first Jesus, then the disciples he sends out (6:7-13), and then those who receive the disciples by hospitality (9:37) and pass the word on (1:28, 45; 5:20). The people in the network expand in outreach and influence.

Relationships in the network are based on reciprocity between those who proclaim and heal and those who give them hospitality. Jesus offers no provisions for establishing stationary communities— no ongoing rituals such as Baptism or Eucharist and no directions for communal organization or discipline. Jesus tells disciples to leave their families and property and to receive new familial relations in the hospitality offered them from one village to the next. The person who is at the extremity of the network—one who simply offers a cup of water to someone who bears the name of Christ—is fully part of the network and will receive a reward (9:41). Solidarity in this network is based, therefore, not on relationships in a stationary community but on the hospitality that followers receive from sympathizers as they move from place to place—"houses, brothers, sisters, mothers, children, and fields" (10:28-30). In contrast to a stationary and protectionist culture, the Jesus movement in Mark is a loose-knit network comprised of people who are reaching out.

Like God, Jesus and his followers are "boundary-crossing" figures. They cross the boundaries established by the culture that protect people from ritual uncleanness. Instead of preserving holiness by avoiding contact, the Markan movement spreads holiness by making contact. Instead of avoiding contact with people outside the group, Jesus' followers give all people the chance to experience the good news of the reign of God (13:10). In every case, instead of Jesus being defiled by the contact, Jesus makes clean that which was unclean by spreading purity, forgiveness, and wholeness.

Nor does the Jesus network depicted in Mark guard boundaries to protect those who are inside from those who are outside. The people in the network sow the seeds of the good news everywhere (4:13-20) and exclude no one from the network or from its benefits. Jesus eats with tax collectors and sinners. Jesus heals all who request healing, including a Gentile woman in Tyre (7:24-30). He feeds four thousand people in Gentile territory who have followed him into the desert (7:31—8:10). The narrative explicitly rejects exclusion. At one point, the disciples prevent a man from exorcising a demon in Jesus' name because he "was not following us." In response, Jesus tells them, "Do not stop him . . . for whoever is not against us is for us" (9:38-40). As such, those inside the network are to do nothing to set the limits of the community. Rather, they simply spread the influence of the network. Those outside the network who reject the followers of Jesus—"whoever is against us"—are the ones who set the limits of the network by their acts of rejection. Jesus tells the disciples that if others do not welcome them they are to leave that locale and shake the dust off their feet as a witness to the rejection (6:11). However, they do so only to confirm a decision already made by the outsiders rejecting them.

Furthermore, Jesus gives no directions for expulsion from the network. In fact, he strictly prohibits any attempt to dominate or exclude "the little ones who have faith" (9:42). Jesus himself, knowing that one of the twelve is about to betray him, nevertheless offers the cup at the last communal meal, and they all drink from it—including Judas (14:23). The Markan Jesus sets the boundary lines, but he prohibits the people in the network from guarding these lines. And because followers do not guard or protect the boundary lines, there is no margin to the boundary. People can get in easily, and once inside they can be at various levels of commitment or betrayal. This prohibition against guarding boundaries serves to prevent anything or anyone from inhibiting the expansion of the network. It is also in conformity with Jesus' moral injunction not to lord over anyone (10:41-45).

Purity and Defilement in Social History

The unique approach to purity and defilement taken by the Gospel of Mark takes its place among the spectrum of Jewish approaches to these issues in first-century Israel—from the exceptional strictness of the Essenes to the popular disregard for many of these regulations by much of the populace. It is difficult to tell how much Mark's approach reflects the time of Jesus or the period after Jesus before the Roman-Jewish War of 66–70 C.E. Perhaps Mark proffered his open attitudes to boundaries in part as a response to the contrasting "quest for holiness as separation" that characterized much of the Judean revolution against the Romans.[29] Or perhaps it was driven mainly by his commitment to see that followers of Jesus proclaimed the good news to the ends of the earth before Jesus returned. In any case, given the fact that Mark has such deeply Jewish sensibilities and does not present the Jesus movement as part of a separate religion, we need to see his narrative in the context of Jewish social history of the time.

But we can also see his Gospel in the context of the social history of early Christianity. In this regard, we do not know if Mark's approach to boundaries reflects the realities of his own community or if he was promoting this open approach for the benefit of a Jesus movement that did not agree with him. The approach to boundaries in Mark is somewhat unusual in early Christianity. Mark offers the vision of a radically open attitude toward boundaries inspired by the mission to bring the good news of healing and wholeness to all. Again, Mark's boundary-crossing approach takes its place among the spectrum of approaches to boundaries and purity in emerging Christianity. In distinction from Mark, many early Christian communities considered Baptism to be an important ritual of entrance. Also, both Paul (1 Cor. 5:3-5) and Matthew (18:15-18) have procedures for expelling people from a Christian community. Some biblical literature, such as 1 Peter, takes a defensive attitude toward boundaries, guarding believers from certain kinds of contact with outsiders in order to preserve the holiness of the community. Thus, even if Christianity did begin as a movement of Jews who were boundary-crossing figures, the early churches soon consolidated and organized in order to survive as they spread into the larger Greco-Roman world.

Conclusion

The extended case study given here illustrates the various approaches presented at the beginning of this chapter. In regard to *social description*, I identified many customs, laws, and practices related to pollution and purity in first-century Israel that informed this analysis of Mark's narrative world. In regard to *social history*, I made some brief suggestions about how the conception of purity in Mark's Gospel fit into the course of Israel's history and in the development of early Christianity. In regard to *sociology of knowledge*, I sought to display the contrasting conceptions of the authorities and the Jesus movement vis-à-vis issues of purity and defilement, as depicted in Mark. We saw how the Markan Jesus sought to "convert" followers from their primary socialization regarding purity, defilement, and boundaries to a new enculturation launched by the arrival of the kingdom of God. In regard to *cultural anthropology*, I used models to help clarify the relation between purity and boundaries evident in the narrative of Mark's Gospel. The overall conclusion was that the Markan attitude toward purity and boundaries at the cosmic level and at the bodily level supported a boundary-crossing Jesus movement that was radically oriented to mission.

7

Performing the Gospel of Mark

Dissatisfied at length with an analysis centered on the text as object, I realized that narrative could not be satisfactorily explored except as the site of an interaction. . . . For performance to be successful, it is not enough for it to have purpose; it must also have energy and effect.

—Marie Maclean, *Narrative as Performance*

The Gospel of Mark is an amazing story full of action and drama. It was written to be recounted aloud to an audience in a lively and powerful way. In the late 1970s I memorized this Gospel in order to present it orally. Since then I have performed it before a wide variety of audiences. In what follows I want to share some of what I have learned from this experience. In the first part I reflect on my experience of performing—the significance of performing, memorizing the Gospel, entering the narrative world, using techniques to tell the story, experiencing the self as medium, and becoming aware of the involvement of the audience. In the second part, I want to show how the demands of performance have led me to a greater understanding of Mark's Gospel. To illustrate this, I discuss the settings, events, characters, oral techniques of narration, and the rhetoric of the episode of the Syrophoenician woman. I end with some brief reflections.

The Dynamics of Performance

The Significance of Performing

When I first began performing Mark, it was a new and somewhat strange experience. Yet, having now performed the Gospel of Mark many times, I am rather stunned to think it has not been done much more often and for a long time. Originating in an oral culture, the Gospel of Mark was meant to be performed in its entirety before a listening/observing audience. Yet our primary experiences of this story is a matter of reading it privately or hearing one episode recounted at worship. Imagine musicologists reading scores without hearing them performed. Or imagine being a Shakespearean scholar without ever having seen a play performed. All interpretation of music and theater comes to expression and testing in the act of performing. Why should it not be the same with the biblical writings?

The act of performing involves several shifts. The first shift is from reading the story to hearing it. Hearing the Gospel is a very different experience from reading it. But the experience of hearing is also different from the experience of performing. So the second shift is from hearing the story to presenting it in dramatic form—the whole Gospel at one time. To do so places the interpreter in the role of the narrator of Mark's Gospel, the one who is telling the story. What a different medium this is as a means to interpret the meaning and power of this Gospel! The word is no longer on the page but alive in yourself, coming to expression as a passionate act of communication with an audience.

Learning the Gospel

In the late 1970s, I heard about the British actor Alec McGowen who performed the King James Version of the Gospel of Mark. He learned a verse a day until he committed the whole Gospel to memory, and he played to packed houses in England and the United States.[1] At the time, I was doing my own translation of Mark for a book on that Gospel. I had done a lot of memorizing as a youth and so I decided to learn Mark. A back injury, which kept me laid up for a month, gave me the opportunity. I initially learned Mark in order to provide an educational experience for my students and to give them a chance to hear the entire Gospel as a story at one time. Soon, I got many opportunities to perform Mark at churches and educational institutions. My aim in memorizing was to be precise and thorough in learning the text by heart so that audiences really heard the Gospel of Mark and not a paraphrase or an elaboration or an abbreviated version of Mark.

At first, I found it very difficult to retain the whole Gospel of Mark in memory. Modern people are biased toward writing something down as a means to remember it, and so we are not very practiced in the skills of recall. Initially, I would spend fifteen to twenty hours practicing the memory work before a presentation. In my experience, unless one has the opportunity to perform a narrative over and over again, it will be quickly forgotten. Each time I recalled it for performance, I committed it more securely to memory. I have performed Mark nearly 200 times. Taking account of practice and memory work, I have probably gone over Mark more than 500 times. Eventually, I got beyond the problem of remembering. I now have the words well in mind, and when I perform, I am no longer trying to remember what words come next.

As this process was taking place, the story came to be liberated from the page. I no longer thought of trying to remember words as they were written on the page; rather, I heard the sounds of the words in my mind as I was recalling them. Now I seldom think in terms of the words themselves so much as the images to which they refer. In the role of narrator of the story, I run pictures through my mind of what I am recounting, and I tell and show the audience what I am seeing in imagination as I perform. I do not think in terms of chapters or verses but about the flow and movement of the story—how it begins, what happens next, and how it turns out. Performing a text is like playing a musical composition. Once the score is committed to memory, neither the artist nor the audience think about notes on a page. Rather, they are caught up in the experience of the music itself, just as the storyteller and the hearer of a biblical story are caught up in the story.

Entering the Story-World

One of the most interesting aspects of performance is the experience of entering the world of the story. At every point, the storyteller uses imagination to re-create the story. You reenact the world of the story in the space on the stage. The act of performing the whole narrative leads a person to be immersed in this world. It takes over two hours to perform the Gospel of Mark. During that time, you have a sense of being inside another world. You enter the whole space and time continuum of this first-century construction of the world. You have a past that goes back to the prophets, David, the patriarchs, and creation, and you have a future that will last only to the end of the generation, when the end will come and a new age will begin. The cosmos is a flat earth with a canopy over it on which the sun and stars are affixed—a cosmos populated by God and Satan, angels and demons, Jews and Gentiles, authorities and peasants. At center stage of this drama is Jesus announcing the kingdom, performing healings, calling and struggling with the disciples, engaging in mortal debate with the leaders of Israel, and moving inexorably toward crucifixion.

To enter this space and time is also to realize what is possible and what is not possible in this story. As Coleridge said, when you enter the world of a story, you "suspend disbelief" and accept what is possible and what is not possible in that world. When the protagonist heals the sick, drives out demons, calms a storm, multiplies loaves in the desert, and expects his disciples to be able to do the same, you realize that this is a world in which everything is possible to one who has faith. Yet, despite these dramatic possibilities, this world is full of strange paradoxes. While Jesus can heal people, he has no authority to control people. He can drive out a demon, but he cannot successfully command someone to keep quiet about it. He can make a deaf man hear, but he cannot make his disciples comprehend what he is teaching them. Here is a world in which it is easier to get a physically blind man to see than the mentally blind disciples to understand. Here too is a world in which someone with authority over illness and demons and nature will come into necessary and violent conflict with

the national leaders and be executed—and, of course, there is resurrection from the dead.

Telling the Story

The task of the performer is to re-create this world on stage and to
draw the hearers into it. How you tell the story is therefore of utmost
importance. After I got beyond the memory problem, I could work on
the interaction with the audience—how to tell the story to an audience in an effective and engaging way. I do not have training in acting,
and I am limited in my capacity to convey the story. I think of my task
less as acting and more as storytelling. Yet I did not want simply to
stand on stage and recount the Gospel, nor did I want to attempt to
replicate how the ancient storytellers might have recounted Mark—
we are uncertain about that in any case.[2] Therefore, I began to use
storytelling techniques drawn from the oral interpretation of literature, and these techniques have helped me to tell Mark's story in a
meaningful way. Here are just a few of these techniques.

When I tell the story as narrator, I make use of an *off-stage focus*
and address the audience directly. Then, when I, as narrator, portray
a character speaking, I show the audience what a character in the
story says by assuming the role of that character. When I portray the
character in this way, I employ an *on-stage focus* and address other
characters in imagination before me on the stage. These shifts must
be made quickly and seamlessly. Such shifts between on-stage and
off-stage focus help the audience to distinguish when I use the voice
of the narrator and when I assume the role of a character. When I do
a characterization of one of the figures in the story, I try to assume
a distinctive posture, voice, gesture, and inflection, meant to be
consonant with the traits and dialogue of the character being portrayed (and there are more than fifty characters with dialogue in
Mark!).

I also *block my movements* by going to different places on the stage
to convey intimacy or mystery or action, or to help the audience recall
similar episodes that occurred earlier in the story (and the number of

scene changes is extraordinary). When similar scenes recur, such as the three passion predictions or three boat scenes, I return to the same place on the stage. In addition, often in coordination with stage movements, I have learned to *pace* the story with urgency, with deliberateness, or with pauses according to the flow of the story.

Finally, in every line, whether speaking as the narrator or as a character, I attend to the *subtext*. Each line of text has the potential meaning of its words, but when delivered orally each line also has a subtext—the message that is conveyed by the "way" a line is delivered—with impatience or indifference or with tolerance. What is the goal of a character in saying this line, and how can that goal be conveyed by the way the character says the line? Every line can be delivered many different ways. Each decision made by the performer about the subtext leads to a change of inflection, the raising of an eyebrow, a distinct shift in posture, or the lowering of the voice, and so on.

In the text, there are explicit and implicit directions for choices about the use of these techniques in performance. When the story says that people were afraid or amazed or alarmed, these are *stage directions* for the performer to signal or express such emotions. When the story says that someone cried out or pleaded, these are guidelines for delivering a line. The change of scene in the story is a guide for movement on stage. The repetition of a word such as "immediately" is an encouragement to pick up the pace of the storytelling. Patterns in the rhetoric, lengths of sentences, the introduction of new information, and the presence of rhetorical questions all affect the pace and rhythm of the storytelling. The consistency of characterization, the intensity of a conflict, and the content of dialogue all become guides to determine subtext. Eventually, a grasp of the whole story guides the decisions one makes about saying each line and portraying each scene.

These and other techniques of oral interpretation give the performer a greater repertoire in self-expression with which to tell the story.[3] They also help the performer place in sharper relief so many dimensions of the story. In so doing, the story is made clearer and more interesting for the audience.

The Performer as Medium

Through these techniques I have become aware that all dimensions of the narrative and its rhetoric pass through the performer. The performer *is* the medium. Performance is not just a mental act of memorizing and retelling. In a performance, your whole psychosomatic reality becomes the vehicle for the presentation of the story. At every point, your self—indeed, your body—is an added presence and the medium of the story. In a sense, you try to make yourself transparent to the story. However, that does not happen, because every dimension of the story is enacted in you. You go to Galilee, you heal the leper, you plot to destroy Jesus, you recount the crucifixion, and so on. In the same way that a text with markings for words on a page mediates a written story, so you become the medium for the story.

A human medium has both limitations and possibilities. In terms of a capacity to tell the story, consider the performer's voice, physical litheness (or lack of it), facial malleability, sense of rhythm, imagination, capacity to mimic, and so on. Even the social location of the performer affects the storytelling. For example, I am a European-American male with a gray beard and a noticeable paunch. I am obviously middle class. People know that I am ordained and that I teach at a seminary. Faithfulness to the story can be a problem, for there is no middle class in Mark's narrative world. This Gospel was written from a peasant perspective. Furthermore, Jesus tells people to leave all they have and be prepared for persecution. My social location makes it difficult for me to convey these marginalized positions from which Mark's Gospel was written. All these factors grant both delightful possibilities and the painful awareness of limitations.

Since the performer is a living medium of the word, decisions about interpretation are embodied in the performer—posture and stance, tone and volume, pace of voice and movement, gestures, facial expressions, and location on stage. All sounds and movements become part of the interpretation. Obviously, the story can be embodied in many different ways. In fact, because the performer changes, no single performance by a player is the same as any other performance by that same player. Performers with different understandings of the story and different gifts for performance will embody the story in a diversity of ways. Some interpretations may be more faithful to Mark's story than others. Nevertheless, within a wide range, there are many legitimate interpretations. Just as every translation is an interpretation, so every performance is an interpretation. Just as every translation captures some aspects of a word or a story and loses other meanings and nuances, so every oral presentation has gains and losses in terms of the meanings and effects of the story. Therefore, experiencing diverse performances of Mark will enhance and deepen people's encounter with Mark's Gospel.

What all this means is that an audience's experience of a performance is not just an aural event. We talk about hearing the gospel rather than reading it. But that is not quite correct, unless we have our eyes closed or are listening to a tape recorder. The experience of a performance is not only aural; it is also very visual, not only in terms of what the audience sees of the performer but also of what the performer leads the audience to see in imagination. In this regard, the presence of a live performer does much to restore the emotive and kinetic dimensions to the text. Without a living presence, words alone can be without passion, awe, delight, or pathos. Given the living, feeling presence of a performer, the audience can be drawn into an emotional identification with characters and a profound emotional reaction to the events being enacted before them—the healing of a man who was blind, the raising of a little child, the crucifixion of a messiah. But the performer also restores the kinetic dimensions to the text—touching a leper, embracing children, pleading in a prostrate position. In light of the presence of the performer, the experience of hearing as distinct from reading is much more than just hearing. Perhaps, it is most appropriate to think about the experience as concert or theater.

Audience as Participant

The performance is the site of an interaction between the presenter and the audience. One of the major dimensions of the shifts from reading to performing is that it is also a shift from a private to a public setting. Public settings can differ significantly in shaping the response of an audience—a church, a classroom, a community theater, a public square, a prison. The shift from reading to performing is also a shift from an individual to a communal experience. The fact that it is a communal setting means that individuals will respond to the story in part in relation to those around them. The common experience of a group in hearing the Gospel also allows for communal conversation with the presenter after the performance—a conversation that may in turn influence subsequent performances.

Furthermore, just as a performer enhances and limits the possibilities of a performance, so also does the audience shape a performance. For example, the life situation of the audience (age, familiarity with Mark, and social location) and the responses of the audience in the course of a performance are factors that make every performance unpredictable. Audiences in educational settings are generally more attuned to the humor in Mark and freer in that context to laugh than audiences in churches. On some occasions, I have gotten "on a roll" with the audience in the humor of Mark's Gospel—how the pig herders flee from Jesus' exorcism and how the disciples are amazed that Jesus asks who touched him in a crowd that is crushing him. On such occasions, I have delivered some lines in ways I had never delivered them before and thereby found new dimensions of the delight in this story. In a different vein, the experience of performing Mark at a medium-security prison changed my understanding of Mark's audience and of the nature of Mark's good news. From them, I realized how crucial the miracles were, how important it was for the disciples to succeed, and how much the good news empowers people to be free of "fornications, thefts, murders, adulteries, works of greed, malicious acts. . ."(7:21-22).

In interaction with the performer, the audience participates in the construction of meaning. In some sense, of course, the story will mean what the audience understands it to mean. Yet, even when the performer gets across a faithful portrayal of the Gospel, much commentary would be necessary for a contemporary audience to understand all the meanings of this ancient story. The author of this story took an enormous amount for granted, because he was addressing an audience with whom he shared common meanings and nuances of words, cultural conventions, community life, historical experiences, and an ancient worldview. Hearing Mark today, without the aid of explanations, is sometimes like hearing an anecdote or a joke from another culture. You have to know the shared assumptions about life in order to "get it." Such gaps in understanding may involve knowledge of the Sabbath laws or the dynamics of purity and defilement or the pattern of telling episodes in a chiastic series. The performer will seek to use various means of self-expression to convey these meanings without in any way adding to the words of the story or seeking to provide an explanation. Yet, given a contemporary audience, this is often difficult or impossible. Nevertheless, much of this story can be grasped well enough to be understood and appreciated without having to fill in the gaps with information from antiquity.

Yet the interaction between performer and audience is much more than communication. The audience participates in more ways than understanding. Words and stories do not just have denotations of meaning. They also have an impact on people. We are not dealing simply with the notion of conveying information about events to an audience. The narrative is not a vehicle for an idea, as if we could get the idea or the theology and then no longer need the story. Nor is the story an example to illustrate an idea. The story itself has energy and power. The story affects the whole person—heart, soul, mind, and body. Words do not just have meaning; they create effects. Words and stories are "speech acts." Something happens to the audience as a result of experiencing the story. The story can confront the hearer, evoke sadness or delight, lead one to identify with some characters and be repelled by others, engender wonder or hope, change one's values, empower for love, or lead one through a catharsis that purges fear and pity. Mark's narrative seeks nothing less than to liberate people from lives of anxious self-concern to be prepared to follow Jesus in a life for others, even to death. Understood this way, an understanding of Mark involves not only what the story *means* but also what the story *does* to transform an audience in its telling.

By the sheer force of the words and the impact of the interaction, the performer seeks to draw hearers into the story-world—as, in a darkened theater, the audience may be drawn into the world of a film. Emerging from a powerful film, you may be a different person or you may be empowered to change your life. The performer of Mark seeks to bring the audience through the whole story so that they are not the same people at the end as they were at the beginning. Yet the performer never controls the outcome. The performer may encounter resistance or indifference or sleepiness. There are hearers who simply do not accept the point of view of the story. The performance may simply be for many people an evening of good or bad entertainment. Some may be offended or hurt by some aspect of the story. On the other hand, people may be changed or affirmed or empowered or forgiven or healed in ways you might never have expected. Regardless of the actual reactions, the performer has a sense of what people *could* experience—given her or his interpretation of the story—and seeks to foster that experience.

Performance and Interpretation

There is a relationship between performance and interpretation that has enabled me to learn more about the Gospel of Mark from the act of performing. Performing Mark has helped me to notice details and dynamics in the story I would not otherwise have seen. As I have indicated, the experience of assuming the role of the narrator and actually telling the story is different from the experience of reading or hearing the Gospel. It is a major act (interaction) of communication. The demands of performance impress upon one the need to make choices about every aspect of the meaning and the rhetoric of the story that a reader or a hearer of the Gospel will probably not make.

For this reason, I find it helpful to make my own translations for performance. Translations are not often made with the idea of story-telling in mind. Translations have been made primarily to convey meaning to a reading audience. Few translations have taken into consideration the oral impact of the rhetoric on an audience. Translations for oral performance can take into account aspects of the text not evident in a translation that is designed for reading—word order, historical presents, elisions, contractions, verbal threads, repetition of sounds, among others. The very experience of learning and telling the story also assists in this process of translation, because I often change and adjust the translation in light of the experience of performance.

To illustrate the interaction between performance and interpretation, I would like to reflect on a single episode from the Gospel of Mark. I have chosen the episode of Jesus' encounter with the Syrophoenician woman. I do not thereby mean to isolate this episode from the story as a whole. Indeed, the episode comes thirty minutes or so into the story, and the episode follows and precedes other episodes that are closely related to it. I have begun the translation a few lines before the episode commences and continued a few lines after it ends (Mark 7:14-35):

> And summoning the crowd again, he said to them, "Hear me everyone and understand. There is nothing from outside people that by going into them is able to defile them. Rather, the things that go out from people are the things that defile people."

> And when he entered into a house from the crowd, his disciples asked him about the parable. And he says to them, "Do you too lack understanding like this? Don't you perceive that everything that enters into people from the outside is not able to defile them because it does not enter into their hearts but into their stomachs and goes on out into the latrine"—thereby rendering clean all foods.

> He said, "What comes out from people is what defiles people. For from inside from the hearts of people come the evil designs: fornications, thefts, murders, adulteries, acts of greed, malicious deeds, deceit, amorality, envious eye, blasphemy, arrogance, reckless folly. All these wicked things come from inside and defile people."

Now from there arising he went off to the territory of Tyre, and entering a house he wanted no one to know about him and he was not able to escape notice. Instead a woman whose little daughter had an unclean spirit at once heard about him, came and fell before him.

Now the woman was Greek, a Syrophoenician by birth, and she asked Jesus to drive out the demon from her daughter.

And he said to her, "Let first the children be satisfied, for it is not good to take the bread for the children and throw it to the little dogs."

But she answers and says to him, "Lord, even the little dogs down under the table eat of the little children's crumbs."

And he said to her, "Because of this word, go on off. The demon has gone out from your daughter."

And going off to her house, she found the little girl thrown on the bed and the demon gone out.

And coming back out from the territory of Tyre, he went through Sidon to the Sea of Galilee up the middle of the territory of the Decapolis.

And people bring to him a deaf and tongue-tied man and plead with Jesus to lay his hand on him.

And taking him apart from the crowd privately, he thrust his fingers into his ears and, spitting, touched the man's tongue. And looking up to heaven, he groaned and he says to him, "Ephphatha!" which means "Be opened!"

And at once his ears were opened and the binding of his tongue was released and he began speaking clearly.

This is a wonderful story full of conflict, drama, surprises, and puzzles, and with interesting characters and a strange setting. As we unpack the dynamics of this episode, we will look at the story-world, the techniques of oral narration, and the rhetoric of the story.

The Story: The Settings

Decisions about movement on stage lead the performer to interpret carefully every spatial detail of Mark's story. You become acutely aware of every place—how it relates to people and events as well as what else happens in the same location in other places in the story. In this episode, I move across the stage and go to the edge of the stage, as a means to signal how far away Tyre is and that it is outside the boundaries of Israel. Jesus goes a long way off to seclude himself. Earlier in the story, people came from Tyre to Galilee because they had heard of Jesus and wanted to see him (3:3-7). That is why Jesus cannot remain hidden for long in Tyre, because his reputation precedes him. As I perform, I enter a house that I imagine to be a typical first-century house. Because it has a gate open to the courtyard, passers-by have access to it. After the encounter between Jesus and the woman in the house, I see, in my mind's eye, the woman going home to her daughter. Hopefully, the audience sees this with me. After that, I move back across part of the stage to convey passing through Sidon, while I recount that Jesus was going "to the Sea of Galilee up the middle of the territory of the Decapolis." Now I have stayed in Gentile territory, gone around the Sea of Galilee from the north, and returned to the place where Jesus had earlier exorcised a "Legion" of demons and had been asked to leave the territory (5:1-20).

In this episode, the physical movements on stage also make me aware of crossing boundaries: Jesus crosses into "the borders" of Tyre into Gentile territory; the woman crosses the boundary to the house; Jesus goes to Sidon and the Decapolis. Jesus' movements into the Gentile territory of Tyre, Sidon, and the Decapolis are significant. If the protagonist of a story were traveling in the United States and then went into Canada or Mexico, the hearer would be very aware of this boundary-crossing, and would remember the events there and recall them when the protagonist returned to Canada or Mexico. A slight pause before the naming of these places may convey something of the significance of this movement.

There are also social boundaries—a Jewish holy man entering impure territory, a female talking to a strange man, and a demon leaving. In addition, the preceding episode involved the overcoming of a bodily boundary when Jesus declared all foods clean. This sequence of episodes is similar to episodes in Acts when Peter's vision of all foods being declared clean led Peter to cross the boundary of the unclean house of Cornelius in Caesarea and convert the first Gentile (Acts 10:1-48). In both cases, the boundary-crossing is a breakthrough in the story. Jesus' encounter with the Syrophoenician woman overcomes the last barrier to Gentiles in a whole series of boundary-crossing episodes in Mark's narrative. Showing a sense of surprise, indeed shock, at the identification of the woman who has approached him as "a Greek, a Syrophoenician by birth" may lead the hearer to realize what a boundary-crossing encounter this episode represents.

The Story: Events

Mark does not often make explicit the connections between events. It is up to the listener to infer the relationships. Mark may not be thinking of cause and effect between events as we might. Yet the performer needs to press the questions of relationship: Is an event contingent upon earlier events? Does an event fulfill an earlier prophecy? Are two events connected by comparison or contrast? Are two events connected by thematic development? Is there a series of events in which a conflict escalates?

About this episode, for example, I wonder why Jesus goes to Tyre in Gentile territory and hides in a house. As a result of performing, it has become clear to me that Mark may be implying multiple causes at once. Based on the whole story, Jesus may be withdrawing after conflict with the Pharisees (earlier, he withdrew after a conflict) or to seek rest from a frantic pace (he did this also) or to escape the disciples and their failure to understand his parable (his impatience with them is growing) or all of the above. Perhaps the narrator is suggesting that Jesus was hiding to avoid Gentiles, since he does tell the Syrophoenician woman that he will not give bread to Gentiles. The performer searches the whole story, especially the immediate context, for causes and connections. The lack of explanation and explicit connections by Mark leaves the story open to different legitimate interpretations. In any case, the performer's decision about this event and how to fill the gaps in the story will bear directly upon performance, whether, for example, in the brief account of Jesus' movement to Tyre, the performer should convey an attitude of eagerness, weariness, secrecy, or discouragement.

The act of narration makes one aware not only of connections between episodes but also of the sequence of action and dialogue within an episode. At every line, the performer asks: Why does this happen next? Why does she say this in response to that? Why does he do that after she says this? You can see the sequence here:

- He goes off and hides (to rest, to escape disciples, to avoid Gentiles?).
- She hears about him and falls at his feet (because of those who had gone from Tyre to see Jesus in Galilee).
- She is Greek, yet she asks Jesus to exorcise the demon (this is new information and creates suspense).
- He refuses her request (a surprise, yet he explains).
- She understands the riddle (a surprise, because even the disciples do not understand; she is clever and persistent).
- He declares the child freed of the demon (again he explains that it is because of her word).
- The woman goes off and finds the daughter healed (the words of Jesus were effective).
- Jesus goes off to the Decapolis (to return to where he had earlier been rejected in Gentile territory).

At every point, therefore, the performer is acutely aware of the flow of the story. Each decision will affect the telling of the story. Sometimes in the middle of a performance, I will see a connection I had not seen before. For example, I know that Jesus calls the woman a "dog" because Jews sometimes referred to Gentiles as dogs. In that time, dogs were not treated as pets, but roamed around scavenging for scraps. Dogs were considered unclean, as were Gentiles. Suddenly, in a performance, I (as Jesus) see this woman begging at my feet for what is not rightfully hers—acting like a scavenger dog! In my mind, I am saying, "Oh, now I see why he says that to her. It's a response to what she is doing. No wonder they exchange proverbs about dogs." At times, the connections leap across the story. When Jesus says, "Because of this word, go on off. The demon has gone out from your daughter," it has the same rhythm as an earlier line of Jesus to a woman healed of a flow of blood: "Your faith has restored you. Go in peace, and be free of your ailment" (5:34).

As oral narrator, one also attends to the pace of events. Here, there is an awareness of the relation between story time and plotted time. How long does an event take in the story-world (story time), and how long does it take to narrate the event (plotted time)? In this episode, there is an acceleration of time when a day's journey to Tyre (story time) takes about four seconds to narrate (plotted time). This statement introduces setting. Then there is a deceleration of time as the woman hears about Jesus and falls at his feet. This introduces a character. Then there is a descriptive pause: No action takes place while the narrator tells us that the woman was a Greek and a Syrophoenician by birth. Descriptive pauses (explanatory asides to the reader) are not unusual in Mark, and they signal the introduction of important information. The narration needs to slow down to let this new information sink in before we go on. What follows in the story will not be understood unless we slow down. The pace becomes equivalent to dialogue in a dramatic scene, in which the recounting of the scene takes about the same time as it takes for the scene to occur in story time. Such scenes often signal the heart of an episode. Here the narration must be deliberate if the audience is to grasp the allegorical proverbs Jesus and the woman exchange in dialogue. Finally, plotted time accelerates again in relation to story time as the woman goes off to her house and finds the child—a consequence of the action and the dialogue. Then a new episode commences and Jesus goes off to the Decapolis, also a consequence of the interchange.

The Story: Characters

Characters are a key dimension of the Markan narration. Some are ongoing characters, such as Jesus, the disciples, and the Pharisees. Most characters simply make cameo appearances and then are gone.

Yet many of these characters are memorable—the leper, the man with the withered hand, Jairus and his daughter, the woman with the flow of blood, the Syrophoenician woman, blind Bartimaeus, and so on. In the course of telling and retelling the Gospel of Mark, I have come to think that each of these minor characters appears at a strategic place in the narrative and is not interchangeable with any other. The episode of the Syrophoenician woman may seem to be just one more miracle story. Yet the Syrophoenician woman appears just after Jesus has declared all foods clean and just before Jesus gives bread to Gentiles. Jesus' encounter with her is the hinge event that leads to his mission in Gentile territory. The narration may in some ways be able to show the development in the flow of these episodes in sequence.

As a performer, you get to know each character well. In the role of narrator, you tell about her in introductions and descriptions. You assume the role of that character in the course of showing what she said or did. You also talk with and react to that character in the roles you play as other characters in the story. With regard to the Syrophoenician woman, for example, the performer tells about her as narrator, pleads with Jesus as the woman herself, and reacts to her request in the role of Jesus.

From performing this episode, I have concluded that the woman is the driving force of the whole scene. This woman is determined to get her daughter restored. Despite Jesus' efforts to hide, she finds him. Despite her origins, she asks him. Despite his refusal, she persists. She goes home only when her request is met. The question for the performer is how to display her actions or say her lines. To decide this, one has to think through the text. When she falls at his feet, is she kneeling or prostrate? What is her attitude in speaking? What is the subtext? Is she a person pleading rather pathetically for her daughter, or is she a feisty inferior who persists and cleverly gets her way? How do you express her attitude by gesture and posture? How can the characterization convey the way she upstages Jesus with her proverbial response to his cryptic allegory? This is a woman determined to get her daughter healed. And she is willing to use every clever device at her disposal to make it happen.

The characterization of Jesus in this episode is also very interesting. At every point, the demands of performance press upon one the need to make decisions that exegetes might not otherwise make. A performer will want to answer the following questions:

- Why does Jesus go to Tyre and hide?
- Why does he reject the Syrophoenician woman's request?
- What is Jesus' time scheme for Jews and Gentiles?
- Why does he speak here in a parabolic allegory?
- What does he mean by this allegory?
- Does he change his mind or has he only been testing the woman?
- Did Jesus heal the woman's daughter? Or was it her faith? Or God?
- Why does he immediately go back to the Decapolis?

Each of these questions can be answered in different ways. However, all of the decisions about them will be reflected in the gestures, inflections, facial expressions, posture, pace, volume, and tone presented in each line.

As performer, I find there is one key question to the characterization of Jesus in this episode: Does he reject the woman's request as a test, or does he really mean it? In other words, does he change his mind? If I perform it one way, Jesus will be playful and coy. If I perform it another way, Jesus will be serious and then surprised. In this last scenario, he will tell the riddle in a way that suggests he really wants her to understand it, and then he will be happily surprised when she does. I find the story makes better sense when we assume that Jesus is not testing her but really does initially reject her request. This interpretation is consistent with the integrity of Jesus' words throughout the story. Also, according to Jesus' explanation, he rejects the woman's request because he will not give bread to the Gentiles (the dogs) before the Jews (the children) are satisfied. After all, when he went into Gentile territory before (in the Decapolis), the people asked him to leave, and he accepted this rejection and left. This interpretation also gives another explanation as to why Jesus was hiding while in Tyre: because he was not intending to heal Gentiles. Furthermore, in what follows this episode, Jesus seems to have changed his mind about not giving bread to the Gentiles before the Jews are satisfied, because he stays in Gentile territory (returning to the Decapolis) and performs healings and provides bread in the desert to Gentiles. Then the question arises: What does it say about Mark's overall characterization that Jesus changes his mind and his mission as a result of the intelligence and persistent faith of this Gentile woman?

In characterization, it is also important to provide continuity through the story. This one vignette takes only about sixty seconds to perform. It passes quickly as part of the flow of the story. The character of Jesus should be consistent with what the audience has seen and heard, even if new insights come. Regarding the role of the woman, it is important to reflect how similar she is to all the other suppliants with faith who come to Jesus for healing. They appear in a recurring type of scene with characters who respond favorably to his proclamation of the kingdom.

Style and Techniques of Oral Narration

The performer attends especially to the rhetoric of the story, or *how* the story is told—style, word order, choice of words, grammar, and so on—in order to create certain effects on the audience. Because the Gospel of Mark was written to be read aloud, it contains many sophisticated features of oral storytelling. I have learned a great deal about Mark by using these features to enhance performance.

One such feature for oral storytelling is Mark's *spare style*. Mark says an enormous amount in few words. His descriptions are suggestive rather than exhaustive: ". . .and entering a house he wanted no one to know about him," "Now the woman was Greek," "she found the little girl thrown on the bed and the demon gone out." Mark does not write with a flourish, varying his vocabulary and seeking dramatic figures of speech or fancy turns of phrase. His choice of words is simple, and he repeats the same words and phrases in many contexts. Repetition is the lifeblood of oral narration, and our narrator employs repetition to great effect, not only to reinforce certain patterns but also to make connections between episodes.

The narrator of this story also seldom tells us what people are like; he does not say explicitly that the woman has faith or that Jesus changes his mind. The narrator does not tell us the meaning of events; he does not say overtly that this episode is a breakthrough to Gentiles or that the words of the woman will change Jesus' subsequent actions. Rather, the narrator *shows* us the actions and the words of the characters, and simply depicts the course of events. The listeners must infer the rest. The listeners are left to experience the traits of the characters in their behavior, the meaning of the events in their recounting, and the effects of the narrative in its telling.

Another feature of Mark's oral storytelling is *word order*. In Greek, nouns are identified by case endings rather than by their place in the sentence. As such, the Greek writer can put the nominative subject almost anywhere in the sentence and the hearers will know it is the subject. Word placement can indicate emphasis, pace, repetition, parallelism, and so on. When we try to be faithful in English to the Greek word order, the sentence is often awkward or unintelligible. Here, the performer of an English text is at an advantage, since it is possible in spoken English to employ a greater variety of word order than in written English (although, in written English, poetry uses word order more freely). Take the different effect of, "Let the children be satisfied first," and, "Let first the children be satisfied." In the former example, the word "first" is in the background and is less important than the feeding of the children. In the second example, the word "first" is foregrounded and emphasizes the temporal order as the reason for Jesus' rejection of the woman's request. In written English, the first example seems most natural and the second seems awkward. However, in spoken English, as part of a performance, either one may be said naturally. The second example, in which the performer stresses the word "first," renders faithfully Mark's word order in Greek and conveys the desired impact.

Word order often expresses *parallelism*. In the Greek text of this episode, the last words of Jesus parallel the subsequent results of his words.

a   . . . go on off,

b   has gone out from your daughter

c   the demon."

a'   And going off to her house,

b'   she found the little girl thrown on the bed

c'   and the demon gone out.

Such parallelism can often be rendered faithfully in the word order of an oral narration, even when it cannot be so rendered in a written style for reading—although this example from our episode may be too awkward in parts even for oral narration. The content and order reveal a one-to-one correlation between what Jesus says and what happens as a result. One can recount the announcement by Jesus and the result of it with certain emphasis and rhythm so as to suggest the correlation. The parallelism emphasizes the authority of Jesus and the power and reliability of his words, as well as the faithful response of a suppliant. When such parallelism recurs after many of Jesus' healings, the accumulative effect is considerable.

Another feature of oral narration in Mark's Gospel is the *historical present*, or the use of the Greek present tense to narrate events of the past. In English, we often use the present tense in popular speech to make an anecdote more vivid and immediate. Yet, in written English, it is awkward to go back and forth between the present and past tenses. As a result, most English translations render the historical present in the simple past. Yet historical presents are an important part of Mark's storytelling and occur in most episodes of the narrative. Historical presents can often be rendered in oral performance without any awkwardness at all. There is one historical present in the episode of the Syrophoenician woman: "But she answers and says to him. . . ." Several historical presents occur in the next episode cited above: "And people bring to him a deaf and tongue-tied man and plead with Jesus to lay his hands on him." These are limited examples. The historical present occurs more extensively in other episodes, such as the raising of Jairus's daughter.[4] In performance, the historical present makes the narrative much more vivid and intensifies the hearer's involvement with the story.

Repetition is a key technique of Mark's oral narration. The repetition of words, lines, types of episodes, structures of episodes, and so on are central to oral narration. One of the most pervasive stylistic elements of Mark's narrative is repetition in *two-step progressions*. First, a word or phrase occurs, and then the same thing is repeated in other, more specific terms. The first element makes a point, and the second element nails it down with greater specificity. In our episode, the two-step progression is evident in the words: "Now the woman was Greek, a Syrophoenician by birth. . . ." This two-step progression, occurring as it does in a descriptive pause, signals important information: (1) she was a Greek (probably not a Jew), (2) a Syrophoenician by birth (definitely not a Jew). The pace at which one narrates this line conveys the two steps with the surprise and even puzzlement that a Gentile would ask Jesus for a healing.

Another stylistic feature that is evident in this episode is Mark's careful use of *diminutives*. I do not think I would ever have noticed the number of diminutives in this episode but for the need in performance to imagine the little girl and the little dogs and the little children's crumbs under the table and the woman on the ground at Jesus' feet. There are six diminutives in this episode: little daughter (1), little pieces (crumbs, 1), little dogs (2), little ones (2). In our episode, there is a play on these diminutives. In Jesus' reference to little dogs (puppies), the woman found an opening in Jesus' rejection of her request, because puppies were allowed to scavenge under the table when the children ate. Also, in the last line, the narrator includes the little girl as one of the children of God by depicting her as one of the "little ones." The repetition of diminutives leads the performer to accent this feature just enough to alert the hearer to this delightful motif.

You may have noticed that virtually all sentences in the episode recounted above begin with the word "and." The act of performing leads one to notice this and to make use of it. *Parataxis* is the habit of stringing lines together, usually with the Greek word *kai* (and). It looks strange in written English to begin every sentence with the word "and." Yet this is Mark's style. In oral narration, this stylistic feature is usually not noticed unless pointed out. Yet the overall effect of such narration is to make the story flow and to make more natural the connections from line to line and from episode to episode. By means of parataxis and other techniques, the author of Mark strings phrases, sentences, clauses, and episodes together in such a way as to create an almost breathless narration.[5] Narrating so that almost every sentence begins with "and" eventually becomes second nature to the performer and an important way to maintain the flow of the narrative.

There are also oral techniques of narration Mark uses to make connections between episodes across the Gospel. There are the series of three episodes (three call scenes, three boat scenes, and three passion predictions), episodes in a chiastic pattern (the five conflict stories in Galilee), similar episodes that frame a section (stories of blind men being healed frame the journey to Jerusalem), the sandwiching of one story between the beginning and ending of another (the woman with the flow wedged inside the story of Jairus' daughter and the denial of Peter within the trial of Jesus), the use of type scenes (healings, exorcisms, and conflict stories), and the repetition of verbal motifs running through the story like threads ("handed over," "the way," "put to death," and "good news"). It is because these structures overlap and interlace the whole story that Joanna Dewey referred to Mark's Gospel as "a seamless interwoven tapestry."[6] In the episode of the Syrophoenician woman, the use of verbal threads from previous episodes ("went off," "unclean spirit," "fell at his feet," "bread," "satisfied," and "house") connect this episode to previous exorcisms and with scenes of feeding in the desert. Also, the recurrence here of a Markan type scene ("the healing of a suppliant with faith") provides echoes of and associations with the healing stories that have occurred previously in the Gospel. The narrator may accentuate these connections between episodes by repetition in blocking, emphasis, gestures, facial expressions, pace, and tone.

The Rhetoric

All the features of the story along with the techniques of narration combine to form the rhetoric of a story—the overall impact of the episode on an audience. The performer seeks to determine the overall impact of Mark's story as well as the impact this one episode might have in the overall rhetoric of the Gospel. Through gestures, voice, movement, facial expressions, emotions, and many other things, the performer seeks to be faithful to the implied impact of this story. In this way, the impact on the audience includes, of course, the presence, words, and actions of the narrator. Such an impact on an audience is not limited to the persuasiveness of the values and beliefs embedded in the story but also includes the emotions evoked by the narration. The performer realizes that stories have power to change and transform, and, as such, the performer works to allow the story to have its way with the audience.

All these considerations figure in the translation and narration of one sixty-second episode in the context of a two-hour performance. The demands of understanding it as a basis for performing it lead one to know the story well and, hopefully, to bear its potential impact faithfully to the audience.[7]

Concluding Reflections

Because of my experience with Mark's narrative, I have learned and performed other narratives as a way to understand a text better—the Sermon on the Mount, scenes from John, Paul's letter to the Galatians, the Epistle of James, 1 Peter, and the book of Revelation. Each is quite different from the other, and each places different demands on the performer as interpreter and on the interpreter as performer. The practice of performance has become a primary tool of interpretation in my research into biblical writings. The practice of performance has also transformed my teaching. I perform texts as a means to engage students, so that they have a fresh experience of biblical works in a new medium. I also involve students in the process of learning and performing biblical texts. In a course on Paul, students present to classmates Paul's letter to Philemon. I have found no better way for students to understand the dynamics of a letter—form, content, rhetoric, and historical context—than to learn and perform one brief letter. In courses on the Gospels, students often learn and perform three or four episodes throughout the semester. In retreats and workshops with pastors and laypersons, participants engage in learning and telling stories. I teach a course called "Scripture by Heart," in which the students work together to offer "storytelling concerts" for the community. Many of these students go on to be pastors who recount from memory the Gospel lesson at worship each Sunday, thereby making the presentation of scripture a significant highlight of the service.[8]

The experience of performing and listening is delightful. It assists in developing faithful interpretations of the Gospel, and it makes learning and worshiping experiences more meaningful at a personal level. Telling biblical stories thus provides a communal experience in which together we can encounter the word in ever fresh and transforming ways.[9]

8

The Ethics of Reading Mark
as Narrative

At every step in the process of reading, readers make decisions that have ethical implications. The discipline of "the ethics of reading" invites us to reflect on the process of reading, so that the *way* we read the Bible has integrity.[1] Reflecting on the ethics of the process of reading is vital, because it leads us to be honest about what we can and cannot do when we interpret a text, and it challenges us to be responsible and to "do no harm" in the way we apply our interpretations in modern contexts.

Ethical reflection on the process of reading has emerged in light of recent developments in biblical scholarship. During the last two centuries in the West, biblical scholars have tended to think that we could overcome our presuppositions in reading and attain an accurate, objective, and fairly complete knowledge of a text from a detached, value-free, and dispassionate perspective. The confidence of such convictions has often led readers to believe that their interpretation of scripture was *the* correct interpretation and that this interpretation should apply universally to all people.

However, in the last half century, the influx into biblical scholarship of readers from diverse social locations—Jewish scholars interpreting the New Testament after the holocaust, European-American women, women and men of color, marginalized readers from base communities, and interpreters from third world countries—have made it clear that *all* interpretation is relative, value-bearing, and particular in nature, whether we are aware of it or not. Furthermore, postmodern reflections on the dynamics of reading have given us a more profound understanding of the ambiguous and indeterminate nature of all texts.[2] These factors have enabled scholars to see that there is not one universal meaning to a text but that there may be many faithful interpretations of meaning. And the recognition that our interpretations are relative carries with it the consequence that our appropriations of a text are also limited in nature. Interpreting with people from different social locations reveals that the appropriation of a biblical text from the perspective of one group may be quite harmful to other groups.

What Is the Ethics of Reading?

The ethics of reading deals with two quite interrelated foci of the act of reading: *interpreting* the potential meanings of a text in its original context and *appropriating* a text for its relevance to a contemporary time and place.[3]

In regard to the act of interpreting a biblical writing in its original context, we now know that meaning does not reside in the text as such. Rather, readers determine potential meanings in interaction with the text.[4] Technically speaking, a text is only marks on a page until readers give meaning to the descriptions and ideas presented in the text. In addition, a narrative like the Gospel of Mark is a particular story, composed for a particular time and place. So readers have to imagine what it might have meant for people in Mark's time to hear such a narrative. Furthermore, all texts are porous because words give a very incomplete representation of the realities being described by the text—thus leaving gaps and fissures and many things taken for granted with the reader. The narrative of Mark, in particular, gives minimal description and takes for granted many cultural assumptions. As a result, readers imagine in various ways what is being

suggested and fill the gaps in different ways. Because readers participate so fully in the construction of the text's meaning, it behooves us
to reflect on the limitations of our interpretations and how we can go
about giving faithful interpretations of a text.

In regard to the act of appropriating a biblical text for our time,
readers do this also in interaction with the text. All texts have power.
As Christian scriptures, the biblical writings, including Mark, have
great power. The Bible has served to transform persons, generate
communities, liberate people, and shape the values of society. The
biblical writings have also been used to support slavery, keep women
in abusive relationships, and engender anti-Judaism.[5] But readers
also have power. Readers can increase the impact of a text by treating
it as scripture and proclaiming it; or readers can ignore it; or readers
can resist its harmful effects. Given the force that the Bible continues
to exert for good and ill in public and private life, it is imperative to
develop an ethics of reading that will acknowledge in honest dialogue
both the possibilities and liabilities of a text—as we seek to appropriate the text in ways that promote life and resist harm.[6]

This essay reflects on the ethics of these two foci of reading—focusing primarily on the ethics of interpreting. The first part deals with
the process of interpreting a text in its original context, taking into
account both the relative perspective of the reader and some methods
we may use to be faithful readers. The second part reflects on the
process of appropriating a biblical text for our own time and place.
Although the following reflections could be applied to any biblical
writing and to each method of interpretation, I will use as my example a literary approach, the process of reading the Gospel of Mark as
a narrative.

The Ethics of Reading:
Interpretation

Because meaning results from interaction between reader and text,
we can think of interpretation as a dialogue.[7] In this analogy, our ethical responsibility to a text is similar to our respect for a person with

whom we are in dialogue. As with the practice of active listening in a dialogue, responsible reading entails a desire "to read carefully, patiently, and scrupulously" in order to understand a text on its own terms as an "other."[8] The ethics of reading has to do with respecting a text "under the elementary assumption that the text being read may say something different from what one wants or expects it to say or from what received opinion says it says."[9] Choosing to address the text in dialogue is an ethical choice based on values of respect for the otherness of the text, openness to be changed by it, honesty in critiquing the text, acceptance of difference in opinion, as well as a refusal to dominate the text or to be dominated by it.

As is true in a dialogue, it is not by detached objectivity that we may best understand a story, but by engagement and empathetic participation.[10] Empathetic participation includes not only the cognitive dimensions of the text but also the emotive (fear, awe, grief, puzzlement), the physical (touch, gesture, pain, movement), and the relational (love, enmity, conflict, kinship) aspects of the story. The Gospel of Mark, for example, invites readers to enter imaginatively into its narrative world, a world in which people are healed by touch, demons are driven out, the quest for status is exposed as destructive, people are frightened or amazed, they yell and scream, soldiers flog and beat Jesus, and people are called to live for the good news even if they must die for it. To read empathetically is to engage the full range of experiences in the world generated by the text. Since we have only our imaginations to do this, the question is: How can we use our imaginations to be faithful to the text as "other" than ourselves?[11]

Given how much readers participate in constructing potential meanings in a text, the effort to engage and understand a text in its own right is especially problematic when the writing is from a different culture in a distant time and addressed to a very different audience. In such a case, the readers have to work hard—reading within ancient frames of reference and using various methods—to allow the text to speak on its own. The need to work hard to determine potential meanings in the original context explains, of course, the last two centuries of biblical scholarship. The disciplines and methods of biblical scholarship reflect a commitment to read the Bible in a way that does not make the writing say what we want it to say or what we think it should say or what will justify our beliefs and values or in a way that does not naively misinterpret what we read. What has often been neglected in this process, however, has been a full awareness of the relative nature of the reader's perspective and of the fact that we cannot get *the* original meaning of a text.

We need to be aware of the relative and contingent nature of our methods as well. Letting a text speak on its own terms only happens within the parameters of the status we have given a text and the methods we have chosen to interpret it. For example, once we have decided to read Mark as a narrative in its ancient context, then there are criteria *within the methods we employ and the contexts we have chosen* for being faithful to the potential meanings of the text. Based on the criteria of our methods, some possible constructions of meaning are more consonant than others with the potential meanings of the Gospel of Mark in its original context. Therefore, it is important for us to reflect ethically also on the methods we choose to employ.

The Subjectivity of the Reader

In what follows, I will look first at some presuppositions we bring to the text from our subjective perspectives and social locations that serve to shape our interpretations. Then I will reflect on some frames and methods we can use to help us read faithfully.

Purposes and Biases in Reading

Aware now that we cannot gain an objective knowledge of a text from a detached, value-free, and dispassionate perspective, we are able to identify more clearly those factors that make our interpretations subjective. In so doing, we actually have a greater likelihood of attaining to faithful interpretations.

Many of our subjective perspectives in reading are rooted in the reasons we choose to read a biblical text in the first place. Why we read Mark, what we look for, and what we select as important for interpretation affect the ways in which different readers interpret. Much of the time we may be unaware of these factors. Coming to the Gospel of Mark, for example, with an implicit purpose or an explicit lens—expecting to appreciate its spiritual power or seeking to discern its political dynamics—may help us see dynamics that have been neglected. Yet such expectations and purposes may also lead us to be blind to other, perhaps negative, aspects of Mark. And because we tend to see what we expect to see or what we want to see, we may make Mark say what we want it to say.

Part of our purpose in reading may be to critique a biblical text from our own experiences and values, and hence read with a hermeneutic of suspicion. In this regard, our resistances to a text will be an important part of our understanding of that text. We may resist Mark's portrayal of women, his apocalyptic dualism, or his emphasis on suffering. Resistances may enable us to notice negative aspects of Mark that have been softened by other interpreters. Yet resistances may also lead us to dismiss positive aspects of the whole story or to exaggerate the problem. Without in any way wishing to compromise our assessment of the negative aspects of the text, we may nevertheless have an ethical responsibility in our dialogue to give the text a fair reading.

The ethics of reading will encourage us to name our conscious purposes and bring to awareness our unconscious biases in the act of reading. And the ethics of reading will lead us to be explicit about our own ethical standards by which we evaluate various aspects of a text as positive or negative. The first step is to seek to be faithful to what the text says on its terms—even if we may then disagree with it or repudiate it.

Interpretive Location and Reading Perspective

Because our approaches to reading are rooted in our social location and personal experiences, it will help to be cognizant of those factors that shape the assumptions, experiences, and commitments we bring to the act of determining meaning in interaction with the text.

National identity: the assumptions of the reader's society, including language and cultural beliefs and patterns of behavior; the continental location (north/south/east/west); the natural setting (climate/desert/mountains/rich or poor resources); privileged or impoverished place in the world community; a colonial power or a (post-)colonized country.

Social location: the place within national identity includes race, ethnicity, dominant or minority culture, gender, sexual orientation, economic level, social class, urban/rural setting, education, age, political convictions, religious commitments and communities, family of origin, and so on—all factors that determine in what ways we may experience privilege and power and in what ways we may be exploited, marginalized, and oppressed.

Historical realities: characteristics of an era such as scientific developments, political trends, media changes, economic prosperity, and so on. Historical events that shape our perspective include such matters as war or peace, political and social oppression, natural or environmental disasters, terrorism or nuclear threat, discrimination and ethnic cleansing, and civil revolution.

Personal Experiences, Beliefs, and Values: personal experiences such as abuse, abandonment, friendships, religious experiences, and illness. We come to reading with our own longings and hopes, with social causes, religious beliefs, political commitments, truths to defend, and moral issues. Such personal factors may sometimes put readers at odds with the values of their own social location.

Interpretive Communities: We read as part of "communities of interpretation"—ethnic, religious, academic, gender, national, economic and social, or in solidarity with groups such as the poor or oppressed—with whom we share common values. We represent these communities and look to these communities as "audiences" for the legitimacy of our interpretations.

Changing and multiple perspectives: There is no essential or static identity of a reader or of a community—no uniform African-American reading or common feminist reading or common lower class reading. People often read against the grain of their communities, and readings differ among those within the same social location. Readers change, communities change, social and historical circumstance change.[12] People usually represent more than one interpretive community, with the result that they interpret at different times with different interpretive audiences in mind, such as the middle class or a denomination or a scholarly community. Many individuals have a "hybrid" identity of more than one cultural community, due to inter-marriage or as the result of migration. Hence, while some readings may characterize certain groups or communities, the identification of such communities cannot ever serve as a basis to stereotype a person or community in any essentialist or static way.[13]

The ethics of reading encourages us to make explicit these factors that shape our reading of the biblical materials. Furthermore, it leads us to be aware of the power dynamics of our place in interpreting, both in relation to the text and in relation to other interpreters. Awareness of someone's social location, however, is never a reason to dismiss an interpretation. On the contrary, as we have said, there are factors in one's reading that can block understanding, and there are factors that can also help one to interpret faithfully. Hence, instead of pretending that we can be objective, we can make use of our relative perspectives as means to enhance the clarity of our vision. Feminist critics have argued that interpreters should not feign objectivity by failing to identify the social traits and personal commitments that shape interpretation.[14] Such openness is a sign to those who read our interpretations that we are aware of the relative and limited nature of our interpretations. In this way, others can take into account our social location in assessing our interpretations.

Reading Faithfully

Given the inevitably subjective nature of our readings, what strategies can we pursue and what methods can we employ to help us overcome the problems of our reading perspective and at the same time to use our reading perspective to give the most faithful interpretations of a text? In what follows, I suggest three approaches: interpreting Mark within ancient frames of reference, using appropriate methods of analysis, and reading in dialogue with others.

Frames of Reference

As a means to overcome our tendency to place Mark into our own modern frames of reference, we can use various first century frames as contexts to provide resources to fill the gaps of the Markan text more faithfully and at the same time to put controls and limits on our interpretations of Mark's Gospel. All three frames that follow are important in our efforts to grasp the meaning of a passage within the Markan text.[15]

The Whole Story as Framework. Like each writing in the New Testament, the Gospel of Mark offers a world to consider—places, people, happenings, beginnings and endings, values and beliefs, a sociopolitical ethos, along with the whole cultural moorings that sustain them. It is Mark's story as a whole that provides the framework for interpreting each of the episodes within that particular story. To read a story on its own terms is to immerse ourselves imaginatively in the whole story-world. Only as we are able to get into the world of the whole story do we have a chance to relativize our own frames of meaning and to read faithfully an episode within Mark.

The Historical/Cultural Context as Framework. Mark is a portrayal of the world by a first-century author; that is, the narrative is itself an historical artifact. Generally, scholars agree that Mark was written in the Palestine/Syria area [or in Rome] during or just after the Roman-Judean War of 66 to 70 C. E., a situation in which followers of Jesus were threatened with persecution from both Judeans and Romans. Any knowledge we can garner about these historical times, places, and circumstances will help us to grasp the narrative of Mark, its purposes, and its potential impact on first century people.

Furthermore, general historical knowledge about material realities, habits of daily life, and institutions in first century Palestine will help us to understand better the depiction of these things in Mark's narrative. In addition, we can take into account the cultural frames of meaning in which Mark was embedded—a preindustrial peasant society, a collectivist honor/shame culture, a society with distinctive kinship patterns, rules for purity and defilement, an economic system of limited goods, and other factors that provide a cultural context for understanding the dynamics of Mark's narrative.

Social Location of Mark as Framework. In addition to identifying author, date, audience, and circumstance, we can read the Gospel of Mark on its own terms by asking about Mark's social location.[16] We might infer, for example, that Mark wrote from a male perspective in solidarity with an economically and socially oppressed class of peasants in a rural region (of Palestine) and that he opposed the use of power over others. Such factors will help us to determine the level of cultural conformity, the political stance, and the social program of the text, as well as to identify interests the text promotes and denigrates. We might also ask what kind of ancient community the story fosters. Aware of social location, we are less likely to transpose Mark from its original social location into modern social locations to which we ourselves belong.

Using such frames enables us to construct more faithfully the potential meanings and the possible rhetorical impacts of Mark's Gospel in its own time and on its own terms. There is need for caution, however, because there is a tendency for us to think that the contextual frames are stable elements against which we measure the uncertainties of the text. Ethically, we need to acknowledge that our choice of frames, our construction of these contexts, and our selection about what is important are also relative, value-laden, and influenced by our perspective.

Methods

To assist us in reading Mark faithfully as a narrative and as a means to help us use material from the frames to interpret Mark, we need to choose methods most appropriate for our focus of study. Simply put, "we need to use all the sophisticated tools at our disposal and use them rigorously."[17] In addition to some traditional methods that are crucial for understanding Mark as narrative (textual criticism, genre criticism, and linguistic criticism), narrative criticism lends itself especially well as the basic method for analyzing the story-world created by Mark's Gospel—the depiction of settings, the development of the characters, the progression and connection of the events, the conflicts in the plot, the norms of judgment, the role of the narrator, the language and literary techniques employed to tell the story, and the overall rhetorical effect.[18] All these tools help the interpreter engage all aspects of the narrative world.

In order to fill Mark's first-century narrative gaps faithfully, however, narrative critics will need to draw upon other methods as well.
Reader-response criticism explores the rhetoric of Mark and its
potential impact on hypothetical first-century readers. Historical
criticism brings extensive knowledge about life in the first century to
inform our understanding of so many details of the world depicted in
Mark's narrative. Using cultural anthropology to understand the
period enables us to grasp many dimensions of the culture of the first
century as portrayed in the narrative.[19] Orality studies and performance criticism situate the dynamics of the Gospel story and its rhetoric in the oral cultures of the first century. Feminist criticism,
liberationist perspectives, postcolonial criticism, and gender studies[20]
show us dynamics of power both within the narrative world and in
regard to the rhetorical impact of Mark's story on readers within
Israel and within the larger hegemony of the Roman Empire.

All methods bear certain power dynamics. They privilege some perspectives and marginalize others. Therefore, methods need to be used
judiciously. Also, all methods are relative. Like other methods, narrative criticism has its strengths and limitations.[21] The strengths of narrative criticism are that it seeks to honor the text as narrative and that
it appreciates the rhetorical power of the text. However, narrative critics
should not claim more for the method than it can do. For example, in
the search for the unity of a text, narrative critics should not overstate
its coherence or fail to appreciate its indeterminate nature. Feminist
and deconstructionist critics have taught us to read against the grain as
a means to make explicit the inconsistencies and repressed dimensions
of a text not evident in efforts to discern coherence.[22] As with other
methods, narrative critics will differ in their interpretations—partly
because their reading perspectives differ and partly because texts are
porous and permit so many ways for readers to configure the meanings, the patterns, the conventions, and the connections of a story. Nevertheless, there will be limits to what might be considered faithful
interpretations within the agreed upon parameters and criteria of the
methods being used to understanding the potential narrative meanings of Mark's Gospel. Given certain frames and the criteria of certain
methods, not all interpretations are possible.

The ethics of reading will encourage us to acknowledge the relative nature of the methods we use and in so doing to be honest about their strengths and limitations and their inherent tendency to focus on some things and to suppress others. Even given these cautions, there is a further safeguard for faithful interpretations—reading in critical dialogue with people from social locations different from our own.

Read with Others from Diverse Locations and Perspectives

The study of various interpretive locations teaches us to avoid reading in isolation or only with people from our own social location. Otherwise, we will have distorted and limited perspectives. Other perspectives may correct our interpretations and illumine our blind spots. Different people can read out of differing cultural locations and mutually inform each other.[23] In this way, the dialogue with the text is expanded to be a dialogue with other interpreters from diverse social locations. Together in dialogue with others, the distinct angles of vision of each culture and reading perspective become positive contributions to reading and understanding.[24] The appropriate ethical maxims might be: "Do not trust others to interpret for you, but do not trust yourself to interpret alone," and "Together we can do better than alone."

As noted earlier, those of us who are academic, white, middle class, European American males have through the centuries so dominated the copying, translating, interpreting, preaching, and publishing of the biblical texts in the West that it has been difficult not to think that agreements about the history and meanings of the New Testament texts were equivalent to objectivity and correctness. Our illusion of objectivity has now been shattered with the recognition of the biases and blindnesses that have pervaded our biblical interpretation.[25] When Jewish scholars began reading the New Testament, they exposed the prejudicial ways Christian scholars read the biblical writings. Women using feminist criticism exposed the patriarchal/antipatriarchal and androcentric dimensions of Mark and showed both positive and negative aspects of Mark's depiction of women. Base communities of peasants from Latin America using liberation interpretation revealed how Mark was written from a peasant perspective. Women of color demonstrated the multiple oppressions evident in Mark's story. Asian interpreters exposed fresh dynamics of honor and shame in Mark. Hispanic scholars showed the double marginalization involved in being a Galilean under other Jews from Judea and under the Romans. Interpreters from cultures closer to those of the Bible are often able to grasp the Markan dynamics of purity and defilement and the collectivist identity in fresh ways. Readers from colonized countries using postcolonial criticism are now laying bare the colonial dynamics in Mark in relation to the colonial power of Rome.[26]

Ideally, such an intercultural approach to reading will help de-center the dominant white male tradition[27] and de-colonize the dominant European-American position.[28] There are, however, such significant asymmetries of power among interpreters that it is difficult to dislodge the dominant tradition. Nevertheless, the hoped-for result is a relativizing of dominant perspectives and a legitimizing of suppressed perspectives. The aim of intercultural interpretation is not to disregard anyone's point of view, not even that of traditional interpreters. Rather, it is to establish a roundtable, in which all are respected for their readings—with no interpretation being privileged and none marginalized.[29] Here we may be engaged in critical interaction with each other whereby we are persuaded and changed at a roundtable dialogue with the text and with different interpreters—all of whom enhance and challenge and amplify our understanding.

One Faithful Interpretation among Many

When we take our ethical responsibilities into account, we will acknowledge that we are really working toward *limited and multiple interpretations from relative and multiple perspectives out of particular social locations that are faithful to certain canons of reading.*

Hence, in light of the indeterminate nature of texts, the relative perspectives of readers, and the limitations of our methods, we conclude that there can be no such thing as a neutral or apolitical or innocent reading of a text. All interpretations are constructions by readers from particular personal and social locations. To recognize our inability to be objective does not mean that we now abandon criteria for faithful interpretations and embrace an attitude of "anyone's opinion is as good as any other." Surely that would be to abandon an ethics of reading. Rather, as ethical readers, we choose methods that we believe to be responsible, and we interpret rigorously according to the criteria of those methods. We may come to be confident in our interpretations even if we cannot be certain about them.[30] For all interpretations are provisional. Aware of the relative and provisional nature both of our methods and of our interpretations, we test our interpretations in dialogue with others, and we acknowledge a plurality of approaches. There are multiple readings, which may be more or less faithful[31] and which will compete with each other but will also inform and complement each other and provide alternative perspectives. Such multiple perspectives—even, and especially, when they are in tension and in contradiction with each other—serve to enlarge our grasp of the Gospel and its potential for meaning.

If we learn anything from the ethics of reading, it should be the importance of humility. Given the number of variables we have outlined, it would be pretentious to claim that one could come up with the correct or the only legitimate or even an objective interpretation of a text in its context. Hence, our goal should be to give faithful and cogent readings of Mark that do justice to the whole story in its historical, cultural, and social contexts.[32]

The Ethics of Reading: Appropriation

Next we reflect briefly on our ethical responsibilities in appropriating an interpretation of Mark for our own time and place—how we act on our interpretations in public and private life and how we communicate our interpretations to others. The act of responsible appropriation is as complex as the act of interpreting. It never involves a one-to-one correlation of the ancient and the modern situation. Rather, there are similarities and differences between the ancient story and our stories, between the ancient context and our context. The task of appropriation involves immersing ourselves in the world of Mark's first-century story in its context and experiencing its rhetorical impact in imagination, and then emerging to ask what might be the potential impact and relevance of the experience for a particular context today.

To be sure, the actual experience of reading is never a straightforward process from the ancient to the present. As we have seen, we always take the present interests and assumptions into our interpretation of the past. Then, when we seek to appropriate the text for our time, we place our imaginative experience of the past into our modern frames of reference. As in any dialogue, we move back and forth between interpretation and appropriation, between our context and situation and that of the past.

Open to Transformation

If the reading of a text is a genuine dialogue in which we are addressed by the text, then our reading will entail a willingness to risk, an openness to be changed by the encounter.[33] Unless we consider, at least in imagination, how we might be changed in response to a particular writing, have we really taken the story on its own terms?[34] If the rhetoric of a story is designed to transform people or to liberate or to change behavior or to create a new society, have we fully read the story unless we entertain these possibilities? Encountering a story is an *event* that happens to us as much as any other event, and we have a choice to allow that event to have a significant impact on us or not. Are we willing in this dialogue with Mark to raise questions about the adequacy of our own story, to allow our own stories to be fractured or transformed or changed by the story we encounter? Genuine dialogue entails such risks.

In response to the reading of Mark, for example, we might ask: How am I different as a result of my experience? What insights have I gained? Do I see the world differently? Do I have greater hope or faith? Do I have more courage? Am I more eager to serve others? Have I been granted a greater vision for humanity? Is my new view more compassionate or more judgmental? All these become possibilities for us when we risk ourselves in dialogue with the text.[35] Even when we resist and reject the possibilities offered by the story, we will be different people for having considered them.

Avoid Universalizing

Despite the importance of being open to the relevance of Mark, we cannot assume that a biblical writing will be relevant or appropriate for every situation. Thus, we need to be aware of the dangers of universalizing a story and of absolutizing its meaning. What happens, for example, when we universalize the statement in Mark that "The poor you always have with you" (14:7)? It is not right to expect a text to do more than it was meant to do. Like all texts, a biblical writing is particular—limited in scope, local in origin, and relative in perspective—even given its place in the canon of scripture. Only as we recognize the particularity of a story as "other" can we begin to see whether a story might relate to our situation or not.

Nor can we assume that because a text might be helpful in one situation, it will be helpful and not harmful in another situation. The transformation that one reader considers to be good may be hurtful to another, especially, for example, if it leads to discrimination or a zealous suppression of others. From Mark, we may encourage some people who have an illness by the affirmation that "Everything is possible to one who has faith" (9:23), but the same advice may be inappropriate and even cruel to others. What happens when people who are not healed are judged for their lack of faith? What if we applied the admonition to "be servant of all" (9:35) to the oppressed rather than to oppressors? Would that advice not sanction a condition of servitude? Therefore, we need to evaluate any positive or negative effects of our response to a text. Just as we may interpret with others from different social locations in an ethnic roundtable, we need to entertain ideas of appropriation with others, so that we recognize the relative and provisional nature of our appropriations and so that what serves to benefit one group does not at the same time work ill for others.

Responsibility for Our Interpretations

In the end, the ethics of reading constrains us to take responsibility not only *to* the writings we read but also responsibility *for* the writings we read.[36] Our public responsibility begins when we speak or write or teach about or act upon our understanding of a biblical writing. Because we act on our readings, they affect us, our relationships, and our social institutions.[37] We might ask: What actions does the writing foster? What would be the differing consequences if certain interpretations were acted upon by different individuals? Or by different churches? Or by society as a whole? Just because we have a faithful interpretation does not mean that our interpretation is neutral. Interpretations can help or harm people, serve the interests of some and counter the interests of others. And, of course, each of us will judge a story as moral or immoral based on differing standards and diverse ethical frames of reference. Again, we need to be explicit and accountable in regard to our own ethical reasons for accepting or rejecting the values urged upon us by a biblical interpretation.

On the one hand, if our understanding is that the story is a good story from our ethical point of view, we have a responsibility to promote that story, to tell it or to encourage others to read it. The telling of Mark may give hope to the poor, the sick, the marginalized, the sinful, the powerless, women, children, and bring about humane personal and social change.

On the other hand, if a biblical story, including Mark, is harmful in certain ways—engenders discrimination or suppresses women or fosters anti-Judaism[38]—we should become readers who resist (that dimension of) the text, who refuse to be changed by it, and who stand in fundamental opposition to it. Then it is not enough for us simply to repeat our interpretation of the story without comment. In such circumstances, we would be remiss to offer an interpretation without stating our disagreement, countering the force of the text, and fostering a liberating and healing alternative. The ethics of reading involves being responsible for the rhetorical effects of the text itself and of our interpretations of it, so that we can counter its potentially harmful effects.[39]

Conclusion

It is essential that reflection on the ethics of reading become an integral part of our relationship to scripture. Otherwise, we risk making the text say what we want it to say and then appropriating it naively in ways that are harmful to others. Of course, the reflections here are themselves relative, value-laden, and limited. Hopefully, however, they will be part of an ongoing conversation with others who share a similar commitment to struggle to read with integrity. Such an ongoing conversation ought to assist us to understand the Bible more faithfully and to proclaim it in ways that bring life and not death to the world.

Notes

1. Narrative Criticism and the Gospel of Mark

1. Wayne Booth, "Distance and Point of View: An Essay in Clarification," xii.

2. Our investigation into narrative includes what M. H. Abrams refers to as "objective criticism," which "describes the literary product as a self-sufficient world in-itself," and "pragmatic criticism" (also rhetorical criticism), which views the literary work as something "constructed in order to achieve certain effects on the audience." M. H. Abrams, *A Glossary of Literary Terms*, 37.

3. A literary critic, writing on Mark, cautions against finding too much unity in a text. Frank Kermode writes that we are "programmed to prefer fulfillment to disappointment, the closed to the open," when in fact fractures and incoherence in a text may "mime the fortuities of real life"; Frank Kermode, *The Genesis of Secrecy*, 54, 64. John C. Meagher, "Die Form- und Redaktionsgeschichtliche Methoden: The Principle of Clumsiness and the Gospel of Mark," 459–72, argues simply that Mark was (sometimes) a careless storyteller who left many loose ends. We will not, however, be in the best position to determine fractures in the Markan text until we have fully explored its integrity.

4. According to Petersen, closure refers to "the sense of literary ending derived from the satisfaction of textually generated expectations. . . . Such satisfactions can be achieved in a variety of ways—explicitly or implicitly, ironically or literally, positively or even negatively." Norman R. Petersen, "When Is an End not the End?" 152.

5. Robert C. Tannehill, "The Disciples in Mark: The Function of a Narrative Role."

6. Norman R. Petersen, "Literary Criticism in Biblical Studies," 21.

7. Norman R. Petersen, *Literary Criticism for New Testament Critics*, 38–39.

8. Hans Frei, *The Eclipse of the Biblical Narrative*; Thomas E. Boomershine, "Mark, the Storyteller: A Rhetorical-Critical Investigation of Mark's Passion and Resurrection Narrative," 12–13.

9. Boris Uspensky, *Poetics of Composition*, 137.

10. See Petersen, *Literary Criticsm for New Testament Critics,* 49–50.

11. Eric S. Rabkin, *Narrative Suspense.*

12. *Coming to Terms: The Rhetoric of Narrative in Fiction and Film;* and *Story and Discourse: Narrative Structure in Fiction and Film.*

13. Joanna Dewey, *Markan Public Debate: Literary Technique, Ring Composition and Theology in Mark 2:1—3:6.*

14. Robert C. Tannehill, "The Gospel of Mark as Narrative Christology."

15. Petersen argues that closure is necessary to the coherence of the narrative. "When is an End not the End?" 161. Yet it may be that some narratives are "deliberately" left unresolved (without closure in some respects) without relinquishing their quality as a coherent narrative.

16. Mary Ann Tolbert, "Response to Robert Tannehill," 7–8.

17. Seymour Chatman, *Story and Discourse*, 107–38.

18. Gordon Allport, "What Is a Trait of Personality?"

19. E. M. Forster, *Aspects of the Novel*, 65–82.

20. Tannehill, "The Gospel of Mark as Narrative Christology," 61–63.

21. Uspensky observes that the motives of a character's behavior are often identified more by the context and situation than by depictions of the character's inner thoughts or feelings. Uspensky, *Poetics of Composition*, 121–22.

22. Anitra Kolenkow, "Beyond Miracles, Suffering, and Eschatology," followed by Dewey, *Markan Public Debate*, 105–6.

23. Tolbert, "Response to Robert Tannehill," 11.

24. Joanna Dewey, "Mark 10:35-40 from the Perspective of the Implied Reader," 9.

25. Tannehill says that the materials related to the opponents and the disciples fits into progressive sequences that begin early and continue to the Gospel's end. By contrast, each miracle story with a supplicant is complete in itself. So, healings and exorcisms are not progressive but iterative; as such, the minor characters do not have an ongoing role as the disciples and the opponents do. "The Gospel of Mark as Narrative Christology," 67–68.

26. John R. Donahue, "A Neglected Factor in the Theology of Mark."

27. Seymour Chatman, *Story and Discourse*, 138–45.

28. Werner Kelber, *The Kingdom in Mark.*

29. Werner Kelber, *Mark's Story of Jesus*.

30. See Wayne Booth, *The Rhetoric of Fiction*.

31. Seymour Chatman, *Story and Discourse*, 146–262; Wayne Booth, *The Rhetoric of Fiction*, 149–63, among others.

32. Norman R. Petersen, "'Point of View' in Mark's Narrative," 97–122.

33. Robert M. Fowler, "The Feeding Stories in the Gospel of Mark," 118–22, 182–215.

34. Petersen, "Literary Criticism in Biblical Studies," 21–22.

35. J. M. Lotman, "Point of View in a Text," 352.

36. Daniel Patte and Aline Patte, *Structural Exegesis: From Theory to Practice*.

37. Petersen, "'Point of View,'" 107.

38. Uspensky, *Poetics of Composition*, 11.

39. Booth, *The Rhetoric of Fiction*, 71–72.

40. Robert Scholes, "Cognition and the Implied Reader," 14.

41. Robert Crosman, "In Defense of Authors and Readers."

42. Booth, *The Rhetoric of Fiction*, 138.

43. Tolbert, "Response to Robert Tannehill," 6.

44. Dewey, "Mark 10:35-40," 8.

45. Wolfgang Iser, *The Implied Reader*, xii.

46. Tannehill, "The Disciples in Mark," 395.

47. Peter M. Wetherill, *The Literary Text: An Examination of Critical Methods*.

48. See the fascinating analysis of Mark's narrative by David Noble, "An Examination of the Structure of Mark's Gospel." Within many episodes, themes are first introduced, then developed, following a pattern usually of a, b, a', b' or a, b, b', a'. Dewey shows repetition in the chiastic structure of a line or several lines within an episode.

49. Mark's verbal threads are quite extensive and guide the reader (or hearer) by word association to recall and relate passages narrated earlier. Thomas Boomershine, "Mark, the Storyteller: A Rhetorical-Critical Investigation of Mark's Passion and Resurrection Narrative."

50. Frans Nierynck, *Duality in Mark,* shows how duality occurs at every level of the narrative. The two-step progressions are also evident in Noble's analysis of episodic structure. Very few scholars have dealt with the rhetorical implications of Nierynck's analysis. Our own suggestion is that, like the blind man who is healed at a second touch, the reader is led to take a second, closer look, to see more clearly—the events, the dialogue, and especially the character of Jesus. See David Rhoads, Joanna Dewey, and Donald Michie, *Mark as Story*, 49–51. On the subliminal suggestiveness of style, see Eric Rabkin, *Narrative Suspense*.

51. Scholars have often noted the triadic patterns that comprise the three passion predictions. Tannehill, *Mirror for the Disciples*, deals with the

three boat scenes and three bread scenes in relation to the disciples. Vernon Robbins, "Summons and Outline in Mark: The Three-Step Progression," analyzed the threefold series of the call, commission, and sending out of the disciples. Other familiar triplets include Jesus' finding his disciples asleep, Peter's denials, and Pilate's interaction with the crowd, perhaps also Jesus' three nights outside Jerusalem and the three references to the women who go to the grave. See also Norman Petersen's analysis of numerous triadic patterns related to the three boat scenes, "The Composition of Mark 4:1–8:26."

52. Howard Kee, *Community of the New Age*, 54–56; William Telford, "The Barren Temple and the Withered Fig Tree."

53. Joanna Dewey, *Markan Public Debate*.

54. There are an extraordinary number of rhetorical questions for such a brief story. The functions of the rhetorical questions differ for the dialogue of each character, and Jesus characteristically addresses his disciples and the opponents with different kinds of rhetorical questions. See Rhoads, Dewey, and Michie, *Mark as Story*, 55–56.

55. Donald Juel, *Messiah and Temple*; Robert Fowler, "The Feeding Stories in the Gospel of Mark"; Wayne Booth, *A Rhetoric of Irony*; D. C. Muecke, *The Compass of Irony*; and idem, *Irony*.

56. Madeleine Boucher, *The Mysterious Parable: A Literary Study*.

2. Narrative Criticism: Practices and Prospects

1. Mark Allan Powell, *What Is Narrative Criticism?* See also, e.g., Stanley E. Porter, "Literary Approaches to the New Testament: From Formalism to Deconstruction and Back," 77–128; and David M. Gunn, "Narrative Criticism," 171–95.

2. Norman R. Petersen, *Literary Criticism for New Testament Critics*.

3. Hans Frei, *The Eclipse of Biblical Narrative*.

4. For an account of these shifts and a helpful critique of their problems, see Stephen D. Moore, *Literary Criticism and the Gospels: The Theoretical Challenge*, and idem, *The Postmodern Bible: The Bible and Culture Collective*. See also "Reconceiving Narrative Criticism" by Raimo Hakola and Petri Merenlahti in *Characterization in the Gospels: Reconceiving Narrative Criticism*, edited by David Rhoads and Kari Syreeni.

5. On this point, see Merenlahti and Hakola, "Reconceiving Narrative Criticism." All the essays in *Characterization in the Gospels* are relevant to the practices and prospects of narrative criticism.

6. See the discussion about limited and cautious inferences we may make about an author in Merenlahti and Hakola, "Reconceiving Narrative Criticism."

7. On the reader's role in the interpretation of character, see John A. Darr, *On Character Building: The Reader and Rhetoric of Characterization in Luke-Acts*; and Fred Burnett, "Characterization and Reader Construction in the Gospels."

8. See Stephen D. Moore, *Poststructuralism and the New Testament: Derrida and Foucault at the Foot of the Cross*. See also Frank Kermode, *The Genesis of Secrecy: On the Interpretation of Narrative*; David Seeley, *Deconstructing the New Testament*; Gary A. Phillips, "The Ethics of Reading Deconstructively"; and A. K. M. Adams, *What Is Postmodern Biblical Interpretation?* See also the bibliographical references above in n. 4.

9. See, e.g., Shlomith Rimmon-Kenan, *Narrative Fiction: Contemporary Poetics;* Mieke Bal, *Narratology: Introduction to the Theory of Narrative;* and Wallace Martin, *Recent Theories of Narrative,* as well as works by Robert Alter, Wayne Booth, Seymour Chatman, Jonathan Culler, Gerard Genette, Wesley A. Kort, Susan Lanser, Gerald Prince, Meir Sternberg, and Boris Uspensky, among many others, on particular issues such as rhetoric, style, irony, and so on. On character studies, see especially Baruch Hochman, *Character in Literature*.

10. See Janice Capel Anderson, *Matthew's Narrative Web: Over, and Over, and Over Again*.

11. See, e.g., Paul D. Duke, *Irony in the Fourth Gospel*, and Jerry Camery-Hoggatt, *Irony in Mark's Gospel: Text and Subtext*.

12. Craig Koester, *Symbolism in the Fourth Gospel: Meaning, Mystery, Community*.

13. See, e.g., Adele Reinhartz, *The Word in the World: The Cosmological Tale of the Fourth Gospel*.

14. For recent developments in character studies of biblical narratives, see Elizabeth Struthers Malbon and A. Berlin, editors, *Characterization in Biblical Literature*.

15. Wesley A. Kort, *Story, Text, and Scripture: Literary Interests in Biblical Narratives*.

16. For recent narrative-critical treatments of whole Gospels, see Mark W. G. Stibbe, *John as Storyteller: Narrative Criticism and the Fourth Gospel*; Warren Carter, *Matthew: Storyteller, Interpreter, Evangelist*; and Stephen Smith, *A Lion with Wings: A Narrative-Critical Approach to Mark's Gospel*.

17. See, e.g., chapter 4 in this volume. Note also the exercises and questions for a narrative analysis of individual episodes in David Rhoads, Joanna Dewey, and Donald Michie, *Mark as Story*, 154–59.

18. See the anthologies of Susan R. Suleiman and Inge Crosman, editors, *The Reader in the Text: Essays on Audience and Interpretation*; and Jane P. Tompkins, editor, *Reader-Response Criticism: From Formalism to Post-Structuralism*. Note also Elizabeth Freund, *The Return of the Reader: Reader-Response Criticism*; as well as works by theorists Wolfgang Iser, Stanley Fish, Wayne Booth, and others.

19. Examples of such constructions include Robert M. Fowler, *Let the Reader Understand: Reader-Response Criticism and the Gospel of Mark*; and Jeffrey Lloyd Staley, *The Print's First Kiss: A Rhetorical Investigation of the Implied Reader in the Fourth Gospel*. See also Fowler's introduction to the subject, "Reader-Response Criticism: Figuring Mark's Reader."

20. Wilhelm Wuellner, "Where Is Rhetorical Criticism Taking Us?"

21. J. L. Austin, *How to Do Things with Words*; and Sandy Petrey, *Speech Acts and Literary Theory*. On biblical studies, see Dietmar Neufeld, *Reconceiving Texts as Speech Acts: An Analysis of 1 John*.

22. See the groundbreaking work of Norman R. Petersen, *Rediscovering Paul: Philemon and the Sociology of Paul's Narrative World*.

23. See David L. Barr, *Tales of the End: A Narrative Commentary on the Book of Revelation*.

24. See parallel guidelines for classical rhetorical analysis in Margaret M. Mitchell, *Paul and the Rhetoric of Argumentation: An Exegetical Investigation of the Language and Composition of I Corinthians*.

25. See, e.g., Mary Ann Tolbert, *Sowing the Gospel: Mark's World in Literary and Historical Perspective*; and Vernon K. Robbins, *Jesus the Teacher: A Socio-Rhetorical Interpretation of Mark*.

26. Adele Berlin, *Poetics and Interpretation of Biblical Narrative*; Robert Alter, *The Art of Biblical Narrative*; Meir Sternberg, *The Poetics of Biblical Narrative*; and Shimon Bar-Efrat, *Narrative Art in the Bible*; Yairah Amit, *Reading Biblical Narratives: Literary Criticism and the Hebrew Bible*; and John Petersen, *Reading Women's Stories: Female Characters in the Hebrew Bible*. There are also many studies now available of individual narrative cycles of the Old Testament.

27. For an articulation of the importance of genre studies, see Tolbert, *Sowing*, 48–84.

28. George Kennedy, *New Testament Interpretation through Rhetorical Criticism*; and Dennis L. Stamps, "Rhetorical Criticism of the New Testament: Ancient and Modern Evaluations of Argumentation."

29. See Burton L. Mack and Vernon K. Robbins, *Patterns of Persuasion and the New Testament*.

30. For an integrative approach to Mark using several disciplines of New Testament study, see Vernon K. Robbins, *Exploring the Texture of Texts: A Guide to Socio-Rhetorical Interpretation*.

31. See the works of Walter Ong, such as *The Presence of the Word: Some Prolegomena for Cultural and Religious History*, and idem, *Orality and Literacy: The Technologizing of the Word*.

32. See, e.g., various articles by Joanna Dewey: "Mark as Interwoven Tapestry: Forecasts and Echoes for a Listening Audience," "Oral Methods of Structuring Narrative in Mark," and "The Gospel of Mark as Oral-Aural Event: Implications for Interpretation." See also P. J. J. Botha, "Mark's Story as Oral Literature: Rethinking the Transmission of Some Traditions about Jesus"; and Christopher Bryan, *A Preface to Mark: Notes on the Gospel in Its Literary and Cultural Settings*, esp. 67–171.

33. Paul J. Achtemeier, "*Omne Verbum Sonat*: The New Testament and the Oral Environment of Late Western Antiquity."

34. Listening to the Greek text was a key methodological procedure in Thomas E. Boomershine's groundbreaking narrative analysis, "Mark the Storyteller: A Rhetorical-Critical Investigation of Mark's Passion and Resurrection Narrative."

35. Bernard Brandon Scott and M. Dean, "A Sound Map of the Sermon on the Mount."

36. See Marie Maclean, *Narrative as Performance: The Baudelairean Experiment*; and R. Moore, "The Gospel and Narrative Performance: The Critical Assessment of Meaning as Correspondence in D. F. Straus and R. Bultmann."

37. See chapter 7 in this volume. Note also how a performance can be influenced by an audience. For information about video presentations of some biblical works by the author, write to SELECT, c/o Trinity Lutheran Seminary, 2199 E. Main Street, Columbus, OH 43209, USA.

38. For example, it is virtually impossible to deliver the line of Jesus to the disciples in Mark praising the poor widow as if it were a negative criticism of her gift to a corrupt Temple system, as some commentators have interpreted it.

39. See Whitney Taylor Shiner, *Proclaiming the Gospel: First-Century Performance of Mark*.

40. See Bruce J. Malina, *The New Testament World: Insights from Cultural Anthropology*; John H. Elliott, *What Is Social-Scientific Criticism?* and Richard L. Rohrbaugh, editor, *The Social Sciences and New Testament Interpretation*.

41. Bruce J. Malina, "Reading Theory Perspective."

42. See all the articles in Jerome H. Neyrey, editor, *The Social World of Luke-Acts*.

43. Labeling and deviance theories in the social-science approach also help to chart the mutual accusations that constitute many of the conflicts in the plot. See Bruce J. Malina and Jerome H. Neyrey, *Calling Jesus Names: The Social Value of Labels in Matthew*.

44. See Halvor Moxnes, *The Economy of the Kingdom: Social Conflict and Economic Relations in Luke's Gospel.*

45. See chapter 6 in this volume.

46. See, e.g., John J. Pilch, "Sickness and Healing in Luke-Acts."

47. See chapter 5 in this volume; and Rhoads, "Mission in the Gospel of Mark."

48. Bruce J. Malina and Richard L. Rohrbaugh, *Social-Science Commentary on the Synoptic Gospels,* and idem, *Social-Science Commentary on the Gospel of John.*

49. For an integration of narrative criticism and social-science criticism in character analysis, see David Gowler, *Host, Guest, Enemy, and Friend: Portraits of Pharisees in Luke and Acts.*

50. See, e.g., Richard L. Rohrbaugh, "The Pre-industrial City in Luke-Acts"; and Douglas E. Oakman, "The Countryside in Luke-Acts."

51. Gerhard Lenski et al., *Human Societies.* This model for preindustrial agrarian society has been criticized for not accounting adequately for greater social mobility.

52. See Richard L. Rohrbaugh, "The Social Location of the Markan Audience"; Vernon K. Robbins, "The Social Location of the Implied Author in Luke-Acts"; and several of the articles in David L. Balch, editor, *Social History of the Matthean Community: Cross-Disciplinary Approaches,* especially the one by Antoinette Clark Wire, "Gender Roles in a Scribal Community," 87–121.

53. See Terry Eagleton, *Ideology: An Introduction*; David Jobling and Tina Pippin, editors, "Ideological Criticism of Biblical Texts," and "Ideological Criticism," in George Alchele, et al., *The Post-modern Bible,* 272–308.

54. See, e.g., Ched Myers, *Binding the Strong Man: A Political Reading of Mark's Story of Jesus*; and Richard J. Cassidy, *John's Gospel in New Perspective.*

55. Recent studies of the ambiguous treatment of women in Luke-Acts are good examples: T. K. Seim, *The Double Message: Patterns of Gender in Luke-Acts*; and Barbara Reid, *Choosing the Better Part? Women in the Gospel of Luke.* See also Elaine Mary Wainwright, *Towards a Feminist Critical Reading of the Gospel according to Matthew*; the commentaries and articles in Elisabeth Schüssler Fiorenza, editor, *Searching the Scriptures*; Janice Capel Anderson, "Feminist Criticism: The Dancing Daughter"; Emily Cheney, *She Can Read: Feminist Strategies for Biblical Narrative*; and Luise Schottroff, Silvia Schroer, and Marie-Terese Wacker, *Feminist Interpretation: The Bible in Women's Perspective.*

56. On the ethics of reading in literary studies, see J. Hillis Miller, *The Ethics of Reading: Kant, de Man, Eliot, Trollope, James, and Benjamin*; and Wayne Booth, *The Company We Keep: The Ethics of Fiction.* In biblical studies, see Elisabeth Schüssler Fiorenza, "The Ethics of Interpretation: De-Centering Biblical Theology"; D. J. Smit, "The Ethics of Interpretation: New Voices from the

USA"; P. J. J. Botha, "The Ethics of New Testament Interpretation," 169–74; and Daniel Patte, *Ethics of Biblical Interpretation: A Reevaluation*.

57. Hans Georg Gadamer, *Truth and Method*.

58. The importance of these dynamics was brought to scholarly attention by feminist critics. See, e.g., Elisabeth Schüssler Fiorenza, *In Memory of Her: A Feminist Reconstruction of Christian Origins*. See also George Aichele et al., *The Postmodern Bible*, passim; and R. S. Sugirtharajah, editor, *The Postcolonial Bible*.

59. For recent studies that emphasize the multivalent dimensions of scripture, see Daniel Patte, *Discipleship according to the Sermon on the Mount: Four Legitimate Readings, Four Plausible Views of Discipleship and their Relevant Values*; Fernando F. Segovia, editor, *What Is John? Readers and Readings of the Fourth Gospel*; and Charles H. Cosgrove, *Elusive Israel: The Puzzle of Election in Romans*.

60. Wesley A. Kort argues that it is precisely this willingness to risk in reading that defines our attitude toward a writing as scripture, in *"Take, Read": Scripture, Textuality, and Cultural Practice*.

61. For an understanding of the way our social location affects interpretation, see Fernando F. Segovia and Mary Ann Tolbert, editors, *Reading from This Place*, vol. 1: *Social Location and Biblical Interpretation in the United States*; and idem, *Reading from This Place*, vol. 2: *Social Location and Biblical Interpretation in Global Perspective*; Brian K. Blount, *Cultural Interpretation*; Daniel Smith-Christopher, editor, *Text and Experience: Towards a Cultural Exegesis of the Bible*; and Mark G. Brett, editor, *Ethnicity and the Bible*. See also the two volumes of Elisabeth Schüssler Fiorenza, editor, *Searching the Scriptures*; and Cain Hope Felder, editor, *Stony the Road We Trod: African-American Biblical Interpretation*.

62. As one specific example of the way in which a contemporary cultural perspective enhances our understanding of a biblical narrative, see Hisako Kinukawa, *Women and Jesus in Mark: A Japanese Feminist Perspective*.

3. Losing Life for Others in the Face of Death: Mark's Standards of Judgment

1. See Thomas E. Boomershine, "Mark, the Storyteller: A Rhetorical-Critical Investigation of Mark's Passion and Resurrection Narrative"; Norman R. Petersen, "Point of View in Mark's Narrative," 97–121; and Dan O. Via, *The Ethics of Mark's Gospel: In the Middle of Time*.

2. See Wayne Booth, *The Rhetoric of Fiction*.

3. On paradox and ambiguity in Mark's narrative, see Robert M. Fowler, *Let the Reader Understand: Reader-Response Criticism and the Gospel of Mark.*

4. On the complex integrity of Mark's narrative, see Joanna Dewey, "Mark as Interwoven Tapestry: Forecasts and Echoes for a Listening Audience," 221–36. The standards of judgment pervade every episode of Mark's narrative. The analysis that follows gives only a portion of the examples from Mark that could be drawn to illustrate and amplify them.

5. On the characters in Mark, see David Rhoads, Joanna Dewey, and Donald Michie, *Mark as Story: An Introduction to the Narrative of a Gospel,* 98–136.

6. It is inappropriate to see Mark's portrayal of the Jewish authorities as fostering anti-Semitism. The character-types in Mark are a rhetorical strategy that present caricatures of moral choices. Like the disciples, real people have good and bad traits. Also, the choice Mark offers to readers is not between Judaism and Christianity, for all the major characters in the narrative are Jewish.

7. See Jack Dean Kingsbury, *Conflict in Mark: Jesus, Authorities, Disciples.*

8. See Joanna Dewey, "The Gospel of Mark."

9. See Christopher Marshall, *Faith as a Theme in Mark's Narrative.*

10. See Jack Dean Kingsbury, *The Christology of Mark's Gospel.*

11. Robert C. Tannehill, "The Disciples in Mark: The Function of a Narrative Role."

12. This story is based on an incident recounted in an autobiographical work about a Japanese concentration camp in Thailand during World War II by Ernest Gordon (*Miracle on the River Kwai* [Wheaton, Ill.: Tyndale, 1962]). The work is a remarkable story of people who discovered a humane way of living that is consonant with the portrait of the kingdom in Mark.

13. The phrase is from Elisabeth Schüssler Fiorenza, *In Memory of Her.* Mark is anti-patriarchal. Disciples leave fathers, but they do not gain them in the new community.

14. For a contemporary psychological analysis of good and evil that offers remarkable parallels to Mark's assessment of the human condition, see Ernest Becker, *The Denial of Death,* and idem, *Escape from Evil.*

15. For a recent treatment, see Joel Marcus, "The Jewish War and the *Sitz im Leben* of Mark."

16. See Ched Myers, *Binding the Strong Man: A Political Reading of Mark's Story of Jesus.*

17. This chapter is only one way to understand the purpose of Mark, based on the use of narrative criticism. For further discussion of variety in perspective and method, see Janice Capel Anderson and Stephen D. Moore, editors, *Mark and Method: New Approaches in Biblical Studies.* On narrative criticism, see Mark Allan Powell, *What Is Narrative Criticism?*

4. Jesus and the Syrophoenician Woman

1. Mark Allan Powell, *What Is Narrative Criticism?*; David Rhoads, Joanna Dewey, and Donald Michie, *Mark as Story: An Introduction to the Narrative of a Gospel*; Stephen D. Moore, "Are the Gospels Unified Narratives?"; Wayne Booth, *The Rhetoric of Fiction*; Seymour Chatman, *Story and Discourse: Narrative Structure in Fiction and Film*; Shlomith Rimmon-Kenan, *Narrative Fiction: Contemporary Poetics*.

2. Norman R. Petersen, *Literary Criticism for New Testament Critics*, and chapter 1 in this volume.

3. Joanna Dewey, "Mark as Interwoven Tapestry: Forecasts and Echoes for a Listening Audience."

4. Robert M. Fowler, *Let the Reader Understand*; Stephen D. Moore, *Literary Criticism and the Gospels: The Theoretical Challenge*.

5. Mary Ann Beavis, "Mark's Teaching on Faith."

6. Robert M. Fowler, *Loaves and Fishes: The Function of the Feeding Stories in the Gospel of Mark*, and idem, *Let the Reader Understand*.

7. I have labeled the episodes in this way not in order to suggest that they form a Markan chiastic pattern but only to show more clearly the progressive and pivotal nature of the central episodes.

8. Robert Alter, *The Art of Biblical Narrative*, 47–61.

9. Robert C. Tannehill, "The Gospel of Mark as Narrative Christology."

10. Eduard Schweizer, "The Portrayal of the Life of Faith in the Gospel of Mark."

11. Cf. Joanna Dewey, *Markan Public Debate: Literary Technique, Concentric Structure, and Theology in Mark 2:1–3:6*.

12. Robert C. Tannehill, "The Disciples in Mark: The Function of a Narrative Role."

13. Frans Nierynck, *Duality in Mark: Contributions to the Study of the Markan Redaction*.

14. Rhoads, Dewey, and Michie, *Mark as Story*, 49–51.

15. T. A. Burkill, "The Syro-Phoenician Woman: The Congruence of Mark 7:24-37," and Gerd Theissen, *The Gospels in Context: Social and Political History in the Synoptic Tradition*. Theissen argues that the two steps explain that a Gentile (a "Hellene") was able to communicate with Jesus because she was bilingual (a native "Syrophoenician by birth"), 69.

16. David Noble, "An Examination of the Structure of Mark's Gospel," 318.

17. Noble, "Structure of Mark's Gospel"; Rhoads, Dewey, and Michie, *Mark as Story*, 47–55.

18. Joanna Dewey, "Oral Methods of Structuring Narrative in Mark."

19. Thomas E. Boomershine, "Mark, The Storyteller: A Rhetorical-Critical Investigation of Mark's Passion and Resurrection Narrative"; compare Eric Rabkin, *Narrative Suspense*; and Meir Sternberg, *The Poetics of Biblical Narrative: Ideological Literature and the Drama of Reading*.

20. See chapter 1 in this volume; and Mary Ann Tolbert, *Sowing the Gospel: Mark's World in Literary Historical Perspective*.

21. J. D. M. Derrett, "Law in the New Testament: The Syrophoenician Woman and the Centurion of Capernaum."

22. Theissen, *The Gospels in Context*, 62

23. T. A. Burkill, "The Historical Development of the Story of the Syrophoenician Woman (Mark vii: 24-37)."

24. Why Jesus went there to retreat is not clear. This uncertainty represents one of the many gaps of causation and motivation evident throughout the Markan narrative. Cf. chapter 7 in this volume. Appreciating such gaps and seeking to interpret them is much of the task of criticism. Frank Kermode, *The Genesis of Secrecy: On the Interpretation of Narrative*; Stephen D. Moore, "Are the Gospels Unified Narratives?"; and idem, *Literary Criticism and the Gospels: The Theoretical Challenge*.

25. Carol Fontaine, "The Use of the Traditional Saying in the Old Testament."

26. Bruce J. Malina, *The New Testament World: Insights from Cultural Anthropology*.

27. E. M. Forster, *Aspects of the Novel*; Seymour Chatman, *Story and Discourse: Narrative Structure in Fiction and Film*, 131–34; cf. further Baruch Hochman, *Character in Literature*.

28. Robert C. Tannehill, "The Gospel of Mark as Narrative Christology."

29. To Galilean or Syrian hearers of Mark's Gospel, Jesus' entrances into the Gentile regions of Tyre and the Decapolis may have been just as memorable as forays into Canada or Mexico from the United States would be to modern readers.

30. See chapter 1 in this volume

31. Boomershine, "Mark, The Storyteller."

32. Jerome H. Neyrey, "The Idea of Purity in Mark's Gospel," and chapter 6 in this volume.

33. Marcus Borg, *Conflict, Holiness, and Politics in the Teaching of Jesus*.

34. Mary Douglas, *Purity and Danger: An Analysis of the Concepts of Pollution and Taboo*, 269.

35. Wayne Booth, *The Rhetoric of Fiction*; Boomershine, "Mark, The Storyteller"; and chapter 3 in this volume.

36. Joanna Dewey, *Disciples of the Way: Mark on Discipleship*; Sharon Ringe, "A Gentile Woman's Story"; Mary Ann Beavis, "Mark's Teaching on Faith";

and Elisabeth Schüssler Fiorenza, *In Memory of Her: A Feminist Theological Reconstruction of Christian Origins.*

37. For a thorough treatment of the negative dimensions of Mark's view of women, see Tat-Siong Benny Liew, *The Politics of Parousia: Reading Mark Inter(con)textually*, 133–49.

38. Richard L. Rohrbaugh, "The Social Location of the Markan Audience."

39. Joel Marcus, "The Jewish War and the *Sitz im Leben* of Mark."

40. Theissen, *The Gospels in Context.*

41. Ibid. Theissen argues that the economic disparity between wealthy Tyrians and Jewish peasants was represented in the story by the depiction of the woman as a cultural Hellene who was wealthy (note reference to the daughter's bed as a "bed" rather than as a peasant's "mat") and therefore a member of the free-citizenry of the city of Tyre, 71.

42. Ibid.

5. Network for Mission:
The Social System of the Jesus Movement in Mark

1. The use of models as a means to explore the social dynamics of early Christianity is only one of many social-science approaches. For a survey of recent studies using methods from the social sciences, see Jonathan Z. Smith, "The Social Description of Early Christianity"; Robin Scroggs, "The Sociological Interpretation of the New Testament: The Present State of Research"; and Carolyn Osiek, *What Are They Saying about the Social Setting of the New Testament?* See also Richard L. Rohrbaugh, "Models and Muddles: Discussion of the Social Facets Seminar." For an extensive bibliography, see Daniel J. Harrington, "Second Testament Exegesis and the Social Sciences: A Bibliography."

2. On the autonomy of the text, see Norman R. Petersen, *Literary Criticism for New Testament Critics.* For a literary-critical study of narrative worlds, see Seymour Chatman, *Story and Discourse: Narrative Structure in Fiction and Film;* and Boris Uspensky, *Poetics of Composition: The Structure of the Artistic Text and Typology of a Compositional Form.* For an analysis of the Markan narrative world, see chapter 1 in this volume; and David Rhoads, Joanna Dewey, and Donald Michie, *Mark as Story: An Introduction to the Narrative of a Gospel.* Obviously, knowledge about the ancient world and the history of Israel is important for understanding this first century narrative. However, the focus here is on using that larger cultural knowledge to inform and understand the story rather than using the story to reconstruct history.

3. Norman R. Petersen, *Rediscovering Paul: Philemon and the Sociology of Paul's Narrative World*, 7. See this work for a creative application of social-scientific models in the narrative world of a New Testament letter.

4. This chapter is based in part on the sociology of knowledge, which focuses on the "knowledge" that a given society takes for granted, the shared meanings and often unexamined cultural assumptions that make possible the ordinary communication of everyday life. I propose to study the social knowledge and shared cultural assumptions in the narrative world of Mark's Gospel. See Peter Berger and Thomas Luckman, *The Social Construction of Reality*; and Peter Berger, *The Sacred Canopy*. Also note the philosophical work of Nelson Goodman, *Ways of Worldmaking*. See also Harold Remus, "Sociology of Knowledge and the Study of Early Christianity."

5. For the discussion of this well-known contrast between text as window and as mirror, see Murray Krieger, *A Window to Criticism: Shakespeare's Sonnets and Modern Poetics*, 3–4.

6. For an excellent treatment of these literary-critical issues and a summary of the relevant theorists, see Elizabeth Freund, *The Return of the Reader: Reader-Response Criticism*.

7. See Clifford Geertz, "Thick Description: Toward an Interpretative Theory of Culture," in idem, *The Interpretation of Cultures*, 3–30. Compare also the remarks of W. T. Jones in "World Views: Their Nature and Their Function," 8.

8. There have been few attempts to unpack the social system of the Jesus movement in Mark. See Howard Clark Kee's *Community of the New Age: Studies in Mark's Gospel*, who tends to confuse the social world of the narrative with the social world of Mark's historical community and to treat narrative elements as indirect, almost allegorical, references to Mark's audience. Nevertheless, his work is important and contains many useful insights. See also the interesting application to Mark of the work of sociologist Bryan Wilson in J. Wilde, "The Social World of Mark's Gospel: A Word about Method." For a fascinating Marxist analysis of the Gospel, see Fernando Belo, *A Materialist Reading of the Gospel of Mark*. Vernon K. Robbins has very helpfully applied social role theory to the teacher-disciple relationship in Mark, in *Jesus the Teacher: A Socio-Rhetorical Interpretation of Mark*.

9. On the relation between social systems and cosmologies that support them, see the works of Mary Douglas, especially *Natural Symbols: Essays in Cosmology*, and idem, *Cultural Bias*. For a critique of Douglas, see Richard L. Rohrbaugh, "'Social Location of Thought' as a Heuristic Construct in New Testament Study."

10. For a fuller explanation of these two stages see Rhoads, Dewey, and Michie, *Mark as Story*, 80–82.

11. On Jesus as holy man, see Marcus Borg, *Conflict, Holiness, and Politics in the Teaching of Jesus* ; and idem, *Jesus, a New Vision: Spirit, Culture, and the Life of Discipleship*, 23–75. For an earlier treatment, see Geza Vermes, *Jesus the Jew*. See also Peter Brown, "The Rise and Function of the Holy Man in Late Antiquity."

12. For an anthropological analysis of networks see J. Boissevain, *Friends of Friends: Networks, Manipulators and Coalitions*. Insights and methods from this study have guided our entire analysis of the Jesus network in Mark.

13. Note here the work of D. Snow, L. Zurcher, and S. E. Olson, "Social Networks and Social Movements: A Micro-structural Approach to Differential Recruitment."

14. Gerd Theissen, in his *Sociology of Early Palestinian Christianity*, views early Palestinian Christianity as a "movement of wandering charismatics," on the model of the Cynic teacher. However, Richard A. Horsley, in *Jesus and the Spiral of Violence*, rightly distinguishes the role of the historical disciples of Jesus from wandering Cynics by emphasizing the mission of the disciples to preach and heal and their acceptance of local hospitality (230–31). This latter study of the historical Jesus as the leader of a renewal movement has some significant parallels to our analysis here of the Jesus movement as depicted in Mark.

15. On dyadic relations, see Bruce J. Malina, *The New Testament World: Insights from Cultural Anthropology*, 58–80. In contrast to the individualism that characterizes modern Western society, a collectivist personality is one who simply "needs another continually in order to know who he or she really is" (62). Such persons are always related to others horizontally and vertically and defined by these relationships. See Malina's entire volume for a study of first-century cultures. On the general Mediterranean personality, see David D. Gilmore, "Anthropology of the Mediterranean Area," 175–205.

16. See Bruce J. Malina, "Patron and Client: The Analogy behind Synoptic Theology." Here he develops the depiction of Jesus as faction leader who plays the role of social broker for God as patron in relation to the people of Israel.

17. For an analysis of ancient hospitality, see Julian Pitt-Rivers, *The Fate of Shechem or the Politics of Sex: Essays on the Anthropology of the Mediterranean*, 94–112. On early Christian hospitality, see Abraham J. Malherbe, *Social Aspects of Early Christianity*, 2d ed.; and Bruce J. Malina, "The Received View and What It Can Do: III John and Hospitality."

18. For the analysis of household language and roles in 1 Peter, see John H. Elliott, *A Home for the Homeless: A Sociological Exegesis of I Peter, Its Situation and Strategy*; and David L. Balch, *Let Wives Be Submissive: The Domestic Code in I Peter*. Note also the review of these works by Antoinette Clark Wire "Review of *A Home for the Homeless* and *Let Wives be Submissive*." Contrast the situation

at Qumran, where communal sharing was not based on fictive kinship, but on the separation of possessions from that which was considered to be unclean. See Michael Newton, *The Concept of Purity at Qumran and in the Letters of Paul*, 19–20. For those scholars who assume that this passage in Mark refers to house churches in a stationary setting, see Ernst Best, *Following Jesus: Discipleship in the Gospel of Mark*, 226–29; and John R. Donahue, *The Theology and Setting of Discipleship in the Gospel of Mark*, 31–50. Also, Elizabeth Struthers Malbon, in *Narrative Space and Mythic Meaning*, notes how the Markan Jesus shifts the locale of his teaching from synagogues to houses, as the plot progresses.

19. The motif of being "on the way" figures prominently in almost every major study of Mark's Gospel.

20. Compare John J. Pilch, "Community Formation in the New Testament," 63–65. The type of society depicted in the narrative lends itself to the formation of competing factions, similar to the Jesus movement depicted in Mark. See Bruce J. Malina, *Christian Origins and Cultural Anthropology: Practical Models for Biblical Interpretation*, 37–44, for a study of different types of societies and the way in which each societal type lends itself to the emergence of certain social movements.

21. See Wilhelm Wuellner, *The Meaning of 'Fishers of Men.'*

22. On Jesus' distinctive relationship with those whom he heals, as portrayed in Mark, see Joanna Dewey, *Disciples of the Way: Mark on Discipleship*, 101–6. From a sociological point of view, Jesus thwarts the usual expectation of open-ended reciprocity between a patron and a client when he admonishes those whom he has healed to be quiet and not to follow him. Note that some commentators consider 5:20 to be an exception to Jesus' commands to silence. On the contrary, Jesus orders the demoniac to "go to your house, to your family." In disobedience to the command, the man went off and "told throughout the Decapolis."

23. In a sense, then, the network itself does not expand, since the number of core disciples who proclaim and heal is limited. Nevertheless, the influence of the core members expands greatly among ever increasing numbers of sympathizers as the disciples go from place to place.

24. Didache 1:1-12; 15:1-3, in Kirsopp Lake, trans., *The Apostolic Fathers*, 1:305–33.

25. Contrast this depiction in Mark with Gerd Theissen's portrait of early Christian historical communities located in villages and exhibiting some kind of organization (*Sociology*, 17–23). Theissen's picture is much closer to that presented in the Didache, where provisions are given for the organization and leadership of local Christian communities. By contrast, Mark's portrayal is much closer to that developed by Richard A. Horsley,

who argues that the historical Jesus sought to renew village life, not gain followers to form separate, distinguishable communities (*Jesus*, 209–84). See also William Arnal, *Jesus and the Village Scribes: Galilean Conflicts and the Setting of Q*.

26. There is uncertainty in the Markan portrayal regarding this continuation of kinship relations after one has left to follow Jesus. It is likely that "Mary the mother of James the lesser [younger] and of Joses" (15:40, 47; 16:1) refers to the mother of Jesus, mentioned earlier in the narrative (6:3). While she may now be part of the Jesus network, she is no longer identified in her role as Jesus' birth mother.

27. In the narrative world, Jesus addresses these predictions only to Peter, James, John, and Andrew. I take them, however, to refer to the persecutions that will be encountered by all the core disciples in the course of proclaiming. By contrast, the admonitions to "keep watch" seem to relate to both core disciples as well as sympathizers ("I say to all").

28. See above, note 18. The notion of house churches in Mark's audience is compatible with the depiction of houses in the narrative world. Strictly speaking, however, there are no house churches in the world of the narrative. In the narrative world, houses are used only for hospitality and teaching by the core group as they go from place to place. Until we are clear first of all about social functions within Mark's narrative, we will not subsequently make valid inferences from the text regarding Mark's audience or the historical Jesus.

29. Despite inferences one might make from the text, there is no explicit admonition to continue Baptism, such as we find, for example, in each of the other Gospels. Traditionally, the young man in the white robe at the grave has been identified with a baptismal initiate. Within the narrative world, however, the white robe seems to symbolize the authority of the young man as a messenger of God.

30. The traditional point of view is that the last supper and the feedings reflect eucharistic formulas. Within the narrative world, however, the language of blessing over the bread and the fish at the desert feedings typifies ordinary meals. At the Passover meal, Jesus relates his impending death on this particular occasion to the intimacy of his last meal with the disciples so as to make it a covenantal meal. But there is no suggestion that it is to be repeated or commemorated. This point is also noted by Donald Senior, *The Passion of Jesus in the Gospel of Mark*, 54.

31. Bruce J. Malina has been very helpful in articulating the nature of revitalization movements (private correspondence).

32. On change agents, see E. Rogers, *Diffusion of Innovations*, 3d ed., 318–19, and elsewhere.

33. On the sociological analysis of boundaries, see the writings of Jonathan Z. Smith, especially "The Influence of Symbols upon Social Change: A Place on Which to Stand"; and idem, "The Wobbling Pivot." Smith argues that the choices to affirm one's place or to be unbounded represent the two basic existential options open to humans. Clearly, the Jesus network portrayed in Mark is a "boundary crossing" movement. Mary Douglas shows how the purity regulations in a society are closely related to attitudes toward boundaries. See *Purity and Danger: An Analysis of the Concepts of Pollution and Taboo*. For an application of these social scientific insights to the Gospel of Mark, see Jerome H. Neyrey, "The Idea of Purity in Mark's Gospel," and David Rhoads, "Boundaries: The Dead Sea Sect and the Jesus Movement in the Gospel of Mark" (unpublished paper).

34. See Snow, et al., "Social Networks and Social Movements," 95.

35. Regarding the model that compares geographical to operational space, see S. Raynor, "The Perception of Time in Egalitarian Sects: A Millenarian Cosmology." On the concept of purity at Qumran, see Newton, *The Concept of Purity*, 10–50, and Jacob Neusner, *The Idea of Purity in Ancient Israel*.

36. Very little scholarly work has been done on the Markan view of the cosmos—shape, extent, understanding of creation, view of nature, idea of history, depiction of the afterlife, and so on. See James M. Robinson, *The Idea of History in Mark*. Elizabeth Struthers Malbon, in *Narrative Space*, has the most illuminating study of Markan space. She does not, however, seek to infer from various clues (e.g., 13:1-37) the shape of the cosmos in Mark's view. An explication of physical cosmology along with a study of the social dynamics of the peasant culture depicted by Mark are crucial for an understanding of the setting and atmosphere of Mark's story-world. On the agrarian society depicted in Mark, see Herman Waetjen, *A Reordering of Power: A Socio-Political Reading of Mark's Gospel*, 4–12.

37. It is not clear in the narrative world to whom this mandate of the Markan Jesus extends. Are the disciples to go to Jews in the diaspora? To Gentiles as well? All Gentile nations? How was this process envisioned by Mark? Does Mark expect that in the end many people will be "saved"? These are fundamental questions about the depiction of the future within the narrative world the answers to which are quite uncertain.

38. For a full discussion of the way Jesus redraws or eliminates purity lines in Mark, see Neyrey, "The Idea of Purity in Mark's Gospel."

39. For this paradigm shift in the view of holiness in relation to the historical Jesus, see Borg, *Conflict*, esp. 123–39.

40. On the function of parables in Mark, see especially Madeleine Boucher, *The Mysterious Parable: A Literary Study*, and Joel Marcus, *The Mystery of the Kingdom of God*.

41. Later, in the historical world of the author, the Gospel itself as a re-enactment of Jesus' life and death becomes a boundary mechanism, eliciting a favorable or an unfavorable response from those who hear it.

42. On rituals of entrance, see van Gennep, *The Rites of Passage*. Actually, the Markan rituals of affiliation are also rituals of separation from family and from certain cultural norms and structures. The entire Jesus network in Mark, from initial call down to the end, is significantly illuminated by the work of Victor Turner. Turner analyzes social movements as expressions of a ritual process involving three stages: separation, liminal transition, and reaggregation. See Turner, "Betwixt and Between," and idem, *The Ritual Process: Structure and Anti-Structure*.

43. Mark's portrait of the attitude of Jesus toward the Law is not entirely clear. Jesus affirms the Law while interpreting it (e.g., 12:28-31; 7:8), yet he also abrogates the laws of uncleanness (7:19). To claim that Jesus is lord of the Sabbath (2:27) is, by extension, to assert that he is lord over the entire Law.

44. For a more thorough analysis of boundary maintenance, see the works of M. Douglas cited above, note 9. See also Rhoads, "Boundaries."

45. See Göran Forkman, *The Limits of the Religious Community: Expulsion from the Religious Community within the Qumran Sect, within Rabbinic Judaism, and within Primitive Christianity*, 65.

46. Note the contrast between Jesus' inclusion of Judas in the sharing of the cup and the restrictions about sharing the cup in the Qumran community. See Michael Newton, *The Concept of Purity*, 10-26.

47. Historically, these figures would then be understood to refer to the various messianic and prophetic figures reported by Josephus to have arisen in Israel before and during the Roman Jewish War of 66-70 C.E. See David Rhoads, *Israel in Revolution 6-74 C.E.: A Political History Based on the Writings of Josephus*, 87-94, and Richard A. Horsley and John S. Hanson, *Bandits, Prophets, and Messiahs: Popular Movements in the Time of Jesus*.

48. For this interpretation, see Werner Kelber, *The Kingdom in Mark: A New Place and a New Time*, 113-16.

49. Even at the end of the narrative, Jesus offers to the disciples, even Peter, the opportunity to be restored from failure (16:7). Hence, all sins will be forgiven the children of humanity, unless a person blasphemes against the Holy Spirit, thereby fundamentally repudiating God (3:28-30; 14:21). Apart from Judas, the disciples have failed to be *for* Jesus, but they have not been *against* him in the sense that they have contributed to his demise.

50. See the works of Mary Douglas cited above, note 9. On the application of these insights to Qumran, see Sheldon Isenberg, "Mary Douglas and Hellenistic Religions: The Case of Qumran."

51. On the teacher-disciple roles, see Robbins, *Jesus the Teacher*.

52. Joanna Dewey has pointed out to me in private correspondence that the women who had been "following Jesus and serving him when he was in Galilee" (15:40-41) are an instance of "portable hospitality."

53. For a discussion of these women as examples of true discipleship in Mark, see Elisabeth Schüssler Fiorenza, *In Memory of Her: A Feminist Theological Reconstruction of Christian Origins*, 316–23.

54. It is likely that those who experienced the Gospel in the first century did so by "hearing" it. The narrator's words, "Let the reader understand" (13:14), are probably instructions to the public presenter of the Gospel.

55. For an analysis of collateral and lineal orientation, see Florence Rockwood Kluckhohn and Fred L. Strodtbeck, *Variations in Value Orientation*, 17–25.

56. Schüssler Fiorenza also considers the absence of "fathers" to be of crucial significance in understanding the Jesus movement. See *In Memory of Her*, 147–51.

57. An ethic that is contra-hierarchical might entail alternating leadership among members of a group, as suggested by Schüssler Fiorenza. However, the narrative of Mark seems to subvert all structures of hierarchical leadership.

58. Note that Simon's wife would have been cared for by his mother-in-law (1:29-31).

59. For a most helpful discussion of authority, see Hannah Arendt, "What Was Authority?" Bruce J. Malina has suggested "authorization" as a primary meaning of the Markan concept of authority (private correspondence). See also Talcott Parsons, *Politics and Social Structure*, 311–472, for a discussion of commitment, influence, power, and inducement. Note Malina's treatment of these concepts in *Christian Origins*, 77–86.

60. On the relation between miracles, power, and the suffering due to persecution, see Anitra Kolenkow, "Beyond Miracles, Suffering and Eschatology."

61. The Jesus network as depicted in Mark fosters a state of "liminality," the transition stage between separation from a society and the subsequent reaggregation into new social forms, a state marked by a relative lack of structure. In Mark, Jesus fosters ongoing liminality until the end. This expression of ongoing mobility/liminality in Mark parallels the founding of the Franciscan Order. According to Victor Turner, St. Francis's prohibitions against property and hierarchy created such a state of "perpetual liminality" as to make it difficult to establish an order (*Ritual Process*, 140–47). For the application of Turner's categories to the Markan narrative, see also Mark McVann, "The Passion in Mark: Transformation Ritual."

6. Crossing Boundaries: Purity and Defilement

1. Peter Berger and Thomas Luckman, *The Social Construction of Reality: A Treatise in the Sociology of Knowledge*. On worldviews, see Michael Kearney, *World View*.

2. Beverly Gaventa, *From Darkness to Light: Aspects of Conversion in the New Testament*.

3. All translations from Mark in this chapter and throughout the book are the author's.

4. Richard L. Rohrbaugh, "'Social Location of Thought' as a Heuristic Construct in New Testament Study."

5. Wayne A. Meeks, "The Man from Heaven in Johannine Sectarianism."

6. Howard Clark Kee, *Community of the New Age: Studies in Mark's Gospel*.

7. Robin Scroggs, "The Earliest Christian Communities as Sectarian Movement," 1–23.

8. John G. Gager, *Kingdom and Community: The Social World of Early Christianity*.

9. Bruce J. Malina, *The New Testament World: Insights from Cultural Anthropology*.

10. Bruce J. Malina, "The Social Sciences and Biblical Interpretation," 229–42.

11. Vernon K. Robbins, *Jesus the Teacher: A Socio-Rhetorical Interpretation of Mark*.

12. John J. Pilch, "Healing in Mark: A Social Science Analysis."

13. Herman Waetjen, *A Reordering of Power: A Socio-Political Reading of Mark's Gospel*.

14. Jerome H. Neyrey, "The Idea of Purity in Mark's Gospel."

15. John H. Elliott, *A Home for the Homeless: A Sociological Exegesis of I Peter, Its Situation and Strategy*.

16. There is disagreement about the location and date of Mark's Gospel. For the view expressed here, see Kee, *Community of the New Age*. For the traditional view, which places the Gospel in Rome during the 60s, see Martin Hengel, *Studies in the Gospel of Mark*.

17. In addition to Neyrey's work, I am especially indebted in this section to the following works: Jacob Neusner, *The Idea of Purity in Ancient Israel*; Jacob Milgrom, "Purity and Impurity"; idem, "Israel's Sanctuary: The Priestly Picture of Dorian Grey"; Baruch Levine, *In the Presence of the Lord: A Study of Cult and Some Cultic Terms in Ancient Israel*; Marcus Borg, *Conflict, Holiness, and Politics in the Teaching of Jesus*. For further bibliography, see Jerome H. Neyrey, "Unclean, Common, Polluted, and Taboo: A Short Reading Guide."

18. Jerome H. Neyrey, "The Idea of Purity in Mark's Gospel." See also idem, "A Symbolic Approach to Mark 7"; and John J. Pilch, "Biblical Leprosy and Body Symbolism."

19. Michael Newton, *The Concept of Purity at Qumran and in the Letters of Paul.*

20. See especially Mary Douglas, *Purity and Danger: An Analysis of the Concepts of Pollution and Taboo*; idem, "Pollution"; idem, *Implicit Meanings: Essays in Anthropology*; and idem, *Natural Symbols: Explorations in Cosmology.*

21. Jonathan Z. Smith, "Animals and Plants"; "The Influence of Symbols upon Social Change: A Place on Which to Stand"; "The Wobbling Point."

22. Smith, "Animals and Plants," 914.

23. Smith, "Influence of Symbols," 467.

24. Smith, "Animals and Plants," 914.

25. Smith, "Influence of Symbols," 467.

26. Douglas, *Natural Symbols,* 70.

27. Douglas, *Implicit Meanings,* 269.

28. See Neyrey, "Idea of Purity," 15.

29. See Borg, *Conflict, Holiness, and Politics in the Teachings of Jesus.*

7. Performing the Gospel of Mark

1. For an account of his experience of performing Mark, see Alec McGowen, *Personal Mark: An Actor's Proclamation of St. Mark's Gospel.*

2. See the fascinating study by Whitney Taylor Shiner, *Proclaiming the Gospels: First-Century Performance of Mark,* in which he culls clues about performance from ancient rhetorical handbooks and offers suggestions about how various passages in Mark may well have been performed in antiquity.

3. For further information on the oral performance of literature, see Ronald Pelias, *Performance Studies: The Interpretation of Aesthetic Texts*; and Charlotte Lee and Timothy Gura, *Oral Interpretation.*

4. Reynolds Price, *A Palpable God: Thirty Stories Translated from the Bible, with an Essay on the Origins and Life of Narrative,* 47–55.

5. See Price, *A Palpable God,* 148–91. More than any other, this translation captures the almost breathless pace of Mark's narration.

6. Joanna Dewey, "Mark as Interwoven Tapestry: Forecasts and Echoes for a Listening Audience."

7. For a thorough literary analysis of this episode in Mark, see chapter 4 in this volume. For an overall literary analysis of Mark's narrative, see David Rhoads, Joanna Dewey, and Donald Michie, *Mark as Story: An Introduction to the Narrative of a Gospel.*

8. For excellent resources to learn and recount biblical stories in various contexts of the Christian life, consult Thomas E. Boomershine, *Story Journey: An Invitation to the Gospel as Story-Telling.*

9. A video of my performance is available under the title, "The Dramatic Performance of the Gospel of Mark," along with several video courses (SELECT, 2199 East Main Street, Columbus, OH 43209). SELECT has videos of performances of some other New Testament works as well.

8. The Ethics of Reading Mark as Narrative

1. On the ethics of reading in literary studies, see J.Hillis Miller, *The Ethics of Reading: Kant, de Man, Eliot, Trollope, James, and Benjamin*; and Wayne Booth, *The Company We Keep: The Ethics of Fiction*. In biblical studies, see Elisabeth Schüssler Fiorenza, "The Ethics of Interpretation: De-Centering Biblical Theology," 3–17; idem, *Rhetoric and Ethics: The Politics of Biblical Studies*; D. J. Smit, "The Ethics of Interpretation: New Voices from the USA," 16–28; J. Botha, "The Ethics of New Testament Interpretation," 169–74; Daniel Patte, *Ethics of Biblical Interpretation: A Reevaluation*; Gary Phillips, "The Ethics of Reading Deconstructively," in *The New Literary Criticism and the New Testament*, 283–325; Stephen Fowl and Gregory Jones, *Reading in Communion: Scripture and Ethics in the Christian Life*; Danna Nolan Fewell and Gary Phillips, editors, *Bible and Ethics of Reading*; Elna Mouton, *Reading a New Testament Document Ethically*; and Gary Phillips and Nicole Wilkinson Duran, editors, *Reading Communities Reading Scripture: Essays in Honor of Daniel Patte*.

2. On the postmodern study of the Bible see Fred Burnett, "Postmodern Biblical Exegesis: The Eve of Historical Criticism," 51–81; George Aichele, et al., *The Postmodern Bible: The Bible and the Culture Collective*; A. K. M. Adam, *What is Postmodern Biblical Criticism?*; A. K. M. Adam, editor, *Handbook of Postmodern Biblical Interpretation*, and idem, *Postmodern Interpretations of the Bible*.

3. The ethics of reading focuses on the ethics *of reading* the New Testament rather than on the ethics *in* the New Testament, although the latter is obviously not irrelevant to the ethics of reading. In recent decades, there has been a renewed interest in the ethics in the New Testament. See, for example, Wayne Meeks, *The Moral World of the First Christians*; Willi Marxsen, *New Testament Foundations for Christian Ethics*; Brian Rosner, editor., *Understanding Paul's Ethics: Twentieth-Century Approaches*; Richard Hayes, *The Moral Vision of the New Testament: A Contemporary Introduction to Christian Ethics*; Eduard Lohse, *Theological Ethics of the New Testament*; Eugene Lovering and Jerry Sumney, *Theology and Ethics in Paul and His Interpreters*; Frank Matera, *New Testament Ethics: The Legacies of Jesus and Paul*.

4. In biblical studies, this point is especially emphasized by reader-response critics. See Edgar McKnight, *Post-Modern Use of the Bible and the Emer-*

gence of Reader-Oriented Criticism; idem, editor, "Reader Perspectives on the New Testament"; Mark Allan Powell, *Chasing the Eastern Star: Adventures in Biblical Reader-Response Criticism*; Robert Fowler, "Reader-Response Criticism: Figuring Mark's Reader." For further study, see works by literary critics Wayne Booth, Stanley Fish, Wolfgang Iser, Susan Sulieman, and Jane Thompkins. On the indeterminacy of texts, their inherent secrets and mysteries, see Frank Kermode, *The Genesis of Secrecy: On the Interpretation of Narrative*, and Anthony Thiselton, *New Horizons in Hermeneutics*. On the meaning potential of language, see Michael Halliday, *Language as Social Semiotic: The Social Interpretation of Language and Meaning*.

5. See Burton Mack, *A Myth of Innocence*, for a portrayal of the significant harm Mark has done by means of his apocalyptic dualism. See also Mary Ann Tolbert, "When Resistance Becomes Repression." Concerning Paul, see "Paul in the Service of Death," in Neil Elliott, *Liberating Paul: The Justice of God and the Politics of the Apostle*, 3–24.

6. See Mary Ann Tolbert, "When Resistance Becomes Repression," 345–46.

7. On the analogy of reading as a dialogue, see Wayne Booth, *The Company We Keep: The Ethics of Fiction,* and J. Hillis Miller, *The Ethics of Reading*, 18–20.

8. J. Hillis Miller, "The Triumph of Theory, the Resistance to Reading, and the Question of the Material Base," 284.

9. Ibid.

10. On the traits of empathic reading, see Stephen Reid, "The Role of Reading in Multicultural Exegesis," in Daniel Smith Christopher, ed. *Text and Experience: Towards a Cultural Exegesis of the Bible*, 210–24.

11. On treating the text as "other," as something "not to be overwhelmed or overridden, but acknowledged, respected, and engaged in its very otherness," see Fernando Segovia, "The Text as Other: Towards an Hispanic American Hermeneutic," in Daniel Smith-Christopher, editor, *Text and Experience*, 287.

12. On the dynamic, interactive relationship between person and place, people and context, see Halvor Moxnes, *Putting Jesus in His Place: A Radical Vision of Household and Kingdom*.

13. For the complexity of an individual social location with its multiple identities, see Mary Ann Tolbert, "The Politics and Poetics of Location," in *Reading from this Place*, volume 2, 305–17.

14. On feminist criticism, see the works of Elisabeth Schüssler Fiorenza, especially *Bread Not Stone: The Challenge of Feminist Biblical Interpretation* and the two volumes edited by her, *Searching the Scriptures*. See also Luise Schottroff, Silvia Schroer, and Marie-Theres Wacker, *Feminist Interpretation: The Bible in Women's Perspective*; Silvia Schroer and Sophia Bietenhard, editors,

Feminist Interpretation of the Bible and the Hermeneutics of Liberation; and Janice Capel Anderson, "Feminist Criticism: The Dancing Daughter," in idem and Stephen Moore, *Mark and Method.*

15. Other frames of reference could be considered, such as the canon or the history of interpreting Mark.

16. On the social location of a Gospel, see Richard Rohrbaugh, "The Social Location of the Markan Audience"; and Vernon Robbins, "The Social Location of the Implied Author in Luke-Acts," in Jerome Neyrey, editor, *The Social World of Luke-Acts,* 305–32.

17. J. Botha. "The Ethics of New Testament Interpretation," 185.

18. On narrative criticism, see David Rhoads, et al., *Mark as Story: An Introduction to the Narrative of a Gospel;* Alan Culpepper, *Anatomy of the Fourth Gospel: A Study in Literary Design*; Mark Powell, *What Is Narrative Criticism?* For further resources, see the first two chapters of this book.

19. For a survey of approaches and resources in the sociocultural study of the New Testament, see Chapter 6 in this volume.

20. On gender studies in Mark, see Stephen D. Moore and Janice Capel Anderson, editors, *New Testament Masculinities.*

21. For critiques of narrative criticism, see Stephen Moore, *Literary Criticism and the Gospels: The Theoretical Challenge*; David Rhoads and Kari Syreeni, editors, *Characterization in the Gospels: Reconceiving Narrative Criticism*; and David Lee, *Luke's Stories of Jesus: Theological Reading of Gospel Narratives and the Legacy of Hans Frei.*

22. Deconstruction, for example, "makes explicit what is hidden, repressed or denied in any ordinary reading." (George Aichele, et al., *Postmodern Bible,* 130). See also Frank Kermode, *Genesis of Secrecy*; Gary Phillips, "The Ethics of Reading"; and Stephen Moore, *Literary Criticism and the Gospels: The Theoretical Challenge.*

23. Fernando Segovia, "Toward Intercultural Criticism: A Reading Strategy from the Diaspora," in *Reading from this Place,* volume 2, 302–30. On communal reading, see Stanley Fish, *Is there a Text in This Class?* and Stephen Fowl and Gregory Jones, *Reading in Communion: Scripture and Ethics in the Christian Life.*

24. For interpretations by people from different social locations, see, for example, the informative articles in books edited by F. Segovia, Mary Ann Tolbert, and Daniel Smith-Christopher. See also, R. S. Sugirtharajah, editor, *Voices from the Margin: Interpreting the Bible in the Third World,* and Cain Hope Felder, *Stony the Road We Trod: African-American Biblical Interpretation*; John R. Levison and Priscilla Pope Levison, *Return to Babel: Global Perspectives on the Bible*; Walter Dietrich and Ulrich Luz, editors, *The Bible in Global Context: An Experiment in Contextual Hermeneutics*; Justin Upkong, et al., *Reading the Bible in*

the Global Village: Capetown; and Vincent Wimbush, editor, *African Americans and the Bible: Sacred texts and Social Structures*. See also Daniel Patte, editor, *The Global Bible Commentary*.

25. For a moving tribute to this awareness, see Daniel Patte, *Ethics of Biblical Interpretation*.

26. On postcolonialism in biblical studies, see Laura Donaldson, editor, "Postcolonialism and Scriptural Reading"; R. S. Sugirtharajah, editor, *The Postcolonial Bible* and idem, *Postcolonial Criticism and Biblical Interpretation*; Fernando Segovia, *Decolonizing Biblical Studies: A View From the Margins*; Musa Dube, *Postcolonial Feminist Interpretation of the Bible*; and Musa Dube and Jeffrey Staley, editors, *John and Postcolonialism: Travel, Space and Power*. On Mark, see Benny Liew, *The Politics of Parousia*.

27. Elisabeth Schüssler Fiorenza, "The Ethics of Interpretation."

28. Fernando Segovia, "Intercultural Criticism," 304–5 and Kathleen O'Brien Wicker, "Teaching Feminist Biblical Studies in a Postcolonial Context," in Elisabeth Schüssler Fiorenza, ed., *Searching the Scriptures, Volume One: A Feminist Introduction*, 367–80.

29. For the image of the roundtable, see Justo Gonzalez, *Out of Every Tribe and Nation: Christian Theology at the Ethnic Roundtable*. It is important to bring to the roundtable for discussion not only the diverse interpretations of biblical texts but also the differing cultural methods, assumptions, and working presuppositions. On the asymmetries of power in intercultural dynamics, see especially James Cochrane, *Circles of Dignity: Community Wisdom and Theological Reflection,* and Miroslav Wolf, *Exclusion and Embrace: A Theological Exploration of Identity, Otherness, and Reconciliation*.

30. Elna Mouton, *Reading a New Testament Document Ethically*, 258.

31. For three recent studies that emphasize the multivalent dimensions of scripture, see J. Botha, *Subject to Whose Authority: Multiple Readings of Romans*; Daniel Patte, *Discipleship according to the Sermon on the Mount: Four Legitimate Readings, Four Plausible Views of Discipleship and Their Relevant Values;* and the two volume series edited by Fernando Segovia, *What Is John?*

32. Elisabeth Schüssler Fiorenza, "De-Centering," 14.

33. Wesley Kort argues that it is precisely this willingness to risk in reading that defines our attitude toward a writing as scripture, in *"Take, Read": Scripture, Textuality, and Cultural Practice*. Compare also Booth, "To decline the Gambit, to remain passive in the face of the author's strongest passions and deepest convictions, is surely condescending, insulting, and finally irresponsible." *The Company We Keep,* 135.

34. J. Hillis Miller identifies literature as a "safe area" where we can imagine what it might be like "if we lived our lives according to a certain moral principle." *The Ethics of Reading*, 30.

35. Robin Scroggs calls this potential transformation "world-switching," in *The Text and the Times*, 282.

36. Wayne Booth, *The Company We Keep*, 9.

37. See Gale Yee, "The Author/Text/Reader and Power: Suggestions for a Critical Framework for Biblical Studies," in *Reading from This Place*, volume 1, 109–18.

38. On the stereotyping of the Pharisees in the Gospels, see Robert Tannehill, "Should We Love Simon the Pharisee: Hermeneutical Reflections on the Pharisees in Luke."

39. In this context, the biblical writing itself becomes relativized, and we assess by our own (relative) values. See Elisabeth Schüssler Fiorenza, "The Ethics of Interpretation," 14.

Bibliography

This bibliography contains all books and articles referred to in the notes of this volume, in addition to some recent works on Mark not mentioned in the notes.

Abrams, M. H. *A Glossary of Literary Terms*. New York: Holt, Rinehart and Winston, 1971.

Achtemeier, Paul J. *"Omne Verbum Sonat*: The New Testament and the Oral Environment of Late Western Antiquity." *JBL* 109 (1990) 3–27.

Adam, A. K. M., editor. *Handbook of Postmodern Biblical Interpretation*. St. Louis: Chalice, 2000.

———. *Postmodern Interpretations of the Bible*. St. Louis: Chalice, 2001.

———. *What Is Postmodern Biblical Criticism?* GBS. Minneapolis: Fortress Press, 1995.

Aichele, George, et al. "Ideological Criticism." In *The Postmodern Bible*, 272–308. The Bible and Culture Collective. New Haven: Yale Univ. Press, 1995.

Allport, Gordon. "What Is a Trait of Personality?" *Journal of Abnormal and Social Psychology* 25 (1931) 368–72.

———, and Henry Odbert. *Trait Names: A Psychological Study*. Psychological Monographs 47. Princeton: Psychological Review Company, 1936.

Alter, Robert. *The Art of Biblical Narrative*. New York: Basic, 1981.

Amit, Yairah. *Reading Biblical Narratives: Literary Criticism and the Hebrew Bible*. Translated by Yael Lotan. Minneapolis: Fortress Press, 2001.

Anderson, Janice Capel. "Feminist Criticism: The Dancing Daughter." In *Mark and Method: New Approaches in Biblical Studies*, edited by Janice Capel Anderson and Stephen D. Moore, 103–34. Minneapolis: Fortress Press, 1992.

——. *Matthew's Narrative Web: Over, and Over, and Over Again.* JSNTSup 91. Sheffield: JSOT Press, 1994.

——, and Stephen D. Moore, editors. *Mark and Method: New Approaches in Biblical Studies.* Minneapolis: Fortress Press, 1992.

Arendt, Hannah. *What Was Authority?* In *Nomos I: Authority*, edited by C. J. Friedrich, 81–112. Cambridge: Harvard Univ. Press, 1958.

Arnal, William E. *Jesus and the Village Scribes: Galilean Conflicts and the Setting of Q.* Minneapolis: Fortress Press, 2001.

Austin, J. L. *How to Do Things with Words.* 2d ed. Cambridge: Harvard Univ. Press, 1975.

Bal, Mieke. *Narratology: Introduction to the Theory of Narrative.* Toronto: Univ. of Toronto Press, 1985.

Balch, David L. *Let Wives Be Submissive: The Domestic Code in I Peter.* SBLMS 26. Atlanta: Scholars, 1981.

——, editor. *Social History of the Matthean Community: Cross-Disciplinary Approaches.* Minneapolis: Fortress Press, 1992.

Bar-Efrat, Shimon. *Narrative Art in the Bible.* Translated by D. Shefer-Vanson and S. Bar-Efrat. JSOTSup 70. Sheffield: Almond, 1989.

Barr, David L. *Tales of the End: A Narrative Commentary on the Book of Revelation.* Santa Rosa, Calif.: Polebridge, 1998.

Beardslee, William A. *Literary Criticism of the New Testament.* GBS. Philadelphia: Fortress Press, 1970.

Beavis, Mary Ann. "Mark's Teaching on Faith." *BTB* 16 (1986) 139–42.

——. "Women as Models of Faith in Mark." *BTB* 18 (1988) 3–9.

Beck, Robert R. *Nonviolent Story: Narrative Conflict Resolution in the Gospel of Mark.* Maryknoll, N.Y.: Orbis, 1996.

Becker, Ernest. *The Denial of Death.* New York: Free Press, 1973.

——. *Escape from Evil.* New York: Free Press, 1975.

Belo, Fernando. *A Materialist Reading of the Gospel of Mark.* Translated by Matthew J. O'Connell. Maryknoll, N.Y.: Orbis, 1981.

Berger, Peter L. *The Sacred Canopy : Elements of a Sociological Theory of Religion.* New York : Anchor, 1990 (1967).

Berger, Peter L., and Thomas Luckman. *The Social Construction of Reality: A Treatise in the Sociology of Knowledge.* Garden City, N.Y.: Doubleday, 1966.

Berlin, Adele. *Poetics and Interpretation of Biblical Narrative.* BLS 9. Sheffield: Almond, 1983.

Best, Ernest. *Following Jesus: Discipleship in the Gospel of Mark.* JSNTSup 4. Sheffield: JSOT Press, 1981.

——. *Mark: The Gospel as Story.* SNTIW. Edinburgh: T. and T. Clark, 1987.

——. *The Temptation and the Passion: Markan Soteriology.* SNTSMS 2. Cambridge: Cambridge Univ. Press, 1990.

Bilezikian, Gilbert G. *The Liberated Gospel: A Comparison of the Gospel of Mark and Greek Tragedy.* Grand Rapids: Baker, 1977.

Black, C. Clifton. *Mark: Images of an Apostolic Interpreter.* PNT. Minneapolis: Fortress Press, 2001.

Blount, Brian K. *Cultural Interpretation: Reorienting New Testament Criticism.* Minneapolis: Fortress Press, 1995.

———. *Go Preach! Mark's Kingdom Message and the Black Church Today.* Maryknoll, N.Y.: Orbis, 1998.

———, and Gary Charles. *Preaching Mark in Two Voices.* Louisville: Westminster John Knox, 2003.

Bock, Darrell. *Blasphemy and Exaltation in Judaism: The Charge against Jesus in Mark.* Grand Rapids: Baker, 2000.

Boissevain, J. *Friends of Friends: Networks, Manipulators and Coalitions.* Oxford: Blackwell, 1974.

Bolt, Peter G. *Jesus' Defeat of Death: Persuading Mark's Early Readers.* SNTSMS 125. Cambridge: Cambridge University, 2003.

Boomershine, Thomas E. "Mark 16:8 and the Apostolic Commission." *JBL* 100 (1981) 225–39.

———. "Mark, the Storyteller: A Rhetorical-Critical Investigation of Mark's Passion and Resurrection Narrative." Ph.D. dissertation, Union Theological Seminary, New York, 1974.

———. *Story Journey: An Invitation to the Gospel as Story-Telling.* Nashville: Abingdon, 1988.

———, and Gilbert Bartholomew. "The Narrative Technique of Mark 16:8." *JBL* 100 (1981) 213–23.

Booth, Wayne. *The Company We Keep: The Ethics of Fiction.* Berkeley: Univ. of California Press, 1988.

———. *Critical Interpretation: The Powers and Limits of Pluralism.* Chicago: Univ. of Chicago Press, 1979.

———. "Distance and Point of View: An Essay in Clarification." *Essays in Criticism* 11 (1961) 60–79.

———. *The Rhetoric of Fiction.* 2d ed. Chicago: Univ. of Chicago Press, 1983.

———. *A Rhetoric of Irony.* Chicago: Univ. of Chicago Press, 1974.

Borg, Marcus. *Conflict, Holiness, and Politics in the Teaching of Jesus.* SBEC 5. New York. Edwin Mellon, 1984.

———. *Jesus, A New Vision: Spirit, Culture, and the Life of Discipleship.* San Francisco: Harper and Row, 1987.

Botha, Jan. *Subject to Whose Authority: Multiple Readings of Romans.* ESEC 4. Atlanta: Scholars, 1994.

Botha, P. J. J. "Mark's Story as Oral Literature: Rethinking the Transmission of Some Traditions about Jesus." *HvTSt* 47 (1991) 304–31.

——. "The Ethics of New Testament Interpretation." *Neot* 26 (1992) 169–74.

Boucher, Madeleine. *The Mysterious Parable: A Literary Study.* CBQMS 6. Washington, D.C.: Catholic Biblical Association, 1977.

Bratcher, Robert, and Eugene A. Nida. *A Translator's Handbook on the Gospel of Mark.* New York: United Bible Societies, 1979.

Brett, Mark G., editor. *Ethnicity and the Bible.* BibIntSer 19. Leiden: Brill, 1996.

Brock, Rita Nakashima. *Journeys by Heart: A Christology of Erotic Power.* New York: Crossroad, 1992.

Brown, Peter. "The Rise and Function of the Holy Man in Late Antiquity." *JRS* 61 (1971) 80–101.

Bryan, Christopher. *A Preface to Mark: Notes on the Gospel in Its Literary and Cultural Settings.* New York: Oxford Univ. Press, 1993.

Burkill, T. A. "The Historical Development of the Story of the Syrophoenician Woman (Mark vii: 24–37)." *NovT* 9 (1967) 161–77.

——. "The Syro-Phoenician Woman: The Congruence of Mark 7:24-37." *ZNW* 57 (1966) 23–37.

Burnett, Fred. "Characterization and Reader Construction in the Gospels." *Semeia* 63 (1993) 1–26.

——. "Postmodern Biblical Exegesis: The Eve of Historical Criticism." In Gary Phillips, ed., *Poststructuralist Criticism and the Bible: Text/History/Discourse, Semeia* 51 (1990) 51–81.

Camery-Hoggatt, Jerry. *Irony in Mark's Gospel: Text and Subtext.* Cambridge: Cambridge Univ. Press, 1992.

Carter, Warren. *Matthew: Storyteller, Interpreter, Evangelist.* Peabody, Mass.: Swiss Studies in English 84. Hendrickson, 1996.

Casparis, Christian Paul. *Tense without Time: The Present Tense in Narration.* Bern: Francke, 1975.

Cassidy, Richard J. *John's Gospel in New Perspective: Christology and the Realities of Roman Power.* Maryknoll, N.Y.: Orbis, 1992.

Chatman, Seymour. *Coming to Terms: The Rhetoric of Narrative in Fiction and Film.* Ithaca, N.Y.: Cornell Univ. Press, 1990.

——. *Story and Discourse: Narrative Structure in Fiction and Film.* Ithaca, N.Y.: Cornell Univ. Press, 1987.

Chávez, Emilio G. *The Theological Significance of Jesus' Temple Action in Mark's Gospel.* Lewiston, N.Y.: Edwin Mellen Press, 2002.

Cheney, Emily. *She Can Read: Feminist Strategies for Biblical Narrative.* Valley Forge, Pa.: Trinity, 1996.

Cochrane, James. *Circles of Dignity: Community Wisdom and Theological Reflection.* Minneapolis: Fortress Press, 1999.

Collins, Adela Yarbro. *The Beginning of the Gospel: Probings of Mark in Context.* Minneapolis: Fortress Press, 1992.

Cook, John G. *The Structure and Persuasive Power of Mark: A Linguistic Approach.* Semeia Studies. Atlanta: Scholars, 1995.

Cosgrove, Charles H. *Elusive Israel: The Puzzle of Election in Romans.* Louisville: Westminster John Knox, 1997.

Crosman, Robert. "In Defense of Authors and Readers." *Novel* 11 (1977) 5–25.

Culpepper, R. Alan. *Anatomy of the Fourth Gospel: A Study in Literary Design.* Philadelphia: Fortress, 1983.

———. "The Passion and the Resurrection in Mark." *RevExp* 75 (1978) 583–600.

Daniel, Harry. "The Transfiguration (Mark 9:2-13 and Parallels): A Redaction-Critical and Traditio-Historical Study." Ph.D. dissertation, Vanderbilt University, 1976.

Danove, Paul L. *The End of Mark's Story: A Methodological Study.* BibIntSer 3. Leiden: Brill, 1993.

———. *Linguistics and Exegesis in the Gospel of Mark: Applications of a Case Frame Analysis and Lexicon.* JSNTSup 218. Sheffield: Sheffield Academic, 2001.

Darr, John A. *On Character Building: The Reader and Rhetoric of Characterization in Luke-Acts.* LCBI. Louisville: Westminster John Knox, 1992.

Dawson, Anne. *Freedom as Liberating Power: A Socio-Political Reading of the* exousia *Texts in the Gospel of Mark.* NTOA 44. Göttingen: Vandenhoeck & Ruprecht, 2000.

Derrett, J. D. M. "Law in the New Testament: The Syrophoenician Woman and the Centurion of Capernaum." *NovT* 15 (1973) 161–186.

Dewey, Joanna. *Disciples of the Way: Mark on Discipleship.* Board of Global Ministries: The United Methodist Church, 1976.

———. "The Gospel of Mark." In *Searching the Scriptures*, vol. 2: *A Feminist-Ecumenical Commentary*, edited by Elisabeth Schüssler Fiorenza, 470–509. New York: Crossroad, 1993.

———. "The Gospel of Mark as Oral-Aural Event: Implications for Interpretation." In *New Literary Criticism and the New Testament*, edited by Edgar V. McKnight and Elizabeth Struthers Malbon, 145–63. Valley Forge: Trinity, 1994.

———. "The Literary Structure of the Controversy Stories in Mark 2:1–3:6." *JBL* 92 (1973) 394–401.

———. "Mark 10:35-40 from the Perspective of the Implied Reader." SBL Seminar Paper, 1979.

———. "Mark as Interwoven Tapestry: Forecasts and Echoes for a Listening Audience." *CBQ* 53 (1991) 221–36.

———. *Markan Public Debate: Literary Technique, Concentric Structure, and Theology in Mark 2:1—3:6.* SBLDS 48. Chico, Calif.: Scholars, 1980.

——, editor. "Orality and Textuality in Early Christian Literature." *Semeia*
    65. Atlanta: Scholars, 1995.

——. "Oral Methods of Structuring Narrative in Mark." *Int* 43 (1989) 32–44.

DeYoung, Curtis. *Coming Together: The Bible's Message in an Age of Diversity*. Val-
    ley Forge, Pa.: Judson, 1995.

Dietrich, Walter, and Ulrich Luz, editors. *The Bible in Global Context: An Exper-
    iment in Contextual Hermeneutics*. Grand Rapids: Eerdmans, 2002.

Dolezel, Lubomir. "The Typology of the Narrator: Point of View in Fiction." In
    *To Honor Roman Jacobson: Essays on the Occasion of His Seventieth Birthday, 11
    October 1966*, 3 vols., 1:541–52. Janua linguarum 31–33. Paris: Mouton,
    1967.

Donahue, John R. *Are You the Christ? The Trial Narrative in the Gospel of Mark*.
    SBLDS 10. Missoula, Mont.: Scholars, 1973.

——. "A Neglected Factor in the Theology of Mark." SBL Seminar Paper,
    1980.

——. *The Theology and Setting of Discipleship in the Gospel of Mark*. 1983 Pere Mar-
    quette Theology Lecture. Milwaukee: Marquette University, 1983.

——, and Daniel J. Harrington. *The Gospel of Mark*. SacPag 2. Collegeville,
    Minn.: Liturgical, 2001.

Donaldson, Laura, editor. "Postcolonialism and Scriptural Reading." *Semeia*
    75 (1996).

Douglas, Mary. *Cultural Bias*. Atlantic Highlands, N.J.: Humanities, 1982.

——. *Implicit Meanings: Essays in Anthropology*. London: Routledge & Kegan
    Paul, 1975.

——. *Natural Symbols: Explorations in Cosmology*. New York: Pantheon, 1982.

——. "Pollution." In *The International Encyclopedia of the Social Sciences,* edited
    by David Sills, 12:336–42. New York: Macmillan, 1968.

——. *Purity and Danger: An Analysis of the Concepts of Pollution and Taboo*. Lon-
    don: Routledge & Kegan Paul, 1966.

Dowd, Sharon. *Reading Mark: A Literary and Theological Commentary*. RNTS.
    Macon, Ga.: Smith and Helwys, 2000.

Dowling, William C. *The Critic's Hornbook: Reading for Interpretation*. New York:
    Crowell, 1977.

Dube, Musa W. *Postcolonial Feminist Interpretation of the Bible*. St. Louis: Chal-
    ice, 2000.

——, and Jeffrey Staley, editors. *John and Postcolonialism: Travel, Space and
    Power*. Bible and Postcolonialism 7. Sheffield: Sheffield Academic, 2002.

Duke, Paul D. *Irony in the Fourth Gospel*. Atlanta: John Knox, 1985.

Eagleton, Terry. *Ideology: An Introduction*. London: Verso, 1991.

Edwards, James R. *The Gospel according to Mark*. Pillar New Testament Com-
    mentary. Grand Rapids: Eerdmans, 2002.

Elliott, Neil. *Liberating Paul: The Justice of God and the Politics of the Apostle.* Maryknoll, N.Y.: Orbis, 1994.

Elliott, John H. *A Home for the Homeless: A Sociological Exegesis of I Peter, Its Situation and Strategy.* 2d ed. Minneapolis: Fortress Press, 1990.

———. *What Is Social-Scientific Criticism?* GBS. Minneapolis: Fortress Press, 1993.

Felder, Cain Hope, editor. *Stony the Road We Trod: African-American Biblical Interpretation.* Minneapolis: Fortress Press, 1991.

Fenton, John. *More About Mark.* London: SPCK, 2001.

Fetterly, Judy. *The Resisting Reader: A Feminist Approach to American Literature.* Bloomington: Indiana Univ. Press, 1978.

Fewell, Danna Nolan, and Gary Phillips. *Bible and Ethics of Reading.* Atlanta: Scholars, 1997.

Fish, Stanley. *Is There a Text in This Class? The Authority of Interpretive Communities.* Cambridge: Harvard University Press, 1980.

Fleddermann, Harry. "The Flight of the Naked Young Man (Mark 14:51-52)." *CBQ* 41 (1979) 41–48.

Fontaine, Carol. "The Use of the Traditional Saying in the Old Testament." Ph.D. dissertation, Duke University, 1979.

Forkman, Göran. *The Limits of the Religious Community: Expulsion from the Religious Community within the Qumran Sect, within Rabbinic Judaism, and within Primitive Christianity.* ConBNT 5. Lund: Gleerup, 1972.

Forster, E. M. *Aspects of the Novel.* Harmondsworth, 1962.

Fowl, Stephen E., and L. Gregory Jones. *Reading in Communion: Scripture and Ethics in the Christian Life.* Biblical Foundations in Theology. Grand Rapids: Eerdmans, 1991.

Fowler, Robert M. "The Feeding Stories in the Gospel of Mark." Ph.D. dissertation, University of Chicago, 1978.

———. *Let the Reader Understand: Reader-Response Criticism and the Gospel of Mark.* Minneapolis: Fortress Press, 1991.

———. *Loaves and Fishes: The Function of the Feeding Stories in the Gospel of Mark.* SBLDS 54. Chico, Calif.: Scholars, 1981.

———. "Reader-Response Criticism: Figuring Mark's Reader." In *Mark and Method: New Approaches in Biblical Studies,* edited by Janice Capel Anderson and Stephen Moore, 50–83. Minneapolis: Fortress Press, 1992.

France, R. T. *The Gospel according to Mark: A Commentary on the Greek Text.* NICNT. Grand Rapids: Eerdmans, 2002.

Freedman, William. "The Literary Motif: A Definition and Evaluation." *Novel* 4 (1971)123–31.

Frei, Hans. *The Eclipse of Biblical Narrative.* New Haven: Yale Univ. Press, 1974.

Freund, Elizabeth. *The Return of the Reader: Reader-Response Criticism.* New York: Methuen, 1987.

Friedman, Norman. "Forms of the Plot." In *The Theory of the Novel,* edited by Philip Stevick, 145–56. New York: Free Press, 1967.

———. "Point of View in Fiction: The Development of a Critical Concept." In *Approaches to the Novel,* edited by Robert Scholes, 113–42. San Francisco: Chandler, 1961.

Frye, Roland Muschat. "A Literary Perspective for the Criticism of the Gospels." In *Jesus and Man's Hope,* vol. 2, edited by Donald Miller, 193–221. Pittsburgh: Pittsburgh Theological Seminary, 1971.

———. "Literary Criticism and Gospel Criticism." *Theology Today* 36 (1979) 207–19.

Gadamer, Hans Georg. *Truth and Method.* Translated by J. Weinsheimer and D. Marshall. Rev. ed. New York: Crossroad, 1989.

Gager, John G. *Kingdom and Community: The Social World of Early Christianity.* Englewood Cliffs, N.J.: Prentice Hall, 1975.

Garrett, Susan R. *The Temptations of Jesus in Mark's Gospel.* Grand Rapids: Eerdmans, 1998.

Gaventa, Beverly Roberts. *From Darkness to Light: Aspects of Conversion in the New Testament.* OBT. Philadelphia: Fortress Press, 1986.

Geertz, Clifford. *The Interpretation of Cultures.* New York: Basic, 1973.

———. "Thick Description: Toward an Interpretative Theory of Culture." In idem, *The Interpretation of Cultures,* 3–30. New York: Basic, 1973.

Genette, Gerard. *Narrative Discourse.* Translated by J. F. Lewin. Ithaca: Cornell Univ. Press, 1980.

Gennep, Arnold van. *The Rites of Passage.* Translated by Monika B. Vizedom and Gabrielle L. Caffee. Chicago: Univ. of Chicago Press, 1960.

Geyer, Douglas W. *Fear, Anomaly, and Uncertainty in the Gospel of Mark.* Lanham, Md.: Scarecrow, 2002.

Gilmore, David D. "Anthropology of the Mediterranean Area." *Annual Review of Anthropology* 11 (1982) 175–205.

Gonzalez, Justo. *Out of Every Tribe and Nation: Christian Theology at the Ethnic Roundtable.* Nashville: Abingdon, 1992.

Goodman, Nelson. *Ways of Worldmaking.* Indianapolis: Hacket, 1978.

Gordon, Ernest. *Miracle on the River Kwai.* Wheaton, Ill.: Tyndale, 1962.

Gottwald, Norman K. "Framing Biblical Interpretation at New York Theological Seminary: A Student Self-Inventory on Biblical Hermeneutics." In *Reading from This Place,* vol. 1, edited by Fernando F. Segovia and Mary Ann Tolbert, 251–61. Minneapolis: Fortress Press, 1995.

Gowler, David. *Host, Guest, Enemy, and Friend: Portraits of Pharisees in Luke and Acts.* ESEC 2. New York: Lang, 1991.

Gunn, David M. "Narrative Criticism." In *To Each Its Own Meaning: An Introduction to Biblical Criticisms and Their Application,* edited by S. McKenzie and S. Hayes, 171–95. Louisville: Westminster John Knox, 1993.

Halliday, Michael. *Language as Social Semiotic: The Social Interpretation of Language and Meaning*. London: Edward Arnold, 1978.

Hanson, James S. *The Endangered Promises: Conflict in Mark*. SBLDS 171. Atlanta: Society of Biblical Literature, 2000.

Hanson, K. C., and Douglas E. Oakman. *Palestine in the Time of Jesus: Social Structures and Social Conflicts*. Minneapolis: Fortress Press, 1998.

Hare, Douglas. *Mark*. Westminster Bible Companion. Louisville: Westminster John Knox, 1996.

Harrington, Daniel J. "Second Testament Exegesis and the Social Sciences: A Bibliography." *BTB* 18 (1989) 77–85.

Harrington, Wilfrid J. *Mark: Realistic Theologian: The Jesus of Mark*. Dublin: Columba, 2002.

Harvey, W. J. *Character and the Novel*. Ithaca: Cornell Univ. Press, 1965.

Hatina, Thomas R. *In Search of a Context: The Function of Scripture in Mark's Narrative*. JSNTSup 232. Sheffield: Sheffield Academic, 2002.

Hayes, Richard B. *The Moral Vision of the New Testament: Community, Cross, New Creation. A Contemporary Introduction to Christian Ethics*. San Francisco: HarperSanFrancisco, 1996.

Hengel, Martin. *Studies in the Gospel of Mark*. Translated by John Bowden. Philadelphia: Fortress Press, 1985.

Hess, Karen. *Appreciating Literature, A Self-Teaching Guide*. New York: Wiley, 1978.

Hochman, Baruch. *Character in Literature*. Ithaca, N.Y.: Cornell Univ. Press, 1985.

Holman, C. Hugh. *A Handbook to Literature*. 3d ed. Indianapolis: Odyssey, 1972.

Holmberg, Bengt. *Sociology and the New Testament: An Appraisal*. Minneapolis: Fortress Press, 1990.

Hooker, Morna. *The Gospel according to Saint Mark*. Black's New Testament Commentaries. Peabody, Mass.: Hendrickson, 1993.

Horsley, Richard. *Hearing the Whole Story: The Politics of Plot in Mark's Story*. Louisville: Westminster John Knox, 2001.

———. *Jesus and the Spiral of Violence*. San Francisco: Harper and Row, 1987.

———. *Sociology and the Jesus Movement*. Philadelphia: Fortress Press, 1989.

———, and John S. Hanson. *Bandits, Prophets, and Messiahs: Popular Movements in the Time of Jesus*. Minneapolis: Winston, 1985.

Howe, Allan. "The Teaching Jesus Figure in the Gospel of Mark: A Redaction-Critical Study in Markan Christology." Ph.D. dissertation, Northwestern University, 1978.

Iersel, Bas M. F. van. *Mark: A Reader-Response Commentary*. Translated by W. H. Bisscheroux. JSNTSup 164. Sheffield: Sheffield Academic, 1998.

Isenberg, Sheldon. "Mary Douglas and Hellenistic Religions: The Case of Qumran." In *Society of Biblical Literature Seminar Papers*, 1: 179–85. Cambridge: Society of Biblical Literature, 1975.

Iser, Wolfgang. *The Act of Reading*. Baltimore: Johns Hopkins Univ. Press, 1978.

———. *The Implied Reader*. Baltimore: Johns Hopkins Univ. Press, 1974.

Jennings, Theodore W. *The Insurrection of the Crucified. The Gospel of Mark as Theological Manifesto*. Chicago: Exploration, 2003.

Jensen, Richard A. *Preaching Mark's Gospel*. Lima, Ohio: CSS, 1996.

Jobling, David, and Tina Pippin, editors. "Ideological Criticism of Biblical Texts." *Semeia* 59 (1992) 272–308.

Jones, Hans Robert. "Levels of Identification of Hero and Audience." *New Literary History* 5 (1974) 283–317.

Jones, W. T. "World Views: Their Nature and Their Function." *Current Anthropology* 13 (1972) 79–109.

Juel, Donald. *The Gospel of Mark*. Interpreting Biblical Texts. Nashville, Abingdon, 1999.

———. *A Master of Surprise: Mark Interpreted*. Minneapolis: Fortress Press, 1994.

———. *Messiah and Temple: The Trial of Jesus in the Gospel of Mark*. SBLDS 31. Missoula: Scholars, 1977.

Kaminouchi, Alberto de Mingo. *But It Is Not So Among You: Echoes of Power in Mark 10:32–45*. New York: Continuum, 2003.

Kearney, Michael. *World View*. Novato, Calif.: Chandler & Sharp, 1984.

Kee, Howard Clark. *Community of the New Age: Studies in Mark's Gospel*. Philadelphia: Westminster, 1977.

———. *Knowing the Truth: A Sociological Approach to the New Testament*. Minneapolis: Fortress Press, 1989.

Keenan, John P. *The Gospel of Mark: A Mahayana Reading*. Maryknoll, N.Y.: Orbis, 1995.

Kelber, Werner. *The Kingdom in Mark: A New Place and A New Time*. Philadelphia: Fortress Press, 1974.

———. "Mark and Orality." *Semeia* 16 (1979) 7–55.

———. *Mark's Story of Jesus*. Philadelphia: Fortress Press, 1979.

———, editor. *The Passion in Mark*. Philadelphia: Fortress Press, 1976.

Kennedy, George. *New Testament Interpretation through Rhetorical Criticism*. Chapel Hill: Univ. of North Carolina Press, 1984.

Kermode, Frank. *The Genesis of Secrecy: On the Interpretation of Narrative*. Cambridge: Harvard Univ. Press, 1979.

———. *The Sense of an Ending*. London: Oxford Univ. Press, 1966.

Kingsbury, Jack Dean. *The Christology of Mark's Gospel*. Philadelphia: Fortress Press, 1983.

———. *Conflict in Mark: Jesus, Authorities, Disciples*. Minneapolis: Fortress Press, 1989.

Kinukawa, Hisako. *Women and Jesus in Mark: A Japanese Feminist Perspective*. Bible and Liberation Series. Maryknoll, N.Y.: Orbis, 1994.

Kittel, Ron. "John the Baptist in the Gospel according to Mark." Ph.D. dissertation, Graduate Theological Union, Berkeley, 1977.

Kluckhohn, Florence Rockwood, and Fred L. Strodtbeck. *Variations in Value Orientation.* Evanston: Row, Peterson, 1961.

Koester, Craig. *Symbolism in the Fourth Gospel: Meaning, Mystery, Community.* 2d ed. Minneapolis: Fortress Press, 2003.

Kolenkow, Anitra. "Beyond Miracles, Suffering and Eschatology." In *SBL 1978 Seminar Papers,* edited by George W. MacRae, vol. 2, 155–202. Cambridge: Scholars, 1978.

Kort, Wesley A. *Narrative Elements and Religious Meanings.* Philadelphia: Fortress Press, 1975.

———. *Story, Text, and Scripture: Literary Interests in Biblical Narratives.* University Park: Pennsylvania State Univ. Press, 1988.

———. *'Take, Read": Scripture, Textuality, and Cultural Practice.* University Park: Pennsylvania State Univ. Press, 1996.

Krieger, Murray. *A Window to Criticism: Shakespeare's Sonnets and Modern Poetics.* Princeton: Princeton Univ. Press, 1964.

Lake, Kirsopp, translator. *The Apostolic Fathers,* vol. 1. Cambridge: Harvard Univ. Press, 1912.

Lattimore, Richard. *The Four Gospels and Revelation.* New York: Farrar, Straus, Giroux, 1979.

Lee, Charlotte, and Timothy Gura. *Oral Interpretation.* 8th ed. Boston: Houghton Mifflin, 1992.

Lee, David. *Luke's Stories of Jesus: Theological Reading of Gospel Narratives and the Legacy of Hans Frei.* Sheffield: Sheffield Academic, 1999.

Leitch, Vincent B. "A Primer of Recent Critical Theories." *College English* 39 (1977) 138–52.

Lemcio, Eugene. "Some New Proposals for Interpreting the Gospel of Mark." Ph.D. dissertation, University of Cambridge, 1974.

Lenski, Gerhard, et al. *Human Societies.* 6th ed. New York: McGraw-Hill, 1991.

Levine, Amy-Jill, editor. *A Feminist Companion to Mark.* Feminist Companion to the New Testament and Early Christian Writings 2. Sheffield: Sheffield Academic, 2001.

Levine, Baruch. *In the Presence of the Lord: A Study of Cult and Some Cultic Terms in Ancient Israel.* SJLA 5. Leiden: Brill, 1974.

Levison, John R., and Priscilla Pope Levison. *Return to Babel: Global Perspectives on the Bible.* Louisville: Westminster John Knox, 1999.

Liddell, Robert. *A Treatise on the Novel.* London: Cape, 1947.

Liew, Tat-Siong Benny. *The Politics of Parousia: Reading Mark Inter(con)textually.* BibIntSer 42. Leiden: Brill, 2000.

Lohse, Eduard. *Theological Ethics of the New Testament.* Translated by M. E. Boring. Minneapolis: Fortress Press, 1991.

Lotman, J. M. "Point of View in a Text." *New Literary History* 6 (1975) 339–52.

Lovering, Eugene H., and Jerry L. Sumney, editors. *Theology and Ethics in Paul and His Interpreters: Essays in Honor of Victor Paul Furnish.* Nashville: Abingdon, 1996.

MacDonald, Dennis R. *The Homeric Epics and the Gospel of Mark.* New Haven: Yale Univ. Press, 2000.

Mack, Burton L. *A Myth of Innocence: Mark and Christian Origins.* Philadelphia: Fortress Press, 1988.

——, and Vernon K. Robbins. *Patterns of Persuasion and the New Testament.* Sonoma, Calif.: Polebridge, 1989.

Maclean, Marie. *Narrative as Performance: The Baudelairean Experiment.* London: Routledge, 1988.

Mailloux, Stephen. "Reader Response Criticism." *Genre* 10 (1977) 413–31.

Malbon, Elizabeth. "Fallible Followers: Women and Men in Mark's Gospel." *Semeia* 23 (1983) 29–48.

——. *Hearing Mark: A Listener's Guide.* Harrisburg, Pa. : Trinity, 2002.

——. *In the Company of Jesus: Characters in Mark's Gospel.* Louisville: Westminster John Knox, 2000.

——. *Narrative Space and Mythic Meaning in Mark.* San Francisco: Harper & Row, 1986.

——, and Adele Berlin, editors. *Characterization in Biblical Literature. Semeia* 63 (1993).

Malherbe, Abraham J. *Social Aspects of Early Christianity.* 2d ed. Philadelphia: Fortress Press, 1983.

Malina, Bruce J. *Christian Origins and Cultural Anthropology: Practical Models for Biblical Interpretation.* Atlanta: John Knox, 1986.

——. *The New Testament World: Insights from Cultural Anthropology.* 3d edition. Atlanta: John Knox, 2001.

——. "Patron and Client: The Analogy behind Synoptic Theology." *Forum* 4 (1988) 2–32.

——. "Reading Theory Perspective." In *The Social World of Luke-Acts: Models for Interpretation,* edited by Jerome H. Neyrey, 3–23. Peabody, Mass.: Hendrickson, 1991.

——. "The Received View and What It Can Do: III John and Hospitality." *Semeia* 35 (1986) 171–94.

——. "The Social Sciences and Biblical Interpretation." *Int* 37 (1982) 229–42.

——, and Jerome H. Neyrey. *Calling Jesus Names: The Social Value of Labels in Matthew.* Sonoma, Calif.: Polebridge, 1988.

——, and Richard L. Rohrbaugh. *Social-Science Commentary on the Gospel of John.* Minneapolis: Fortress, 1998.

——, and Richard L. Rohrbaugh. *Social-Science Commentary on the Synoptic Gospels.* 2d edition. Minneapolis: Fortress Press, 2003.

Maloney, Elliott. *Jesus' Urgent Message for Today: The Kingdom of God in Mark's Gospel.* New York: Continuum, 2004.

Marcus, Joel. "The Jewish War and the *Sitz im Leben* of Mark." *JBL* 111(1992) 441–62.

——. *Mark 1–7.* AB 27A. New York: Doubleday, 2000.

——. *The Mystery of the Kingdom of God.* SBLDS 90. Atlanta: Scholars, 1986.

——. *The Way of the Lord: Christological Exegesis of the Old Testament in the Gospel of Mark.* Louisville: Westminster John Knox, 1992.

Marshall, Christopher. *Faith as a Theme in Mark's Narrative.* SNTSMS 64. New York: Cambridge Univ. Press, 1989.

Martin, Clarice. "The Myth of New Testament Introductory Texts as 'Ideologically Neutral'—and Other Myths." Unpublished paper, 1994.

Martin, Wallace. *Recent Theories of Narrative.* Ithaca, N.Y.: Cornell Univ. Press, 1986.

Marxsen, Willi. *New Testament Foundations for Christian Ethics.* Translated by O. C. Dean Jr. Minneapolis: Fortress Press, 1993.

Matera, Frank J. *New Testament Ethics: The Legacies of Jesus and Paul.* Louisville: Westminster John Knox, 1996.

McGowen, Alec. *Personal Mark: An Actor's Proclamation of St. Mark's Gospel.* New York: Crossroad, 1985.

McKnight, Edgar V. *Post-Modern Use of the Bible and the Emergence of Reader-Oriented Criticism.* Nashville: Abingdon, 1988.

——, editor. "Reader Perspectives on the New Testament." *Semeia* 48 (1989).

McVann, Mark. "The Passion in Mark: Transformation Ritual." *BTB* 18 (1988) 96–101.

Meagher, John C. "Die Form- und Redaktionsgeschichtliche Methoden: The Principle of Clumsiness and the Gospel of Mark." *JAAR* 43 (1975) 459–72.

Meeks, Wayne A. "The Man from Heaven in Johannine Sectarianism." *JBL* 91(1972) 44–72.

——. *The First Urban Christians: The Social World of the Apostle Paul.* New Haven: Yale Univ. Press, 1983.

——. *The Moral World of the First Christians.* Library of Early Christianity. Philadelphia: Westminster, 1986.

Mendilow, A. A. *Time and the Novel.* New York: Nevill, 1952.

Merenlahti, Petri. *Poetics for the Gospels? Rethinking Narrative Criticism.* London: T. and T. Clark, 2002.

——, and Raimo Hakola. "Reconceiving Narrative Criticism." In *Characterization in the Gospels: Reconceiving Narrative Criticism,* edited by David Rhoads and Kari Syreeni, 13–48. JSNTSup 184. Sheffield: Sheffield Academic, 1999.

Michie, Donald, and David Rhoads. "Study Guide on the Gospel of Mark as Literature." Unpublished booklet, 1978.

Milgrom, Jacob. "Israel's Sanctuary: The Priestly Picture of Dorian Grey." *RB* 93 (1976) 370–99.

———. "Purity and Impurity." In *Encyclopedia Judaica,* 13:1405–14. Jerusalem: Keter, 1972.

Miller, J. Hillis. *The Ethics of Reading: Kant, de Man, Eliot, Trollope, James, and Benjamin.* New York: Columbia Univ. Press, 1987.

———. "The Triumph of Theory, the Resistance to Reading, and the Question of the Material Base." *PMLA* 102 (1987) 281–91.

Mills, Watson E. *The Gospel of Mark.* Bibliographies for Biblical Research. Lewiston, New York: Mellen Biblical Press, 2002.

Minor, Mitzi. *The Power of Mark's Story.* St. Louis: Chalice, 2001.

———. *The Spirituality of Mark: Responding to God.* Louisville: Westminster John Knox, 1996.

Mitchell, Joan L. *Beyond Fear and Silence: A Feminist-Literary Approach to the Gospel of Mark.* New York: Continuum, 2001.

Mitchell, Margaret M. *Paul and the Rhetoric of Reconciliation: An Exegetical Investigation of the Language and Composition of I Corinthians.* HUT 28. Tübingen: Mohr/Siebeck, 1991.

Moeser, Marion C. *The Anecdote in Mark, the Classical World and the Rabbis.* JSNTSup 227. Sheffield: Sheffield Academic, 2002.

Moloney, Francis J. *The Gospel of Mark: A Commentary.* Peabody, Mass.: Hendrickson, 2002.

———. *Mark: Storyteller, Interpreter, Evangelist.* Peabody, Mass.: Hendrickson, 2004.

Moore, R. "The Gospel and Narrative Performance: The Critical Assessment of Meaning as Correspondence in D. F. Straus and R. Bultmann." Ph.D. dissertation, Rice University, 1992.

Moore, Stephen D. "Are the Gospels Unified Narratives?" In *Society of Biblical Literature 1987 Seminar Papers,* edited by Kent H. Richards, 443–58. Atlanta: Scholars, 1987.

———. *Literary Criticism and the Gospels: The Theoretical Challenge.* New Haven: Yale Univ. Press, 1989.

———. *Mark and Luke in Poststructuralist Perspectives: Jesus Begins to Write.* New Haven: Yale Univ. Press, 1992.

———. *Poststructuralism and the New Testament: Derrida and Foucault at the Foot of the Cross.* Minneapolis: Fortress Press, 1994.

———. *The Postmodern Bible: The Bible and Culture Collective.* New Haven: Yale Univ. Press, 1995.

———, and Janice Capel Anderson, editors. *New Testament Masculinities.* Semeia Studies 45. Atlanta: Society of Biblical Literature, 2003.

Mouton, Elna. *Reading a New Testament Document Ethically.* Academic Biblica 1. Leiden: Brill, 2002.

Moxnes, Halvor. *The Economy of the Kingdom: Social Conflict and Economic Relations in Luke's Gospel.* OBT. Philadelphia: Fortress Press, 1988.

———. *Putting Jesus in His Place: A Radical Vision of Household and Kingdom.* Louisville: Westminster John Knox, 2003.

Muecke, D. C. *The Compass of Irony.* London: Methuen, 1969.

———. *Irony.* The Critical Idiom 13. London: Methuen, 1970.

Mulholland, Robert. "The Markan Opponents of Jesus." Ph.D. dissertation, Harvard University, 1977.

Myers, Ched. *Binding the Strong Man: A Political Reading of Mark's Story of Jesus.* Maryknoll, N.Y.: Orbis, 1988.

———. *"Say to This Mountain": Mark's Story of Discipleship.* Maryknoll, N.Y.: Orbis, 1996.

———. *Who Will Roll Away the Stone? Discipleship Queries for First World Christians.* Maryknoll, N.Y.: Orbis, 1994.

Myers, Eric M., and James F. Strange. *Archaeology, the Rabbis, and Early Christianity.* Nashville: Abingdon, 1981.

Neufeld, Dietmar. *Reconceiving Texts as Speech Acts: An Analysis of 1 John.* BibIntSer 7. Leiden: Brill, 1994.

Neusner, Jacob. *The Idea of Purity in Ancient Israel.* SJLA 1. Leiden: Brill, 1973.

Newton, Michael. *The Concept of Purity at Qumran and in the Letters of Paul.* SNTSMS 53. Cambridge: Cambridge Univ. Press, 1985.

Neyrey, Jerome H. "The Idea of Purity in Mark's Gospel." *Semeia* 35 (1986) 91–128.

———. *Paul, in Other Words: A Cultural Reading in His Letters.* Louisville: Westminster John Knox, 1990.

———, editor. *The Social World of Luke-Acts: Models for Interpretation.* Peabody, Mass. : Hendrickson, c1991.

———. "A Symbolic Approach to Mark 7." *Forum* 4.3 (1988) 63–91.

———. "Unclean, Common, Polluted, and Taboo: A Short Reading Guide." *Forum* 4.4 (1988) 72–82.

Nickelsburg, George W. E. "The Genre and Function of the Markan Passion Narrative." *HTR* 73 (1980) 153–84.

Nierynck, Frans. *Duality in Mark: Contributions to the Study of the Markan Redaction.* BETL 31. Leuven: Leuven Univ. Press, 1972.

Noble, David. "An Examination of the Structure of Mark's Gospel." Ph.D. dissertation, University of Edinburgh, 1972.

Oakman, Douglas E. "The Countryside in Luke-Acts." In *The Social World of Luke-Acts: Models for Interpretation,* edited by Jerome H. Neyrey, 151–79. Peabody, Mass.: Hendrickson, 1991.

Ong, Walter. *Orality and Literacy: The Technologizing of the Word.* New York: Methuen, 1982.

———. *The Presence of the Word: Some Prolegomena for Cultural and Religious History.* Minneapolis: Univ. of Minnesota Press, 1967.

Osiek, Carolyn. "The New Handmaid: The Bible and the Social Sciences." *TS* 50 (1989) 26–78.

———. *What Are They Saying about the Social Setting of the New Testament?* New York: Paulist, 1984.

Ossom-Batsa, George. *The Institution of the Eucharist in the Gospel of Mark: A Study of the Function of Mark 14:22-25 within the Gospel Narrative.* European University Studies, Theology 727. New York: Peter Lang, 2001.

Painter, John. *Mark's Gospel: Worlds in Conflict.* New York: Routledge, 1997.

Parsons, Talcott. *Politics and Social Structure.* New York: Free Press, 1969.

Paton, John, and Vernon K. Robbins. "Rhetorical and Biblical Criticism." Private paper, 1980.

Patte, Daniel. *Discipleship according to the Sermon on the Mount: Four Legitimate Readings, Four Plausible Views of Discipleship and their Relevant Values.* Valley Forge, Pa.: Trinity, 1996.

———. *Ethics of Biblical Interpretation: A Reevaluation.* Louisville: Westminster John Knox, 1995.

———, editor. *The Global Bible Commentary.* Nashville: Abingdon, 2004.

———, and Aline Patte. *Structural Exegesis: From Theory to Practice.* Philadelphia: Fortress Press, 1978.

Patten, Priscilla. "Parable and Secret in the Gospel of Mark in Light of Select Apocryphal Literature." Ph.D. dissertation, Drew University, 1976.

Patten, Rebecca. "The Thaumaturgical Element in the Gospel of Mark." Ph.D. dissertation, Drew University, 1976.

Pelias, Ronald. *Performance Studies: The Interpretation of Aesthetic Texts.* New York: St. Martin's, 1992.

Perrin, Norman. "The Evangelist as Author: Reflections on Method in the Study and Interpretation of the Synoptic Gospels and Acts." *Biblical Research* 15 (1972) 5–18. Reprinted in idem, *Parable and Gospel,* edited by K. C. Hanson, 51–63. FCBS. Minneapolis: Fortress Press, 2003.

Perrine, Laurence. *Story and Structure.* New York: Harcourt, 1966.

Petersen, John. *Reading Women's Stories: Female Characters in the Hebrew Bible.* Minneapolis: Fortress Press, 2003.

Petersen, Norman R. "The Composition of Mark 4:1–8:26." *HTR* 73 (1980) 194–217.

———. *Literary Criticism for New Testament Critics.* GBS. Philadelphia: Fortress Press, 1978.

———. "Literary Criticism in Biblical Studies." In *Orientation by Disorientation: Studies in Literary Criticism and Biblical Literary Criticism, Presented in Honor of William A. Beardslee,* edited by Richard A. Spencer, 3–24. PTMS 35. Pittsburgh: Pickwick, 1980.

———. "Point of View in Mark's Narrative." *Semeia* 12 (1978) 97–121.

——. *Rediscovering Paul: Philemon and the Sociology of Paul's Narrative World.* Philadelphia: Fortress Press, 1985.

——. "When Is an End not the End?" *Int* 34 (1980) 151–66.

Peterson, Dwight N. *The Origins of Mark: The Markan Community in Current Debate.* BibIntSer 48. Leiden: Brill, 2000.

Petrey, Sandy. *Speech Acts and Literary Theory.* New York: Routledge, 1990.

Phillips, Gary A. "The Ethics of Reading Deconstructively." In *The New Literary Criticism and the New Testament,* edited by Edgar V. McKnight and Elizabeth Struthers Malbon, 283–325. Valley Forge, Pa.: Trinity, 1994.

Phillips, Gary, and Nicole Wilkinson Duran, editors. *Reading Communities Reading Scripture: Essays in Honor of Daniel Patte.* Harrisburg: Trinity, 2002.

Pilch, John J. "Biblical Leprosy and Body Symbolism." *BTB* 11 (1981) 102–6.

——. "Community Formation in the New Testament." *New Catholic World* 226 (1983) 63–65.

——. "Healing in Mark: A Social Science Analysis." *BTB* 15 (1985) 142–50.

——. *Healing in the New Testament: Insights from Medical and Mediterranean Anthropology.* Minneapolis: Fortress Press, 2000.

——. "Sickness and Healing in Luke-Acts." In *The Social World of Luke-Acts: Models for Interpretation,* edited by Jerome H. Neyrey, 181–209. Peabody, Mass.: Hendrickson, 1991.

Pitt-Rivers, Julian. *The Fate of Shechem or the Politics of Sex: Essays on the Anthropology of the Mediterranean.* Cambridge Studies in Social Anthropology 19. Cambridge: Cambridge Univ. Press, 1977.

Placher, William. *Narratives of a Vulnerable God: Christ, Theology, and Scripture.* Louisville: Westminster John Knox, 1994.

Porter, Stanley E. "Literary Approaches to the New Testament: From Formalism to Deconstruction and Back." In *Approaches to New Testament Study,* edited by Stanley E. Porter and David Tombs, 77–128. JSNTSup 120. Sheffield: Sheffield Academic, 1995.

Powell, Mark Allan. *Chasing the Eastern Star: Adventures in Biblical Reader-Response Criticism.* Louisville: Westminster John Knox, 2001.

——. *What Is Narrative Criticism?* GBS. Minneapolis: Fortress Press, 1990.

Price, Reynolds. *A Palpable God: Thirty Stories Translated from the Bible, with an Essay on the Origins and Life of Narrative.* New York: Atheneum, 1978.

Prince, Gerald. "Notes towards a Categorization of Fictional 'Narratees.'" *Genre* 4 (1971) 100–105.

Pryke, E. J. *Redactional Style in the Marcan Narrative: A Study of Syntax and Vocabulary as Guides to Redaction in Mark.* SNTSMS 33. Cambridge: Cambridge Univ. Press, 1978.

Rabkin, Eric S. *Narrative Suspense.* Ann Arbor: Univ. of Michigan Press, 1973.

Raynor, Steve. "The Perception of Time and Space in Egalitarian Sects: A Millenarian Cosmology." In *Essays in the Sociology of Perception,* edited by Mary Douglas, 247–74. London: Routledge and Kegan Paul, 1986.

Reid, Barbara E. *Choosing the Better Part? Women in the Gospel of Luke.* Collegeville, Minn.: Liturgical, 1996.

Reid, Robert Stephen. *Preaching Mark.* St. Louis: Chalice, 1999.

Reid, Stephen Breck. "The Role of Reading in Multicultural Exegesis." In *Text and Experience: Towards a Cultural Exegesis of the Bible,* edited by Daniel Smith-Christopher, 210–24. BibSem 35. Sheffield: Sheffield Academic, 1995.

Reinhartz, Adele. *The Word in the World: The Cosmological Tale of the Fourth Gospel.* SBLMS 45. Atlanta: Scholars, 1992.

Reiser, William. *Jesus in Solidarity with His People: A Theologian Looks at Mark.* Collegeville, Minn.: Liturgical, 2000.

Remus, Harold. "Sociology of Knowledge and the Study of Early Christianity." *Studies in Religion* 11 (1982) 45–56.

Rhoads, David. "Boundaries: The Dead Sea Sect and the Jesus Movement in the Gospel of Mark." Unpublished paper.

———. *The Challenge of Diversity: The Witness of Paul and the Gospels.* Minneapolis: Fortress Press, 1996.

———. *Israel in Revolution 6–74 C.E.: A Political History Based on the Writings of Josephus.* Philadelphia: Fortress Press, 1976.

———. "Losing Life for Others in the Face of Death: Mark's Standards of Judgment." *Int* 47 (1993) 358–69.

———. "Mission in the Gospel of Mark." *CurTM* 22 (1995) 340–55.

———. "Narrative Criticism and the Gospel of Mark." *JAAR* 50 (1982) 411–34.

———. "Performing the Gospel of Mark." In *Body and Bible,* edited by B. Krondorfer, 102–19. Philadelphia: Trinity, 1992.

———. "Social Criticism: Crossing Boundaries." In *Mark and Method: New Approaches in Biblical Studies,* edited by Janice Capel Anderson and Stephen D. Moore, 135–61. Minneapolis: Fortress Press, 1992.

———. "The Social System of the Jesus Movement as Depicted in the Narrative of the Gospel of Mark." In *ANRW* 26.2: 1692–729.

———. "The Syrophoenician Woman in Mark: A Narrative-Critical Study." *JAAR* 62 (1992) 342–75.

———, and Donald Michie. *Mark as Story: An Introduction to the Narrative of a Gospel.* 1st ed. Philadelphia: Fortress Press, 1982.

———, Joanna Dewey, and Donald Michie. *Mark as Story: An Introduction to the Narrative of a Gospel.* Rev. ed. Minneapolis: Fortress Press, 1999.

———, and Kari Syreeni, editors. *Characterization in the Gospels: Reconceiving Narrative Criticism.* JSNTSup 184. Sheffield: Sheffield Academic, 1999.

Riches, John. *Conflicting Mythologies: Identity Formation in the Gospels of Mark and Matthew.* SNTIW. Edinburgh: T. and T. Clark, 2000.

Rimmon-Kenan, Shlomith. *Narrative Fiction: Contemporary Poetics.* New York: Methuen, 1983.

Ringe, Sharon. "A Gentile Woman's Story." In *Feminist Interpretation of the Bible,* edited by Letty M. Russell, 65–72. Philadelphia: Westminster, 1985.

Robbins, Vernon. K. *Exploring the Texture of Texts: A Guide to Socio-Rhetorical Interpretation.* Valley Forge, Pa.: Trinity, 1996.

———. *Jesus the Teacher: A Socio-Rhetorical Interpretation of Mark.* Minneapolis: Fortress Press, 1992 [1984].

———. "The Social Location of the Implied Author in Luke-Acts." In *The Social World of Luke-Acts: Models for Interpretation,* edited by Jerome H. Neyrey, 305–32. Peabody, Mass.: Hendrickson, 1991.

———. "Summons and Outline in Mark: The Three-Step Progression." *NovT* 23 (1981) 97–114.

Robinson, James M. *The Problem of History in Mark.* SBT 1/21. London: SCM, 1957.

Rogers, Everett M. *Diffusion of Innovations.* 5th ed. New York: Free Press, 2003.

Rohrbaugh, Richard L. "Models and Muddles: Discussion of the Social Facets Seminar." *Forum* 3.2 (1987) 23–33.

———. "The Pre-industrial City in Luke-Acts." In *The Social World of Luke-Acts: Models for Interpretation,* edited by Jerome H. Neyrey, 125–49. Peabody, Mass.: Hendrickson, 1991.

———. "The Social Location of the Markan Audience." *Int* 47 (1993) 380–95.

———. "'Social Location of Thought' as a Heuristic Construct in New Testament Study." *JSNT* 30 (1987) 103–19.

———, editor. *The Social Sciences and New Testament Interpretation.* Peabody, Mass.: Hendrickson, 1996.

Rosner, Brian S., editor. *Understanding Paul's Ethics: Twentieth-Century Approaches.* Grand Rapids: Eerdmans, 1995.

Rowe, Robert D. *God's Kingdom and God's Son: The Background to Mark's Christology from the Concepts of Kingship in the Psalms.* Leiden; Boston: Brill, 2002.

Sabin, Marie Noonan. *Reopening the Word: Reading Mark as Theology in the Context of Early Judaism.* Oxford: Oxford Univ. Press, 2002.

Schierling, Marla. "Woman, Cult, and Miracle Recital: Mark 5:24-34." Ph.D. dissertation, St. Louis University, 1980.

Schildgen, Brenda Deen. *Power and Prejudice: The Reception of the Gospel of Mark.* Detroit: Wayne State Univ. Press, 1999.

Scholes, Robert. "Cognition and the Implied Reader." *Diacritics* 5 (1975) 13–15.

———, and Robert Kellogg. *The Nature of Narrative.* New York: Oxford Univ. Press, 1966.

Schottroff, Luise, Silvia Schroer, and Marie-Terese Wacker. *Feminist Interpretation: The Bible in Women's Perspective.* Translated by Martin Rumscheidt and Barbara Rumscheidt. Minneapolis: Fortress Press, 1998.

Schroer, Silvia, and Sophia Bietenhard, editors. *Feminist Interpretation of the Bible and the Hermeneutics of Liberation.* New York: Continuum, 2003.

Schüssler Fiorenza, Elisabeth. *Bread Not Stone: The Challenge of Feminist Biblical Interpretation.* Boston: Beacon, 1984.

———. "The Ethics of Interpretation: De-Centering Biblical Theology." *JBL* 107 (1988) 3–17.

———. *In Memory of Her: A Feminist Theological Reconstruction of Christian Origins.* New York: Crossroad, 1983.

———. *Rhetoric and Ethics: The Politics of Biblical Studies.* Minneapolis: Fortress Press, 1999.

———, editor. *Searching the Scriptures.* 2 vols. New York: Crossroad, 1993.

Schweizer, Eduard. "The Portrayal of the Life of Faith in the Gospel of Mark." *Int* 32 (1978) 387–99.

Scott, Bernard Brandon, and M. Dean. "A Sound Map of the Sermon on the Mount." In *Seminar Papers of the Society of Biblical Literature, 1993,* 672–725. Atlanta: Scholars, 1993.

Scroggs, Robin. "The Earliest Christian Communities as Sectarian Movement." In *Christianity, Judaism, and Other Greco-Roman Cults: Studies for Morton Smith at Sixty,* edited by Jacob Neusner; part 2, *Early Christianity,* 1–23. Leiden: Brill, 1975.

———. "The Sociological Interpretation of the New Testament: The Present State of Research." *NTS* 26 (1979–80) 164–179;

———. *The Text and the Times: New Testament Essays for Today.* Minneapolis: Fortress Press, 1993.

Seeley, David. *Deconstructing the New Testament.* BibIntSer 5. Leiden: Brill, 1994.

Segovia, Fernando F. *Decolonizing Biblical Studies: A View From the Margins.* Maryknoll, N.Y.: Orbis, 2000.

———. "Intercultural Criticism." In *Searching the Scriptures,* vol. 1: *A Feminist Introduction,* edited by Elisabeth Schüssler Fiorenza, 304–5. New York: Crossroad, 1995.

———. "The Text as Other: Towards an Hispanic American Hermeneutic" In *Text and Experience: Towards a Cultural Exegesis of the Bible* edited by Daniel Smith-Christopher, 276–98. BibSem 35. Sheffield: Sheffield Academic, 1995.

———. "Toward Intercultural Criticism: A Reading Strategy from the Diaspora." In *Reading from this Place,* Vol. 2, 302–30. Minneapolis: Fortress Press, 1995.

———, editor. *What Is John? Readers and Readings of the Fourth Gospel.* SBLSS 3. Atlanta: Scholars, 1996.

———, and Mary Ann Tolbert, editors. *Reading from This Place.* Vol. 1: *Social Location and Biblical Interpretation in the United States.* Minneapolis: Fortress Press, 1995.

——, and Mary Ann Tolbert, editors. *Reading From This Place.* Vol. 2. *Social Location and Biblical Interpretation in Global Perspective.* Minneapolis: Fortress Press, 1995.

Seim, Turid Karlsen. *The Double Message: Patterns of Gender in Luke-Acts.* Nashville: Abingdon, 1994.

Senior, Donald. *The Passion of Jesus in the Gospel of Mark.* Passion Series 2. Wilmington, Del.: Glazier, 1984.

Shiner, Whitney Taylor. *Follow Me! Disciples in Markan Rhetoric.* SBLDS 145. Atlanta: Scholars, 1995.

——. *Proclaiming the Gospel: First-Century Performance of Mark.* Harrisburg, Pa.: Trinity, 2003.

Smit, D. J. "The Ethics of Interpretation: New Voices from the USA." *Scriptura* 33 (1990) 16–28.

Smith, Barbara Hernstein. *Poetic Closure.* Chicago: Univ. of Chicago Press, 1968.

Smith, Jonathan Z. "Animals and Plants." In *Encyclopedia Britannica* 15th ed. 1:911–18.

——. "The Influence of Symbols upon Social Change: A Place on Which to Stand." *Worship* 44 (1970) 457–74.

——. "The Social Description of Early Christianity." *Religious Studies Review* 19 (1975) 19–25.

——. "The Wobbling Pivot." *JR* 52 (1972) 34–49.

Smith, Stephen. *A Lion with Wings: A Narrative-Critical Approach to Mark's Gospel.* BibSem 38. Sheffield: Sheffield Academic, 1996.

Smith-Christopher, Daniel. *Text and Experience: Towards a Cultural Exegesis of the Bible.* BibSem 35. Sheffield: Sheffield Academic, 1995.

Snow, D., L. Zurcher, and S. E. Olson. "Social Networks and Social Movements: A Micro-structural Approach to Differential Recruitment." *American Sociological Review* 45 (1980) 787–801.

Staley, Jeffrey Lloyd. *The Print's First Kiss: A Rhetorical Investigation of the Implied Reader in the Fourth Gospel.* SBLDS 82. Atlanta: Scholars, 1988.

Stambaugh, John E., and David L. Balch. *The New Testament in Its Social Environment.* Library of Early Christianity 2. Philadelphia: Westminster, 1986.

Stamps, Dennis L. "Rhetorical Criticism of the New Testament: Ancient and Modern Evaluations of Argumentation." In *Approaches to New Testament Study,* edited by Stanley E. Porter and David Tombs, 129–69. JSNTSup 120. Sheffield: Sheffield Academic, 1995.

Starobinski, Jean. "The Struggle with Legion: A Literary Analysis of Mark 5:1-20." Translated by Dan Via. *New Literary History* 4 (1973) 331–56.

Stegemann, Ekkehard, and Wolfgang Stegemann. *The Jesus Movement: A Social History of Its First Century.* Translated by O. C. Dean Jr. Minneapolis: Fortress Press, 1999.

Stegemann, Wolfgang, Bruce J. Malina, and Gerd Theissen, editors. *The Social Setting of Jesus and the Gospels*. Minneapolis: Fortress Press, 2002.

Steiner, George. "'Critic'/'Reader'." *New Literary History* 10 (1979) 23–52.

Sternberg, Meir. *The Poetics of Biblical Narrative: Ideological Literature and the Drama of Reading*. ILBS. Bloomington: Indiana Univ. Press, 1985.

Stibbe, Mark W. G. *John as Storyteller: Narrative Criticism and the Fourth Gospel*. SNTSMS 73. Cambridge: Cambridge Univ. Press, 1992.

Stock, Augustine. *The Method and Message of Mark*. Wilmington, Del.: Glazier, 1989.

Sugirtharajah, R. S., editor. *The Postcolonial Bible*. The Bible and Postcolonialism 1. Sheffield: Sheffield Academic, 1998.

———. *Postcolonial Criticism and Biblical Interpretation*. Oxford: Oxford University Press, 2002.

———, editor. *Voices from the Margin: Interpreting the Bible in the Third World*. Rev. ed. Maryknoll, N.Y.: Orbis, 1995.

Suleiman, Susan R., and Inge Crosman, editors. *The Reader in the Text: Essays on Audience and Interpretation*. Princeton: Princeton Univ. Press, 1980.

Swartley, Willard. "A Study of Markan Structure: The Influence of Holy History upon the Structure of the Gospel of Mark." Ph.D. dissertation, Princeton Theological Seminary, 1973.

Sweetland, Dennis. *Mark: From Death to Life*. Spiritual Commentaries. Hyde Park, N.Y.: New City, 2000.

Tannehill, Robert C. "The Disciples in Mark: The Function of a Narrative Role." *JR* 57 (1977) 386–405.

———. "The Gospel of Mark as Narrative Christology." *Semeia* 16 (1979) 57–95.

———. *Mirror for the Disciples: Following Jesus through Mark*. Nashville: Discipleship Resources, 1977.

———. "Should We Love Simon the Pharisee: Hermeneutical Reflections on the Pharisees in Luke." *CurTM* 21 (1994) 424–33.

Telford, William R. "The Barren Temple and the Withered Fig Tree." Ph.D. dissertation, University of Cambridge, 1976.

———. *The Theology of the Gospel of Mark*. New Testament Theology. Cambridge: Cambridge Univ. Press, 1999.

Theissen, Gerd. *The Gospels in Context: Social and Political History in the Synoptic Tradition*. Translated by Linda M. Maloney. Minneapolis: Fortress, 1991.

———. *The Sociology of Early Palestinian Christianity*. Philadelphia: Fortress Press, 1978.

Thiselton, Anthony C. *New Horizons in Hermeneutics*. Grand Rapids: Zondervan, 1992.

Thurston, Bonnie. *Preaching Mark*. Minneapolis: Fortress Press, 2001.

Tidball, Derek. *An Introduction to the Sociology of the New Testament.* Exeter: Pater Noster, 1983.

Tolbert, Mary Ann. *Perspectives on the Parables: An Approach to Multiple Interpretations.* Philadelphia: Fortress Press, 1979.

——. "The Politics and Poetics of Location." In *Reading from This Place,* vol. 2, 305–17. Minneapolis: Fortress Press, 1995.

——. "Response to Robert Tannehill." SBL Seminar Paper, 1978.

——. *Sowing the Gospel: Mark's World in Literary Historical Perspective.* Philadelphia: Fortress Press, 1989.

——. "When Resistance Becomes Repression: Mark 13:9-27 and the Poetics of Location." In *Reading from this Place,* vol. 2, 331–46. Minneapolis: Fortress Press, 1995.

Tompkins Jane P., editor. *Reader-Response Criticism: From Formalism to Post-Structuralism.* Baltimore: Johns Hopkins Univ. Press, 1980.

Tracy, David. *Dialogue with the Other: The Inter-Religious Dialogue.* Grand Rapids: Eerdmans, 1990.

Trainor, Mark F. *The Quest for Home: The Household in Mark's Community.* Collegeville, Minn.: Liturgical, 2001.

Trakatellis, Demetrios. *Authority and Passion: Christological Aspects of the Gospel according to Mark.* Translated by George Duvall and Harry Vulopas. Brookline: Holy Cross Orthodox, 1987.

Turner, Victor Witter. "Betwixt and Between." In idem, *The Forest of Symbols: Aspects of Ndembu Ritual,* 93–111. Ithaca, N.Y.: Cornell Univ. Press, 1967.

——. *The Forest of Symbols: Aspects of Ndembu Ritual.* Ithaca, N.Y.: Cornell Univ. Press, 1967.

——. *The Ritual Process: Structure and Anti-Structure.* Ithaca, N.Y.: Cornell Univ. Press, 1969.

Upkong, Justin, et al. *Reading the Bible in the Global Village: Capetown.* Atlanta: Society of Biblical Literature, 2002.

Uspensky, Boris. *Poetics of Composition: The Structure of the Artistic Text and Typology of a Compositional Form.* Translated by V. Zavarin and S. Wittig. Berkeley: Univ. of California Press, 1973.

Vermes, Geza. *Jesus the Jew: A Historian's Reading of the Gospels.* Minneapolis: Fortress Press, 1981.

Via, Dan O. *The Ethics of Mark's Gospel: In the Middle of Time.* Philadelphia: Fortress Press, 1985.

——. *Kerygma and Comedy in the New Testament.* Philadelphia: Fortress Press, 1975.

Vines, Michael E. *The Problem of Markan Genre: The Gospel of Mark and the Jewish Novel.* Atlanta: Scholars, 2002.

Waetjen, Herman. *A Reordering of Power: A Socio-Political Reading of Mark's Gospel*. Philadelphia: Fortress Press, 1989.

Wainwright, Elaine Mary. *Towards a Feminist Critical Reading of the Gospel according to Matthew*. BZNW 60. Berlin: de Gruyter, 1991.

Weeden, Theodore J. *Mark: Traditions in Conflict*. Philadelphia: Fortress Press, 1971.

Weimann, Robert. "Narrative Perspective: Point of View Reconsidered." In idem, *Structure and Society in Literary History*, 234–66. Charlottesville: Univ. Press of Virginia, 1976.

Wetherill, Peter M. *The Literary Text: An Examination of Critical Methods*. Berkeley: Univ. of California Press, 1974.

Wicker, Kathleen O'Brien. "Teaching Feminist Biblical Studies in a Postcolonial Context." In *Searching the Scriptures*, vol. 1: *A Feminist Introduction*, edited by Elisabeth Schüssler Fiorenza, 367–80. New York: Crossroad, 1995.

Wilde, James. "The Social World of Mark's Gospel: A Word about Method." In *Society of Biblical Literature Seminar Papers 1972*, 47–67. Missoula, Mont.: Scholars, 1972.

Wilder, Amos. *Early Christian Rhetoric*. Cambridge: Harvard Univ. Press, 1971.

Williams, Joel. *Other Followers of Jesus: Minor Characters as Major Figures in Mark's Gospel*. JSNTSup 102. Sheffield: JSOT Press, 1994.

Wimbush, Vincent L., editor. *African Americans and the Bible: Sacred Texts and Social Structures*. New York: Continuum, 2000.

Wire, Antoinette Clark. "Gender Roles in a Scribal Community." In *Social History of the Matthean Community: Cross-Disciplinary Approaches*, edited by David L. Balch, 87–121. Minneapolis: Fortress Press, 1992.

———. "Review of *A Home for the Homeless* and *Let Wives Be Submissive*." *Religion Studies Review* 10 (1984) 209–16.

Witherington, Ben. *The Gospel of Mark: A Socio-Rhetorical Commentary*. Grand Rapids: Eerdmans, 2001.

Wolf, Miroslav. *Exclusion and Embrace: A Theological Exploration of Identity, Otherness, and Reconciliation*. Nashville: Abingdon, 1996.

Wuellner, Wilhelm. *The Meaning of "Fishers of Men."* NTL. Philadelphia: Westminster, 1967.

———. "Where Is Rhetorical Criticism Taking Us?" *CBQ* 49 (1987) 448–63.

Yee, Gale A. "The Author/Text/Reader and Power: Suggestions for a Critical Framework for Biblical Studies." In *Reading from this Place*, vol. 1: 109–18. Minneapolis: Fortress Press, 1995.